POVERTY AND EXCLUSION IN A GLOBAL WORLD

Also by A. S. Bhalla

BLENDING OF NEW AND TRADITIONAL TECHNOLOGIES (*co-editor*)

* ECONOMIC TRANSITION IN HUNAN AND SOUTHERN CHINA

ENVIRONMENT, EMPLOYMENT AND DEVELOPMENT (*editor – also in Portuguese*)

* FACING THE TECHNOLOGICAL CHALLENGE

* GLOBALIZATION, GROWTH AND MARGINALIZATION (*editor – also in French*)

NEW TECHNOLOGIES AND DEVELOPMENT (*co-editor*)

* REGIONAL BLOCS: Building Blocks or Stumbling Blocks?

SMALL AND MEDIUM ENTERPRISES: Technology Policies and Options (*editor*)

TECHNOLOGICAL TRANSFORMATION OF RURAL INDIA (*co-editor*)

TECHNOLOGY AND EMPLOYMENT IN INDUSTRY (*editor – also in Spanish*)

TOWARDS GLOBAL ACTION FOR APPROPRIATE TECHNOLOGY (*editor*)

* UNEVEN DEVELOPMENT IN THE THIRD WORLD

* *from the same publishers*

Poverty and Exclusion in a Global World

A. S. Bhalla
David Thomson Senior Research Fellow
Sidney Sussex College
University of Cambridge
England

and

Frédéric Lapeyre
Member, Institute of Development Studies
Catholic University of Louvain
Belgium

First published in Great Britain 1999 by
MACMILLAN PRESS LTD
Houndmills, Basingstoke, Hampshire RG21 6XS and London
Companies and representatives throughout the world

A catalogue record for this book is available from the British Library.

ISBN 0–333–71549–7

First published in the United States of America 1999 by
ST. MARTIN'S PRESS, INC.,
Scholarly and Reference Division,
175 Fifth Avenue, New York, N.Y. 10010

ISBN 0–312–21825–7

Library of Congress Cataloging-in-Publication Data
Bhalla, A. S.
Poverty and exclusion in a global world / A.S. Bhalla and Frédéric Lapeyre.
p. cm.
Includes bibliographical references and index.
ISBN 0–312–21825–7 (cloth)
1. Poverty. 2. Social isolation. 3. Marginality, Social.
4. Socially handicapped. I. Lapeyre, Frédéric, 1967– .
II. Title.
HC79.P6B483 1998
305.5'68—dc21 98–38452
CIP

This book is printed on paper suitable for recycling and made from fully managed and sustained forest sources.

10 9 8 7 6 5 4 3 2
08 07 06 05 04 03 02 01

Printed and bound in Great Britain by
Antony Rowe Ltd, Chippenham, Wiltshire

Contents

List of Tables

List of Figures

Preface

The notion of social exclusion is new in the Anglo-Saxon literature on economic, social and political debates but is rapidly gaining currency. Evidence of this is the fact that the New Labour government in the United Kingdom established in December 1997 a Social Exclusion Unit in the Cabinet Office reporting directly to the Prime Minister. When launching this unit, Prime Minister Tony Blair succinctly noted the problems of social exclusion in the following words, which sum up the message of this monograph:

> social exclusion is about income bit but it is about more. It is about prospects and networks and life chances. It is a very modern problem, and one that is more harmful to the individual, more damaging to self-esteem, more corrosive for society as a whole, more likely to be passed down from generation to generation, than material poverty.[1]

Developed originally in France, the notion of social exclusion was subsequently promoted by the European Commission within its political debates and research programmes. The concept now seems to have come of age at least within Europe if not globally. Since the crisis of the welfare state in Western Europe (and in the former Soviet Union and Central and Eastern Europe for that matter), new forms of poverty, inequalities and exclusion from social rights are occurring more frequently than before. These problems are being aggravated by fundamental structural changes necessitated by the emerging global economy.

Our objective is not so much to analyse social exclusion *per se* as to examine its specific forms in the ongoing processes of globalization, labour market flexibility, the crisis of the welfare state, and the rise of individualism.

It is pertinent to ask whether the notion of social exclusion is mainly Eurocentric, or whether it has global relevance. Might a fresh look at social questions offer a new approach to structural problems in both high-income and low-income countries? And how can social exclusion be addressed in policy-making and implementation? We believe social exclusion is of universal validity even if its prevalence in individual countries and social and cultural contexts may be location-specific.

The North and South are beginning to converge on such issues as unemployment and poverty, which for the first time have become common features of both. Marginalization, poverty and exclusion have been on the agenda for a long time in developing countries, and have become more acute, particularly in the 1990s. It may, therefore, be relevant to ask why these countries have not considered the notion of social exclusion. Does it have something to do with the levels of development and different perceptions of the relative weights to be attached to economic, social and political dimensions of poverty and deprivation? Or does it have to do with the absence of a welfare state and social safety nets? Does lack of political, civil and/or social rights or inability to exercise those rights also contribute to, or aggravate, social exclusion?

Poverty as at present defined includes not only economic but also social dimensions (for example, popular participation – see Chapter 1). Is social exclusion, therefore, simply an extension of the poverty concept? We believe that the relationship between *distributional* and *relational* questions lies at the heart of social exclusion. These two dimensions capture the economic, social, political, cultural and related aspects of the problem. Long-term unemployment and job precariousness are the two main elements of the links between the above dimensions. Studies show a positive correlation between economic and social indicators, for example, between economic vulnerability, social-relations deprivation, bad housing, health conditions and weak social participation on the one hand, and employment status on the other. We develop an analytical framework that focuses not so much on social exclusion as a final state of economic and social deprivation as on the dynamic processes that create such a state and push individuals into precariousness, vulnerability, and finally, exclusion.

The above issues are by no means easy to tackle. This monograph, therefore, attempts to give only some tentative pointers towards a definition of social exclusion, an analytical framework and an operational and policy approach. We examine the concrete cases of France, Hungary and Poland in the North and Brazil in the South. The notion of the underclass in the United Kingdom and the United States is also discussed and compared with that of social exclusion. Generally, new institutions are required or old ones need to be modified to promote access to public goods and services, the labour market, decent livelihoods, social and political participation, and so on. But how can institutions improve their performance in the light of such criteria as economic efficiency and social justice? How are social actors affected by a particular institutional setting? Answers to these questions are crucial for an understanding of the different patterns of exclusion and the design of policies to promote social cohesion.

Several years ago, Dudley Seers (1969, p. 3) noted:

> The questions to ask about a country's development are: What has been happening to poverty? What has been happening to inequality? What has been happening to unemployment? If all three of these have become less severe, then beyond doubt this has been a period of development of a country concerned. If one or two of these central problems have been growing worse, especially if all three have, it would be strange to call the result 'development', even if per capita income doubled.

Thus, what has been happening to exclusion (as a new social question) is a fundamental question that needs to be posed about the style and pattern of development.

Chapter 1 opens with a critical review of recent poverty concepts that have evolved from a narrow income focus to a broader one embracing social and, to some extent, political aspects. We then discuss the economic, social and political dimensions of exclusion. The role of the state in overcoming exclusion is analysed as an extension of the political dimension. The last section deals with the question of global relevance of the concept. We conclude that the concept has global appeal even though its particular features may differ between the North and South.

Chapter 2 provides building blocks for an analytical and operational framework by exploring the relationship between *distributional* and *relational* questions in both industrialized and developing countries. A framework is useful only if it can be utilized for practical purposes. Therefore, the second part of the chapter examines the feasibility of applying the framework to concrete situations. Appropriate indicators, which can help measure the extent of exclusion over time, are discussed and the limitations of such indicators are examined. Chapter 3 considers two particular indicators, namely, long-term unemployment and job precariousness, and discusses their reliability and suitability for assessing exclusion.

Chapters 4 and 5 test the framework outlined in Chapter 2 through case studies of France, Hungary, Poland and Brazil. Finally, Chapter 6 discusses the implications of the process of economic globalization on the state of exclusion and marginalization at the national level in both industrialized and developing countries.

We have drawn on our article on social exclusion published in *Development and Change* (July 1997), especially in the writing of Chapter 2. Part of the research and writing work was done at the International Development Research Centre (IDRC) in Ottawa when one of us, A. S. B., was Special Adviser to the President of the Centre. Part of it was completed at the International Institute of Labour Studies in Geneva, at the Institute of Development Studies at the Catholic University of Louvain, and at Sidney Sussex College, Cambridge. We are indebted to all these institutions for their generous support.

We have benefited a great deal from discussions with a number of friends and colleagues, notably Charles Gore of UNCTAD (formerly, of the International Institute for Labour Studies, Geneva); José Figueiredo of the International Institute of Labour Studies in Geneva; and Gerry Rodgers, Director, ILO Multidisciplinary Team in Santiago, who also generously helped by supplying papers on exclusion in Latin America. Many people were kind enough to read draft chapters and offer critical and useful comments: Dr Mohamed Bensaid and Professor Ignacy Sachs, Ecole des Hautes Etudes en Sciences Sociales (EHESS), Paris; Professor Jean-Philippe Peemans, Institute of Development Studies, Catholic University of Louvain, Louvain; Dr A. Ricciardi, CGIL, Avellino, Italy; Judith Maxwell, President of the Canadian Policy Research Networks (CPRN), Ottawa; Professor Subbiah Kannappan of the Economics Department, Michigan State University; and Professor Scott Sernau of the Sociology Department, Indiana University South Bend. Eshete Hailu of the International Development Research Centre prepared diagrams for Chapter 3. To all of them, we are most grateful.

Cambridge, England A.S. Bhalla
Louvain, Belgium Frédéric Lapeyre

Acknowledgements

The authors and publishers thank the following for permission to reproduce copyright material: Basil Blackwell, Oxford, for drawing on our article 'Social Exclusion: Towards an Analytical and Operational Framework', *Development and Change* (July 1997); The Brookings Institution, Washington, DC, for reproducing Tables 5.5 to 5.7; The United Nations Economic Commission for Latin America and the Caribbean (UNECLAC), for using Table 5.8 and Figure 5.1; and The International Development Research Centre (IDRC), Ottawa, for financing the translation of several papers from Portuguese into English for the preparation of Chapter 5; The United Nations Development Programme (UNDP) for Table 1.3; Policy Press (Bristol) for reproducing Table 1.1 from Berghman (1995), Scandinavian University Press for using Figure 1.1 from Andersen (1996); Centre d'Etude des Revenus et des Coûts (CERC) for Tables 4.2 and 4.7; Institut National de la Statistique et des Etudes Economiques (INSEE) for Table 4.5; Organisation for Economic Cooperation and Development (OECD) for Tables 3.3, 4.6 and 4.10; and la Documentation française for using Tables 4.3 and 4.4 from du Boullay (1997).

List of Abbreviations

AFDC	Aid to Families with Dependent Children
AID	Automatic Interaction Detection
CERC	*Centre d'Etude des Revenus et des Coûts*
DIEESE	Brazilian Labour Unions' Statistical Office
EBRD	European Bank of Reconstruction and Development
EU	European Union
GUS	Polish National Office of Statistics
HDI	Human Development Index
IBGE	Brazilian Institute of Statistics and Geography
ICDC (UNICEF)	International Child Development Centre
IDRC	International Development Research Centre
IILS	International Institute of Labour Studies
INSEE	*Institut National de la Statistique et des Etudes Economiques*
IUED	*Institut Universitaire d'Etudes du Développment*
LIL	Low Income Line
NEPP	*Nûcleo de Estudos de Politicas Publicas*
OECD	Organization of Economic Cooperation and Development
PDI	Political Development Index
PL	Poverty Line
RMI	*Revenu Minimum d'Insertion*
SEADE	State Data Analysis System Foundation (São Paulo State, Brazil)
SMIG	*Salaire Mininum Intersectoriel Garanti*
SOT	Socially Oriented Trust
UCL	University College London
UCLA	University of California Los Angeles
UNCTAD	United Nations Conference on Trade and Development
UNDP	United Nations Development Programme
UNECLAC	(CEPAL) United Nations Economic Commission for Latin America and the Caribbean
UNICEF	United Nations Childrens' Fund
UNRISD	United Nations Research Institute for Social Development

1 Defining Exclusion

It was in the first part of the nineteenth century that the social issues related to pauperism emerged explicitly for the first time. At that time a new type of poverty resulting from modernization and industrialization was affecting the working class. Social tensions produced by industrialization and liberalism were threatening the social order. The conflictual dynamics of social forces and the risk of social breakdown were at the heart of the debate. Exclusion was viewed mostly as a political phenomenon resulting from the under-representation of the working class in political institutions. The problem was seen in the context of class struggle. Thus, the social question was relevant to the integration of the working class into the political process. On the basis of an analysis of capitalism in the nineteenth century, Polanyi (1957) has shown that a self-regulating market, where the economy is disembedded from society, so as to allow the market to function without social and political constraints, had in fact failed, as society reacted to enforce factory legislation, social insurance and the institutionalization of industrial relations. This was the origin of the modern welfare state.

The step-by-step building of the welfare state from the end of the nineteenth century to the 1960s reduced social tensions and conflicts in the industrialized countries. A broad set of social institutions emerged which enabled accumulation to proceed unfettered while maintaining social cohesion through temporary resolution of crises endemic in the capitalist accumulation process. During the golden age of the post-Second World War era, social integration resulted from economic growth, development of the wage-earning society, quasi-full employment and improvement in workers' living conditions. The welfare state contributed significantly to this process of integration through a redistributive policy; poverty issues were no longer top of the political agenda in the industrialized countries.

CONCEPT AND DEFINITIONS

Richard Lenoir (1974) is considered pioneer in the use of the term 'social exclusion'. In *Les Exclus: un français sur dix*, he developed a stigmatizing view of the excluded; those who have no access to the fruit of economic growth. Indeed, the socially excluded were the mentally and physically handicapped, suicidal people, the aged and invalid, drug abusers, delinquents, asocial persons, and so on. What this wide variety of people had in common was that they did not fit into the norms fixed by industrial society; they were socially disadvantaged groups. However, the term social exclusion had a very restricted connotation and acceptance at that time,[1] as it was related to a marginal phenomenon which did not affect the whole of society.

But the capitalist system in the late 1970s and the 1980s has been followed by a deep restructuring of the entire social relationship. Globalization of capital and the restructuring of labour markets were accompanied by new types of social and economic regulation and new strategies with supranational dimensions. In this process many institutions, which worked in harmony during the period of Fordist industrial organization to maintain sustainable growth, have been destroyed. These were institutions which promoted social cohesion by finding a relevant compromise between contradictory but interdependent forces (Boyer, 1995). The 1980s experienced a drastic ideological shift towards the supremacy of self-adjusting free market mechanisms aimed at dissolving or circumventing most of the institutional forms inherited from the compromises of the Fordist growth regime. The new trend led to privatization, deregulation, reduction of public services, a shift towards targeted assistance and deregulation of the labour market. According to the neoliberal consensus that emerged in the 1980s, those reforms were crucial for restoring vigorous world economic growth.

The emerging new social problems in the 1980s concerned the deprivation of individuals who had formerly been well integrated in society. Precariousness affected some members of the labour market who had once enjoyed secure jobs and good social networks. Thus the new poverty problem did not pertain to marginals (the disabled or those excluded from social norms) but to an increasing proportion of the population suffering from such multidimensional problems as precarious jobs and unemployment, the weakening of family and extra-family networks and a loss of social status. Thus, the notion of social exclusion relates to socioeconomic structural changes rather than to individuals' behaviour or characteristics.

The new forms of poverty, mass vulnerability and long-term unemployment have led to new concerns relating to the processes of social polarization with rising income gaps between the top and the bottom segments of the social scale. At the heart of the new social question is the return of mass social vulnerability, marked by a growing number of people trapped in precarious forms of work or becoming permanently superfluous, irrelevant or a hindrance to the functioning of the global economy. Social and spatial restructuring, and precarious employment and unemployment are inherent to the dynamics of capital accumulation. In future every nation will have to face the problem of what to do with the millions of people whose labour is needed less or not at all and who lack social recognition in the emerging global economy.

In the past, the exploiters and exploited were linked by a conflictual and interdependent relationship, the exploited being integrated into the productive system and being useful to the exploiters as producers and consumers. Through social conflicts and collective bargaining, the working class fought to improve its living conditions. By contrast, today's excluded are on the fringes of society and do not or cannot participate in either the productive system or the consumption system.

The emerging global economy is characterized by strong tendencies towards a fragmentation of the social fabric and the occupational structure. The labour markets of the wealthiest industrialized economics continue to be plagued by high and persistent rates of unemployment and rising income inequality. The crucial issue then is how to ensure social cohesion in a fragmented society where a significant portion of the population is excluded in the name of economic efficiency and flexibility.

The new social question is related to the crisis of wage-earning society and the loss of social protection (Castel, 1995a). It is also the crisis of solidarity associated with the welfare state that seems inefficient in fighting the new poverty and the processes of social disintegration that emerged in the 1980s (Rosanvallon, 1994). Strobel (1996) notes that the debate on exclusion poses a fundamental question of the social bond and the means that society has of ensuring solidarity among its members. This is becoming an increasingly important political debate.

From a Durkheimian perspective, the development of an industrial society and social division of labour in the nineteenth century led to a transition from mechanical to organic solidarity. Indeed, in the mechanical model of solidarity associated with traditional societies, collective consciousness embraced individual consciousness. This led to strong internal cohesion of the community. In the organic model of solidarity associated with modern societies, collective consciousness was largely overshadowed by individual consciousness. The emergence of this new model of solidarity resulted from the growing interdependence of individuals within the framework of the social division of labour. Solidarity was no longer mechanical, as it implied that each individual was conscious of his or her role in the proper functioning of society.

A growing number of individuals are now suffering from economic and social deprivation. They are wholly or partially excluded from the society in which they live (Galtung, 1995).They are trapped in a kind of 'social no man's land', which risks becoming a social ghetto of people dependent on social benefits and deprived of positive social recognition. Thus, more and more people are not only becoming exluded from an economic, social or geographical point of view but also from a symbolic one. Fragmentation of society, the development of informal activities, and the emergence of different and conflicting models of solidarity are deeply affecting social cohesion. As the Commission on Wealth Creation and Social Cohesion has noted, social cohesion is under stress. Mass vulnerability and exclusion go hand in hand with the new economic opportunities offered by globalization. The process is producing a fractured society with fewer and fewer shared values and common interests (Dahrendorf *et al.*, 1995, p. 16).

Different Definitions and Paradigms

The notion of social exclusion, as developed in the beginning of the 1980s in France (see Chapter 4), emphasizes the risk associated with the breakdown of the social fabric and ensuing loss of collective values. It forms the basis of the global debate on the mechanisms of national solidarity and social exclusion which has become the mainstream paradigm in the 1990s, for a new approach to both the social crisis and the social policies needed to overcome it. For example, through the Revenu Minimum d'Insertion (RMI) programme, the State has acknowledged the fact that new forms of poverty result from structural processes, related in particular to the rise of unemployment.

Society has become more fragile.The debate on social exclusion is concerned with the restructuring of society necessitated by the emerging socioeconomic global order. Exclusion from the productive system and social deprivation are the two crucial processes leading to social exclusion, whereas a job and an effective social network are the main elements of social integration. However, exclusion is not irreversible. It is generally the result of structural processes (such as deep socioeconomic changes) that involve the individual's situation and personal characteristics (for example, age, lack of qualifications, separation and divorce, and alcoholism) and individuals' responses to them. Social exclusion is thus a multidimensional structural process, embracing precariousness of labour and unemployment on the one hand, and the breakdown of social bonds through the crisis of the welfare state, the rise of individualism and the weakening of primary solidarity (of family networks, for example) on the other.

Below we discuss the different interpretations and dimensions of social exclusion.

1. Unemployment and Job Precariousness

Unemployment and precarious forms of work are underlying factors to social exclusion discussed in this monograph. We, therefore, believe that an analysis of the labour market can improve our understanding of social exclusion, and indeed, it is the rise in unemployment and the changing structure of employment involving an increase in atypical jobs, which represent the main source of uncertainty. They contribute to a decline in the process of citizenship-building that characterizes the European social model. Here, two main processes contribute to exclusion: (i) high unemployment and job precariousness for groups of people who were fully integrated before, and (ii) difficulty in entering the labour market to enjoy the social bonds associated with it particularly for younger people (Castel, 1995a). Thus, emphasizing precariousness in the labour market is very useful for a better understanding of the processes leading to social vulnerability and deprivation.

The term 'social exclusion' has been spreading rapidly in Europe during the last few decades. The debate on the subject, which started in France, has gradually spread to other countries through the European Union (EU) channels, in particular through the EU anti-poverty programmes. In fact, the phrase has become part of the political vocabulary in Europe; replacing 'poverty' in official EU terminology. Moreover, long-term unemployment, precarious employment, the breakdown of the social fabric, urban poverty and related social problems have stimulated new areas of research in social sciences. Exclusion is increasingly discussed as a threat to social cohesion in European societies (Spicker, 1997).

Nowadays, the social exclusion is used in many different national contexts. It is also associated with different values and viewpoints (Silver, 1995). It is, therefore, important to understand the theoretical and ideological paradigms underlying the different national debates on the subject.

2. *French vs. Anglo-Saxon Interpretations*

Social exclusion refers to a process of 'social disqualification' (Paugam, 1993) or 'social disaffiliation' (Castel, 1995a), leading to a breakdown of the relationship between society and the individual. This notion refers to the Durkheimian concept of a specific social bond or solidarity, as mentioned above. The social order is conceived as *normative*, based on a core of shared values and rights. It presupposes a national consensus or, in other words, a collective conscience that ties individuals to society whatever their differences and interests. The traditional moral debate on solidarity is concerned with the building up of the national community going beyond individual, group or class interests.

The solidarity debate rejects social class conflict, Christian charity and liberal individualism. It is based on the relationship between two types of responsibility: individual responsibility and collective responsibility (Bourgeois, 1931). In this context, the State has a key role to play to preserve the social bond between individuals and society; and promote social integration (Ion, 1995, p. 67). The responsibility of the State is to alleviate poverty and protect individuals against the risks associated with industrial society (the roots of systems of social protection). But at the same time, individual responsibility also is important: individuals must respect social norms, particularly, through their participation in the labour market, if they want to enjoy social protection.The French debate on exclusion is deeply rooted in this relationship between individual responsibility and collective responsibility. As we will see in Chapter 4, the RMI programme in France was elaborated from this perspective. As Donzelot (1996, p. 94) points out, the State must both protect individuals against society and protect society against individuals.

In the official French debate, exclusion is seen as a rupture of this bond of solidarity and thus as a failure of the State to protect social cohesion. According to Aglietta (1997), the right to not be excluded should be at the heart of the political debate and should become the minimum basis for a new social contract.

Unlike French Republican thought, the Anglo-Saxon tradition views social integration in terms of freely chosen relationships between the individual and society (Silver, 1994, p. 18). This Anglo-Saxon thinking is rooted in the liberal paradigm under which society is viewed as a mass of atomised individuals in competition within the market place.The liberal debate emphasizes individuals' rights and obligations. It assumes that there is no social bond other than the voluntary contractual exchange between free individuals. We must point out, however, that the Liberal paradigm rejects the ideas of domination or exploitation. Therefore, exclusion may reflect voluntary individual choices or a contractual relationship between actors, or 'distortions' to the system, such as discrimination, market failures and/or unenforced rights. From a strictly meritocratic point of view, in a society characterized by democratic institutions and equal opportunities for all, individuals have what they merit. There is no question of social justice, there are no structural processes of exploitation or exclusion, and no one could be seen as directly responsible for situations in which individuals find themselves (Walzer, 1995). The Liberal paradigm does not envisage society's responsibility since it views the main causes of poverty as individual shortcomings and behavioural deficiencies. Nevertheless, there are two different groups of the excluded according to that normative view. First, those who suffer discrimination or who do not have the required abilities because they are handicapped or disadvantaged for one reason or another. Second, those who choose not to take advantage of the opportunities to participate actively in social and economic life because of the disincentive effects of public assistance.

In this context, in an influential contribution, Charles Murray (1984), provoked a liberal debate by suggesting that the underclass was a consequence of State intervention which creates a dependency culture by making public assistance more attractive than work. The underclass is viewed as consisting of deviant individuals behaving rationally in response to the policies of the welfare state.

Thus, policy should be concerned with overcoming the perverse effects of social insurance systems through the withdrawal of the welfare state. The State should intervene only to protect individual rights, prevent discrimination, help individuals to realize their potential and concentrate limited resources on those who really need help rather than on those characterized by deviant values and behaviour.

3. The European Union Approach

The European Commission (which attaches high priority to dealing with social exclusion in Europe) defines social exclusion in terms of the denial or non-realization of social rights. It emphasizes each citizen's right to a certain basic standard of living and to participate in the major social and occupational institutions, for example, employment, housing, health care, education, and so on. Social exclusion occurs when citizens are disadvantaged and unable to secure these social rights.

The Observatory on National Policies to Combat Social Exclusion, funded by the European Commission, has developed a Marshallian view of exclusion. Indeed, according to Marshall's (1950) classic formulation of citizenship rights in industrial society, the coexistence of civil, political and social rights is a necessary condition for full citizenship. Democratic societies should preserve a good balance in the provision of these rights. In this context, the denial of social rights constitutes a major failure, even if civil and political rights are effective; where citizens are unable to secure their social rights, they will suffer from generalized and persistent disadvantages and their social and occupational participation will be undermined (Room *et al.*, 1992).

The European approach to social exclusion focuses attention on new and emerging social problems by highlighting the processes that exclude social groups, individuals or regions in Europe. In particular, in the context of globalization and changing economic conditions, social exclusion is viewed as a consequence of economic restructuring necessitated by growing competition in the emerging global economy (see Chapter 6). The European Commission presents the challenge posed by social exclusion as follows:

> Looking beyond the diversity of national situations, the debate will emphasise the structural nature of a phenomenon which is tending to establish within society a mechanism which excludes part of the population from economic and social life and from their share of the general prosperity. More particularly, they point to an important change over the past 15 years in the nature of the challenge itself; the problem is now not only one of disparity between the top and the bottom of the social scale (up/down), but also between those comfortably placed within society and those on the fringe (in/out). (European Commission, 1992, p. 7)

Social exclusion is a complex and multifaceted notion, because it refers to both individuals and societies, and to disadvantage, alienation and lack of freedom. While it may refer to disadvantage that individuals may perceive, at the more aggregate societal level it concerns inequities among social groups. It is, therefore, not surprising that many people have used the term rather loosely.

4. *Underlying Theoretical Paradigms*

Hillary Silver (1995) defines three major paradigms on exclusion: (i) the *solidarity paradigm*, which explains exclusion in terms of lack of social ties between individuals and society; this paradigm is deeply rooted in French Republican thought as noted above; (ii) the *specialization paradigm*, under which exclusion is described in terms of various distortions, namely, discrimination, market failures and unenforced rights. This paradigm is rooted in the school of Liberal thought that is dominant in the United States, and (iii) the *monopoly paradigm*, under which exclusion is explained in terms of some groups (so-called insiders) controlling or monopolizing resources to their advantage (Silver, 1994); this paradigm is dominant in Western Europe. These explanations of exclusion may of course overlap. For example, the solidarity paradigm or solidarism à la Parkin as a collective response to exclusion may also suffer from some limitations. As Parkin (1979, footnote 5, pp. 71–2) notes, 'solidaristic behaviour can itself be used for blatantly exclusionary ends'.

The monopoly paradigm noted above is quite close to Weber's theory of 'social closure' (see Parkin, 1979). Here social groups interact according to their material interests, with each trying to monopolize advantages. Closure means exclusion of economic and social opportunities to outsiders: one group maximizing rewards by restricting access of other economic or social groups to social and economic opportunities. This invites a collective response by the excluded to win some recognition or share of the resources. Parkin (1979) interprets social closure in terms of exclusion and usurpation, the latter being an inevitable consequence of the former; indeed social closure is the process by which social bodies or clubs seek to maximize rewards by restricting access to a limited number of eligibles; usurpation is the process through which outsiders resist and seek to overcome their exclusion. Depending on the size of such excluded groups of outsiders, their collective action may challenge the prevailing system of resource allocation and distributive justice. Protests and strikes by organized labour, the growth of women's movements, and groups formed by ethnic minorities to seek recognition are all symptomatic of the relationships between the two processes of 'social closure'. These two aspects of closure differ in one significant sense. Exclusionary closure involves the use of power in a 'downward' direction ... whereas the countervailing action by the 'negatively privileged', on the other hand, represents the use of power in an upward direction' (Parkin, 1979, p. 45).

Having introduced the notion of social exclusion, our next task is to distinguish it from the more conventional notions of poverty, deprivation or marginalization. Indeed, it is important to examine whether social exclusion is only a relabelling of old and long-standing problems or whether it emphasizes new social problems.

ON POVERTY AND DEPRIVATION

In this section, we review briefly the existing concepts of poverty and deprivation to determine whether social exclusion is simply a broader *social* analysis of poverty and destitution.

In the context of industrialized countries (mainly the United Kingdom), Townsend (1979, 1993) defines poverty and deprivation in both economic and social terms. Noting that the 'subsistence' concept of poverty and deprivation 'minimises the range and depth of human need just as the 'basic needs' concept is restricted primarily to the physical facilities', Townsend (1993, p. 79) defines poverty in terms of 'relative deprivation' as:

> A state of observable and demonstrable disadvantage relative to the local community or the wider society or nation to which an individual, family or group belongs. The idea has come to be applied to conditions (that is, physical, environmental and social states and circumstances) rather than resources.

Townsend distinguishes between two types of deprivation: *material* (relating to food, clothing, housing, and so on) and *social* (associated with family, recreation and education). The latter kind is noted as providing 'a useful means of generalizing the condition of those who do not or cannot enter into ordinary forms of family and other social relationships' (p. 82). The major focus of Townsend's approach to poverty is on social interaction rather than on material aspects. His interest lies in examining who in the UK is excluded from 'ordinary living patterns, customs and activities' (Townsend, 1979, p. 15).

Non-economists generally believe that the economists' concept of poverty is focused too narrowly on material aspects such as the level, size or distribution of incomes. While this may have been true in the 1970s, it is no longer the case in the 1990s. Lipton and Maxwell (1992) show how the new conceptualization of poverty embraces such elements as the importance of civil society (besides just NGOs) and security of livelihood. To quote them:

> There has been significant change ... since the 1970s – less weight is put in the current literature on income and consumption and more on the complex, multi-dimensional concepts of livelihood and livelihood security ... the perceptions of poor people themselves are also prominent in this definition ... This new perspective allows us to measure and evaluate the level of vulnerability – and freedom from bias by gender and age – of individuals' access to privately and publicly provided goods and services and to common property. (pp. 6 and 10)

Sen (1992a) has also developed a comprehensive approach to poverty which goes beyond economics. At the heart of Sen's theory is the notion of individuals' 'capabilities', which are opportunities to achieve valuable 'functionings' or 'states of being'. Thus 'living may be seen as consisting of a set of interrelated 'functionings', consisting of beings and doings' (p. 38). In addressing poverty issues, Sen focuses on valuable functionings which represent different factors of well-being. Functionings may include both physical elements such as being adequately fed and sheltered, and 'more complex social achievements, such as taking part in the life of the community, being able to appear in public without shame, and so on'. (Sen, 1992a, p. 110). Taking women as a disadvantaged group, Sen adds that

> disadvantages may apply to the capability of being nourished (for example, because of the demands of pregnancy and neonatal care), achieving security (for example, in single-parent families), having fulfilling work (for example, because of stereotyping of women's jobs), establishing one's professional reputation early on in one's career (for example, because of the asymmetric demands of family life). (p. 113)

As the capabilities set reflects the various combinations of functionings individuals can achieve – and so their positive freedom to choose between different ways of living – it embraces the political and social dimensions of poverty. On this point Sen (1981 p. 6) has noted that

> In understanding general poverty, or regular starvation, or outbursts of famines, it is necessary to look at both ownership patterns and exchange entitlements, and at the forces that lie behind them. This requires a careful consideration of the nature of the modes of production and the structure of economic classes as well as their interrelations.

In the context of rich countries defined in terms of GNP per capita (for example, the United States), Sen (1992a) notes that low income is merely one factor among others that influence poverty. The diverse social circumstances and characteristics (inadequate health facilities, violence in inner cities, and the absence of social care as factors in the social environment that influence poverty) also need to be taken into account. In an effort to apply Sen's concept of capabilities empirically, Meghnad Desai (1995) adds the dimension of resource requirements for guaranteeing capabilities, which will vary from society to society depending on social norms and practices. These requirements need to be considered along with the availability of resources at the disposal of individuals.

Another pioneering piece of work on poverty and destitution by Dasgupta (1993) examines the influences of equal and unequal asset distributions on the functioning of the labour market and on those seeking employment. His concept of *economic disenfranchisement* is somewhat similar to Sen's concepts of entitlement and capabilities discussed above. The poor who have no actual labour power (or those like landless people without any ownership of assets) suffer from a failure of entitlements, owing to lack of income, assets or employment. Their capabilities to command employment and access to resources can be enhanced only if their consumption levels are raised; this applies particularly in the case of food, which must satisfy a minimum nutritional requirement if people are to convert their *potential* asset of labour power into *actual* labour power. On the other hand, some people in agrarian societies (the analysis is mainly concerned with these) have some assets in the form of land and unearned income and they enjoy a comparative advantage in the labour market because they can convert their potential labour power into actual labour power without having to work. In the labour market, those with assets can undercut those without any, unless social norms prevent such wage undercutting. Thus, it is the assetless people such as landless labourers, who are particularly vulnerable.

Poverty vs. Exclusion

It is clear from the above discussion that recent concepts of poverty, hunger and destitution, as defined by Dasgupta, Lipton and Sen, capture their economic, social and, to some extent, political dimensions. As such, they provide a useful starting-point for the analysis of social exclusion.

Sen's concept of capabilities can be extended to cover social interaction and political expression, besides standard of living. However, while social exclusion has characteristics similar to those of poverty broadly defined, it goes beyond its economic and social dimensions. While poverty and social exclusion are interrelated, we will argue that the latter is a distinct concept, emphasizing new social problems.

Using a social exclusion approach, rather than a poverty one, implies focusing not only on *distributional* but also on *relational* aspects of exclusion. Thus, we need to assess 'social-relations deprivation' (Penz, 1986), including structural (rather than cyclical) aspects of exclusion besides material deprivation. Most recent studies on exclusion (particularly in developing countries, for example, Kaijage and Tibaijuka, 1996; Appasamy *et al.*, 1996) are, however, concerned mainly with material deprivation. A study on Thailand (Phongpaichit *et al.*, 1996) is perhaps the only one to consider social exclusion explicitly as different from poverty and to define it in terms of claims of rights and citizenship instead (for a detailed analysis of exclusion in the context of developing societies, see Chapter 5).

Poverty may not always be a good indicator of exclusion of people from goods and services. People can be poor and not be excluded from certain basic needs; they may continue to enjoy some access to the labour market, to some physical resources and to political rights and obligations. The same levels of achievement in life expectancy and access to social services can be attained by countries with widely varying incomes per capita (Sen, 1983a). For example, China and Sri Lanka have performed well in the improvement of living standards despite a relatively low GNP per capita (Dasgupta, 1993). In 1992, Sri Lanka had a life expectancy at birth of over 71 years, whereas the Republic of Korea, which is more than three times richer in terms of GNP per capita, has not yet overtaken this level (see UNDP, 1994). Thus social change seems to be highly dependent on the particular pattern of development chosen. Implementation of social policies within the framework of a people-centred development strategy is more likely to lead to an increase in the capabilities of disadvantaged people than is a rapid growth strategy based on a trickledown effect.

The state of poverty is not a condition for exclusion from certain social networks. In developing countries, an increasing number of organizations of the poor support our contention that poverty does not necessarily mean exclusion from social relations. These organizations may actually offer bargaining strength to the poor and ensure social cohesion and solidarity instead of accentuating exclusion, as a number of authors on 'social clubs' have argued (for a discussion of the role of exclusive groups, see Buchanan, 1965; Olson, 1965).

The dimension of civil and political rights and citizenship (a political asset) further distinguishes exclusion from poverty. The traditional concept of poverty is restricted to a lack of disposable income, whereas the more comprehensive concept of social exclusion refers also to a breakdown or malfunctioning of the major social systems that should guarantee full citizenship (Berghman, 1995). This is not to exclude the possibility that economic status (being rich or poor) may influence the extent of exclusion from or access to certain political rights. (Economic clout undoubtedly influences access to political goods and rights.) But some developing societies, like that of India provide constitutional rights. The 'fundamental rights' provision in the Indian constitution guarantees to all citizens nondiscriminatory access to legal process, education, and public employment, as well as basic civil liberties. The constitution goes even further, and provides for compensatory discrimination (affirmative action) in favour of the particularly disadvantaged social groups ('scheduled castes and tribes'), religious and cultural minorities (see Appasamy *et al.,* 1996). However, while the constitution can legally enforce these 'negative' rights and freedoms, it cannot legally ensure 'positive freedoms' or economic welfare in the form of guaranteed employment and a guaranteed minimum income.

In the context of industrialized countries, the shift in thinking in Western European countries, for example, from poverty to social exclusion, was the result of increasing concern with the structural and multidimensional nature of processes by which individuals or specific areas are actually excluded from 'the social exchanges, practices and rights which are an intrinsic part of social and economic integration' (European Commission, 1989, p. 43).

In Europe, the concept of social exclusion was adopted for both political and conceptual reasons. On political grounds, member states expressed reservation about the use of the term 'poverty'. The concept of exclusion was considered less disparaging of the structural social problems experienced (Berghman, 1994). Moreover, the concept of poverty was deemed inadequate considering that the welfare states in Europe guaranteed minimum income and access to basic services. Also, an income-based notion of poverty was considered too static and narrow an approach to social problems.

The European notion of exclusion embraces multidimensional processes and points to the malfunctioning of the *institutions* that should guarantee social integration. Thus the focus of analysis shifts from individuals to communities and institutions to which the individuals belong or from which they are excluded. The shift from a debate on poverty to one on social exclusion is justified by the European Commission as follows:

> The concept of social exclusion is a dynamic one ... referring both to processes and consequent situations. It is therefore a particularly appropriate designation for structural changes. More clearly than the concept of poverty, understood far too often as referring exclusively to income, it also states the multi-dimensional nature of mechanisms whereby individuals and groups are excluded from taking part in the social exchange, from the component practices and rights of social integration and identity ... More generally, by highlighting the risks of cracks appearing in the social fabric, it suggests something more than social inequality and carries with it the risk of a fragmented society. (European Commission, 1992, p. 8)

The concept of social exclusion may be superior to that of poverty in two main respects. First, it focuses on the multidimensional character of deprivation (see below) and can thus provide an insight into the cumulative factors that keep people deprived. Second, it enables an analysis of deprivation as a result of dynamic causal factors. The conceptual differences between poverty and social exclusion are illustrated in Table 1.1.

Table 1.1 Conceptual differences between poverty and social exclusion

	Static outcome	*Dynamic process*
Unidimensional (income)	Poverty	Impoverishment
Multidimensional	Deprivation	Social exclusion

Source: Berghman (1995).

To conclude, we can argue that social exclusion is a new approach to the analysis of social issues. It has stimulated the development of longitudinal research for a better understanding of the multi-dimensional processes causing vulnerability and deprivation for an increasing portion of the population not previously affected by this phenomenon. In the latter part of the 1980s, research in the social sciences has shifted from the static definition of poverty, based on a monetary approach, to the processes leading, at least in some cases, to the extreme situation of social exclusion through the cumulation of disadvantages and a progressive rupture of social bonds. As Mingione (1996b) explains, it is necessary to look at dynamic processes and their perception within changing systems of social integration. From this perspective, the notion of exclusion both promotes the debate and motivates social science research. Further, there has occurred in the 1990s a new phase of research programmes guided explicitly or implicitly by the concept of social exclusion, so that in France, for instance, a large consensus exists on the actual framework for analysing social exclusion and questioning social issues and policy.

SOCIAL EXCLUSION: A MULTIDIMENSIONAL CONCEPT

It follows from the above discussion that both *distributional* (economic) and *relational* (social) issues lie at the heart of the concept of social exclusion (see Chapter 2). The concept goes beyond the economic and social aspects of poverty. It also embraces the political aspects such as civil and political rights and citizenship that determine a relationship between individuals and the state as well as between the society and the individual. Besides rights and citizenship, the emergence of new social organizations and groups can also indicate a new relationship between individuals (through their social group) and the state. This is best illustrated with examples from such transition economies as the Chinese. Under the economic reforms – decollectivization, decentralization of planning and production, and the growth of different forms of ownership (state, collective, private, joint ventures and joint stock companies, and so on) – State control and the old social organizations have been weakened. A number of new social organizations (*shetuan*) have emerged, some spontaneously and others encouraged by the State and the single party.[2]

Apart from social and cultural differences, do economic and technological gaps between the nations of the North and the South necessitate a different approach to marginalization and destitution? In this context two distinct aspects of exclusion, namely *analytical* and *normative* (or prescriptive) need to be considered separately. Economic and technological differences between nations are reflected in different stages of development, which are likely to influence the nature and pattern of exclusion. In the case of normative prescriptions for overcoming exclusion, the differences in the economic as well as the administrative/organizational capacity in the two groups of countries are also of practical significance. Both types of resources are more scarce in developing countries. Therefore, it is not evident whether these countries have the capacity to ensure social inclusion of everyone in society at the same time. Resource and organizational constraints may, *inter alia,* make sequencing and targeting inevitable, at least in the short term. Even countries that have these capabilities are not able to assure social exclusion of everyone!

Having considered the concept of exclusion in general terms, we discuss below its three main aspects, namely, economic, social and political.

1. The Economic Dimension

The economic approach to exclusion is concerned with the questions of income and production and access to goods and services (or commodity bundles *à la* Sen) from which some people are excluded and others are not. That is to say, they may be excluded from income from employment and/or from the satisfaction of such basic needs as housing/shelter, health and education. In a study, *Employment, Technology and Development*, Sen (1975) defined the employment concept in terms of (a) income, (b) production and (c) recognition. The economic approach to exclusion seems to cover mainly the first two aspects. The third aspect refers to the idea that 'employment gives a person the recognition of being engaged in something worth his while' (p. 5). Thus, the recognition aspect of Sen's concept of employment can be interpreted as providing a social dimension to the concept of exclusion (see below).

Dasgupta's concept of economic disenfranchisement, discussed above, more explicitly approximates exclusion from the labour market, which, however, also incorporates such social aspects as malnutrition and ill-health. Both these concepts emphasize ownership of assets (social structure and organization) and access to resources as important factors preventing or minimizing exclusion.

Another economic aspect of exclusion concerns resource allocation and accumulation. The very notion of exclusion implies something that is bad and needs to be overcome by enabling inclusion. But as we noted above, scarce resources often prevent the inclusion of everyone simultaneously. Allocating resources for improving the lot of one set of groups may leave fewer resources for other groups. Hence the need for priorities for different socioeconomic groups (the issue of targeting) and different time dimensions.

In practice, symptoms of economic exclusion can be found in income inequality and worsening of income distribution over time (see Table 1.2). Many countries around the world are experiencing widening gaps between rich and poor. In the 1980s, inequalities of income distribution increased in the eight major industrial countries (namely, France, Germany, Italy, Japan, the Netherlands, Sweden, the UK and the US) and this trend is continuing (Ghai, 1994). Between 1984 and 1987, the proportion of income of the top quintiles of tax payers in France rose from 44 per cent to 46 per cent (Davidson, 1989). Between 1979 and 1989 in the UK and the US, the shares of income of the top quintiles increased from 36 per cent to 42 per cent and from 39 per cent to 42 per cent respectively (see Table 1.2). During the same period, the proportion of households living below the poverty line in the UK (defined as having less than the average income) rose from 9.4 per cent in 1974 to 11.9 per cent in 1983, and to 20 per cent in 1988, with the numbers of the poor jumping from 5 to 12 million between 1974 and 1988 (Ghai, 1994). In the UK and the US, income inequalities have never been so high since the crisis of the 1930s. Between 1969 and 1992, the Gini coefficient in the US rose from 0.35 to 0.40 (*The Economist*, 1994b). For the UK, Goodman *et al.* (1997) emphasized the historical trend – as regards its intensity and length – that is, the continuous rise in the level of inequality which rose, as measured by the Gini, from 0.25 to 0.34 between 1979 and 1993.

Table 1.2 Changing GNP per capita and income distribution

	GNP per capita (US $)	*Households (% of income)*	
		Share of top 20%	*Share of bottom 20%*
Argentina			
1970–5	2 470	50	4
1987–92	6 050	51	5
Brazil			
1970–5	1 070	62	3
1987–92	2 770	68	2
Mexico			
1970–5	1 460	61	3
1987–92	3 470	56	4
Guatemala			
1970–5	570	60	5
1987–92	980	63	2
Côte d'Ivoire			
1970–5	530	50	9
1987–92	670	42	7
Kenya			
1970–5	230	60	3
1987–92	310	62	3
Thailand			
1970–5	360	50	6
1987–92	1 840	51	6
Malaysia			
1970–5	820	56	4
1987–92	2 790	54	5
China			
1980–5	380	39	7
1995	620	47.5	2.2
India			
1970–5	160	49	6
1992	310	42.6	3.7
Poland			
1980–5	2 100	34	10
1992	1 910	36.6	9.3
Early 1980s	2 100 (1981)	32.3	11.3
1993	3 350	36.6	9.5
United States			
1979	10 630	39	6.4
1989	20 910	42.1	5.6
United Kingdom			
1979	6 320	36	9
1989	14 610	42	8

Table 1.2 (continued)

	GNP per capita (US $)	*Households (% of income)*	
		Share of top 20%	*Share of bottom 20%*
France			
Late 1970s	9 950 (1979)	42.4	6.1
1989	17 820	41.9	5.6
Sweden			
Late 1970s	11 930 (1979)	30.2	11.2
Mid-1980s	13 160 (1986)	30.9	11.1

Sources: World Bank (1994, 1997); Boltho (1992); Townsend (1993). For Poland and Hungary for 1992 and 1993, data are from the Hungarian and Polish Household Income Surveys.

In developing countries, the available evidence points to similar trends. In the case of Latin America, in eight countries (Argentina, Bolivia, Brazil, Guatemala, Honduras, Mexico, Panama and Venezuela), the top 10 per cent were the biggest or only winners during the 1980s, whereas in four countries (Bolivia, Guatemala, Panama and Peru) the bottom 20 per cent were hurt disproportionately (Psacharapoulos *et al.*, 1993). During the early 1990s, in Eastern Europe and Russia, poverty increased massively and income distribution became more uneven – except in the Czech Republic, Slovakia and Hungary. For example, in Poland the population living in poverty is estimated to have increased from 20.5 per cent in 1989 to 42.5 per cent in 1992, and during the same period the Gini coefficient of net per capita household income rose from 0.19 per cent to 0.24 per cent (UNICEF, 1993). Increasing poverty among the majority of the population led to a decrease in the average calories consumed daily per capita from 2891 to 2744 between 1989 and 1992 in Poland and from 3499 to 3218 between 1989 and 1991 in Hungary (UNICEF, 1993). This decline in calorie consumption gives some indication that policies implemented within the framework of systemic economic transition can be socially unjust.

When growth is associated with an increase in the income shares of the top 20 per cent, while the income share of the bottom 20 per cent declines, one cannot argue that economic exclusion has been overcome. On the contrary, in the case of a skewed income distribution, the benefits of growth do not trickle down to the poor and the excluded. This is clearly shown in Table 1.2.

2. The Social Dimension

The concept of social exclusion is rooted in the social tradition of giving a greater weight to *relational* issues, while Sen's concept of entitlements is rooted mainly (but not exclusively) in the economic tradition of giving a greater weight to *distribution*. As we noted above, Sen has extended this concept of his to cover functionings and capabilities. Though related to entitlements, these latter concepts go well beyond the purely economic tradition. An extension of Sen's concept of entitlements to a study of social exclusion requires, *inter alia*, the incorporation of a theory of social or group action (besides changes in relative prices) to change the original distribution of incomes and assets or entitlements to commodities. Gore (1993) examines the concept of entitlements and extends it to a moral economy of provisioning in times of hunger and famine. He argues that socially enforced moral rules can constrain or expand entitlement to food and its distribution in conditions of famine. Interactions between social norms determined by non-governmental institutions and State-enforced legal rules extend beyond gender relations.

Let us take a specific case of access to employment to overcome the exclusion of those who are not integrated into the labour market. Sen's concept of employment mentioned above demonstrates that lack of employment not only denies income and output to those who are excluded; it also fails to recognize their productive role as human beings in society. In other words, employment provides social legitimacy and social status as well as access to income. Access to the labour market entitles individuals to rewards and economic rights that are essential entitlements to full citizenship. It brings with it human dignity, which alleviates the negative effects of exclusion on human beings and increases the scope for social integration (Gorz, 1994).

Other social dimensions included in the entitlement concept concern participation of certain social groups in decision-making as well as the marginalization of such disadvantaged groups as women and ethnic minorities. Studies in India (for example, Tilak, 1987) show considerable gender and caste bias in education. Access to education for men and for higher castes is noted to be higher than for women and for backward castes. At the higher levels of educational attainment, access of backward castes becomes even more restricted. This social phenomenon of unequal opportunities and lack of access is explained by both economic and cultural factors.

In industrialized countries, increasing violence and crime is a reflection of the weakening of relations between individuals on the one hand and between individuals and the state and society on the other. Table 1.3 shows that in many countries the number of prisoners has increased substantially. The incidence of drug-related crimes and adult rapes is also high in several countries.

It is useful to recognize that the term 'social' is rather ambiguous and is used differently by different people. This is especially true when one distinguishes between 'economic' and 'social' well-being. The most commonly used indicators of social well-being relate to access to health and education. This is partly because data on these sectors are easily available although the quality or robustness of these data may be dubious. When it comes to *relational* issues as discussed above, it is difficult to be specific and quantitative. However, indicators of civil and political liberties, which represent relations between the State and individuals as well as among individuals, can give some indication of the strength and weakness of such relations (see Chapter 2).

Three main aspects of the social dimension of exclusion are particularly important: (i) access to social services (for example, health and education, drinking water and sanitation facilities), (ii) access to the labour market (precariousness of employment as distinct from low pay) and (iii) extent of social participation reflected in the extent of weakening of the social fabric, as measured by greater crime, juvenile delinquency and homelessness, and so on). This last category captures relational aspects – relations among individuals as well as between the citizens and the State.

3. The Political Dimension

One of the advantages claimed for the concept of social exclusion is that it includes political dimension. That is, it concerns the denial of certain human and political rights to certain groups of the population. The UNDP (1992, p. 29) notes these rights as: personal security, rule of law, freedom of expression, political participation and equality of opportunity. One can extend this list by including trade union rights (or freedom of association) and the process of democratization in general. After all, democracy provides institutions and opportunities for the fulfilment of political rights and freedoms. According to Marshall (1964), these rights can be grouped into three main categories of

Table 1.3 Violence and crime in industrial countries

Countries by HDI Rank	Prisoners (per 100,000 people)		International homicide by men (per 100,000 people)	Drug crimes (per 100,000 people)	Reported adult rapes (000s)	Suicides (per 100,000 people)	
						Male	*Female*
	1987	*1993*	*1985–90*	*1980–6*	*1986*	*1989–93*	
OECD countries							
Canada	–	45	2.7	225	20.5	21	6
USA	–	–	12.4	234	90.4	20	5
Japan	–	–	0.9	31	1.8	22	11
Netherlands	37	51	1.2	38	1.2	14	7
Norway	46	60	1.6	116	0.3	21	8
Finland	–	62	4.1	–	0.3	45	11
France	89	86	1.4	–	2.9	30	11
Iceland	28	39	0.6	–	–	–	–
Sweden	51	66	1.7	–	1.0	22	10
Spain	70	115	1.7	15	1.5	11	4
Australia	–	–	2.5	–	2.3	21	5
Belgium	67	72	2.3	40	–	–	–
Luxembourg	96	108	1.6	–	–	–	–
Austria	98	91	1.4	77	0.5	32	11
New Zealand	–	–	2.6	–	0.5	24	6
Switzerland	–	81	1.1	129	0.4	30	11
United Kingdom	96	92	1.6	–	–	–	–

Table 1.3 (continued)

Countries by HDI Rank	*Prisoners (per 100,000 people)*		*International homicide by men (per 100,000 people)*	*Drug crimes (per 100,000 people)*	*Reported adult rapes (000s)*	*Suicides (per 100,000 people)*	
						Male	*Female*
	1987	*1993*	*1985–90*	*1980–6*	*1986*	*1989–93*	
Denmark	62	71	1.4	176	0.6	29	16
Germany	85	81	1.2	–	–	23	9
Ireland	55	60	1.2	–	–	17	3
Italy	61	89	2.5	6	0.7	12	4
Greece	41	68	1.2	–	0.6	6	2
Portugal	84	111	2.3	13	0.2	12	4
Central & Eastern Europe							
Czech Republic	–	165	1.3	–	–	28	10
Slovakia	–	136	–	–	–	–	–
Hungary	–	132	3.5	–	1.1	55	18
Latvia	–	–	–	–	–	72	17
Poland	–	160	2.5	–	1.9	25	5
Russian Federation	–	–	9.0	–	–	66	13
Belarus	–	–	–	–	–	49	10
Bulgaria	–	99	4.0	–	0.7	25	10
Estonia	–	–	–	–	–	64	15

Table 1.3 (continued)

Countries by HDI Rank	*Prisoners (per 100,000 people)*		*International homicide by men (per 100,000 people)*	*Drug crimes (per 100,000 people)*	*Reported adult rapes (000s)*	*Suicides (per 100,000 people)*	
						Male	*Female*
	1987	*1993*	*1985–90*	*1980–6*	*1986*	*1989–93*	
Kazakhstan	–	–	–	–	–	38	9
Romania	–	200	–	–	–	–	–
Ukraine	–	–	–	–	–	38	9
Lithuania	–	–	–	–	–	74	14
Albania	–	–	2	1			
Tajikistan	–	–	–	–	–	5	2
North America,	–	–	11.4	233	111	20	5
Western and Southern							
Europe	73	85	1.7	–	10	20	8
OECD	80	88	4.8	–	129	21	7
European Union	77	87	1.7	10	20	7	
Nordic Countries	53	65	2.1	–	2	28	11
Eastern Europe and CIS	–	–	–	–	–	47	10

HDI – human development index.
Source: UNDP (1997), p. 213.
– = not available

citizenship rights: (a) *civil* (freedom of expression, rule of law or right to justice), (b) *political* (right to participate in the exercise of political power) and (c) *socioeconomic* (personal security and equality of opportunity, right to minimum health care and to unemployment benefits, and so on). However, these three sets of rights may not be offered to all citizens. Moreover, citizens may be assured of socioeconomic rights but not political rights (as seems to be the case in China). Thus, progression from civil rights and liberties to political rights and social rights proposed by Marshall is not necessarily valid in practice.

Social exclusion can be interpreted in terms of a denial of the above rights or in terms of *incomplete* citizenship. Deficiencies in citizenship rights may be due to poor enforcement of these rights by the State and the inability of the individuals, social groups and organizations to defend their rights.[3] (For a discussion of citizenship rights in relation to social exclusion, see Gore, 1995.)

We will discuss below the global relevance of the concept of social exclusion, but we can already point out here that the problem of political exclusion takes very different forms in democratic and non-democratic countries. Indeed, in Europe, for instance, political exclusion results less from restrictions in political or human rights than from the lack of political representation and influence of the excluded. The excluded have no voice, because there is no politically relevant representation of their specific interests that would make them a social force. By inhibiting participation, social exclusion creates permanently outvoted minorities. Moreover, social fragmentation has a debilitating effect on institutions and modes of political participation. One of the consequences of this is a fragmentation of social forces together with a growing gap between the masses and political leadership. In contrast, in many other countries, overcoming political exclusion involves a democratic transition to the enforcement of political rights.

The spread of social and economic deprivation in the 1980s has deeply threatened social cohesion. As Mingione (1996b, p. 12) notes about the crisis of full citizenship, the problem is not the revolt of the excluded, because they have no political representation, but rather the weakening of the social bond as a whole in a situation where solidarity and certainties are fading away even for those who are not poor. Nowadays, both employment and family are becoming less stable and thus more problematic and selective in protecting individuals from falling into a cumulative process of deprivation. Mass unemployment, the development of precarious forms of work and the weakening of the systems of kinship and community solidarity are all bringing new forms of vulnerability for an increasing number of people. The concept is based on the processes through which individuals who were formerly well-integrated into society are now facing social and economic vulnerability or exclusion. As a consequence of social fragmentation and the lack of social and political representation of the excluded, mechanisms of solidarity between the fully integrated and the vulnerable or the excluded may break down. The crisis of social cohesion may involve political exclusion and the development of hostile attitudes among the different segments of society. This is illustrated in Figure 1.1.

Figure 1.1 Relationship between economic marginalization, social disintegration and political polarization

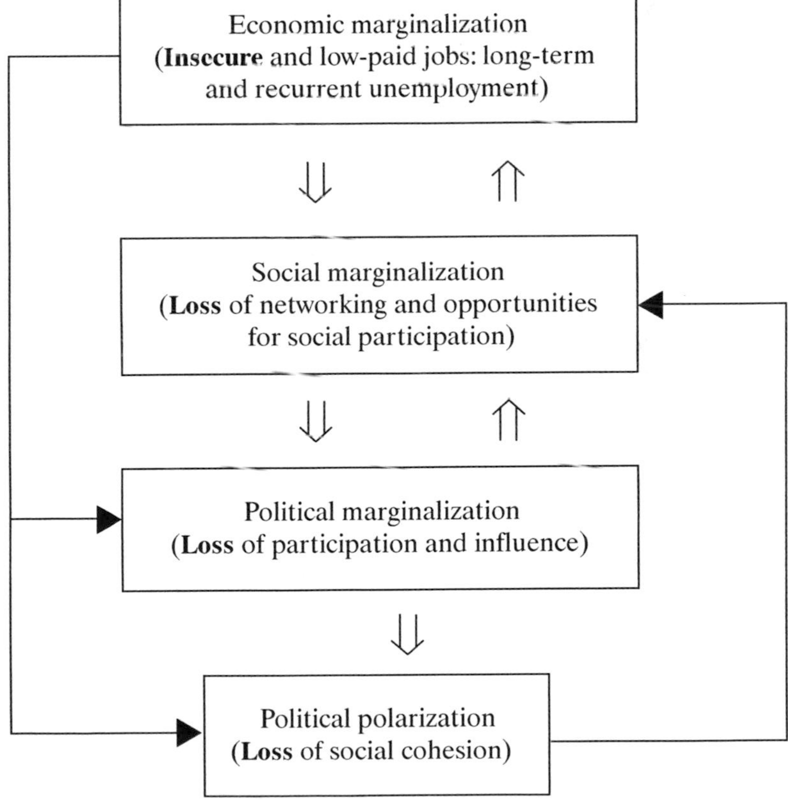

Source: Adapted from Andersen (1996), p. 158.

The economic, social and political dimensions of exclusion discussed above are interrelated. For example, political and civil rights and liberties can draw the best out of people, raising their productivity and thereby contributing to growth and thus overcoming economic exclusion. Are political liberties a necessary condition for overcoming economic and social forms of exclusion? One can argue that these liberties *vis-à-vis* the State give bargaining strength to the excluded to claim inclusion. Violence and wars may be manifestations of this strength 'for the purposes of righting wrongs' (Dasgupta, 1993, p. 122). Freedom also provides a person 'with the *ability* ... to *function* and it values a person's access to and command over certain specific commodities solely because they are a *means* to this ability' (Dasgupta, 1986). Thus, there is clear interdependence between the economic and political aspects of exclusion. Exclusion can be reduced when access to economic and political goods is increased.

The Role of the State

The political dimension of exclusion discussed above involves the notion that the state, which grants basic rights and civil liberties, is not a neutral agency but a vehicle of the dominant classes in a society. Its support for particular classes is reflected in prevailing policies and programmes. Such a bias may be rationalized on pragmatic economic grounds (for example, capital accumulation) or political expediency (as with support of rich farmers and industrialists).

Thus, the role of the State is important for overcoming social exclusion. But this role is being redefined in a new framework of political economy under which markets and the private sector are replacing many of the old functions of the government sector. The emergence of social organizations may help achieve simultaneously the objectives of improved state performance, increased social welfare and greater participation in decision-making. But these organizations may not emerge spontaneously; the State may have an important role to play in their creation and use as intermediaries between government and people.

Social exclusion may also be overcome more directly through government intervention and legislation. Special admissions quotas for educational institutions granted to minorities in China and to backward castes in India are examples of positive discrimination in favour of the underprivileged or socially excluded (Bhalla, 1995; Appasamy *et al.*, 1996). Similarly, in the US, affirmative action programmes and 'bussing' have the objectives of improving access of Afro-Americans and other racial minorities (historically excluded and underprivileged groups) to education and employment. But whether these actions to include some social groups lead to the exclusion of others (because of competing claims on limited resources as noted above) is also a relevant and practical policy issue which underlines the importance of the economic factor. These actions may nevertheless be necessary to overcome deep-seated prejudices that deliberately exclude certain segments of society.

Overcoming social exclusion requires a new approach to the role of the State. In the hegemonic Liberal doctrine, active public policies reflect vested interests, which lead to economic waste, which in turn, involve a welfare cost. A minimal state associated with economic growth policies is often recommended in the expectation that growth will increase the well-being of the population without the need for any state intervention.

One can explain the weakening of the welfare state in Europe in terms of the rising cost of providing social protection, and the failure of the State to raise sufficient resources to include everyone in the welfare system. The resource base for such a system is being eroded by rising unemployment and shrinking social security contributions, as well as by an ageing population. (The baby boomers are close to retirement, which leaves a heavy burden on the social security system, with fewer wage-earners contributing to it.) In discussing the myopia of the political process (discounting of the future costs and benefits), Wolf (1990) explains how the growth of redistributive welfare programmes in Europe and the United States in the 1960s and 1970s was due to an overestimation of the social and political benefits from such programmes, and an underestimation of their long-term costs.

Control of exclusion calls for a proactive social policy based on (i) an understanding of the mechanisms causing exclusion and (ii) democratic institutions of social control. The State needs to play a major role in defining such policy. Institutional creativeness is required to empower excluded groups and promote their effective representation in the process of policy definition. Social policies may involve the creation of new institutions or the modification of existing ones in order to build social consensus. To ensure that such consensus is achieved, these policies need to be rooted in people's own analysis of their situation and needs. The notion of a concerted economy developed by the pioneers of French planning after the Second World War (Massé, 1991) is particularly interesting because it emphasizes the role of the State in order to allow a positive dialogue between the different social actors. By reinforcing the links between individuals and society, information and consultation processes can reduce failures in the implementation of public policies.

RELEVANCE OF THE CONCEPT TO DEVELOPING COUNTRIES

The term 'social exclusion' has not been widely used in social or economic debate in developing countries. Nevertheless, the concept is not Eurocentric; it has wide applicability, since by focusing on the processes of impoverishment and non-material aspects of deprivation it provides a broader view of deprivation and disadvantage than does a traditional poverty approach. A vast literature exists on structural processes generating poverty, deprivation or inequality, which is relevant to our understanding of the processes and practices of exclusion and social institutions that regulate or monitor it in developing countries. Work by the International Institute of Labour Studies (IILS) suggests that an important feature of the concept is that it drives attention away from attributing poverty to personal failings and directs it towards societal structures. Secondly, it focuses on the 'destructive synergies' between different kinds of disadvantages, whereby disadvantages in one sphere spill over into others, rendering some social groups to be what Walzer calls 'radically disadvantaged' (Gore and Figueiredo, 1997, pp. 30–1).

While this new analytical framework has global relevance, we should note that specificities in terms of culture and history will shape particular forms of exclusion and and any policies that may be implemented to fight them. Innovative empirical research within the framework of the IILS programme on social exclusion was conducted in selected developing countries and countries in transition to explore the global relevance of the concept and practice of exclusion. Work under the programme has shown that social exclusion occurs within all societies, even if it results from different processes, if it manifests itself in different forms or even if the perceptions about it are changing according to the societal systems and the mode of integration of the country in question into the global economy. This is the reason why adopting a social exclusion approach implies analysing this macro–micro relationship and proposing meso-level and institution-centred policies (Gore and Figueiredo, 1997, p. 7).

Moreover, as Maxwell (1998) argued, there are two types of convergence between the North and the South in the context of globalization, namely, convergence of: (i) characteristics, and (ii) issues discussed. Perhaps for the first time since the 1930s, the phenomena of unemployment and poverty have become common to both the developed and the developing countries. We noted above that Europe today is characterized by growing poverty and high rates of long-term unemployment (see Chapter 3). In North America, although long-term unemployment is not growing, poverty and inequality are. The poverty situation in many developing countries has also become more acute than ever. Furthermore, the world economy is changing very rapidly; the process of globalization underway (see Chapter 6) calls for major structural changes in both North and South.

A plea for making exclusion a global rather than a European concept is based on the assumption that the analytical concepts and categories are universal even if their operationalization in specific social and cultural contexts may be different. Furthermore, the *distributional* and *relational* problems mentioned above are relevant to both industrialized and developing countries, although distributional equity may be particularly important for low-income countries with very unequal income distribution and the absence of welfare measures and social security systems. The protagonists of a global approach to exclusion suggest that it provides an organizing theme that can help integrate into a general framework different loosely connected notions such as poverty, the lack of access to goods and services and absence of social and political rights (Faria, 1995).

In the *normative* perspective, the protagonists invoke the transfer of experiments tried in developing countries to situations in industrialized countries as an argument in favour of the universality of the concept. Some of the innovative approaches experimented in low-income countries for poverty alleviation – such as non-formal credit systems – are becoming more and more relevant for industrialized countries facing problems of unemployment, poverty and exclusion.[4] The increase in unemployment in Europe – especially of long-term unemployment – has led to a debate on the exclusion of individuals or groups from access to credit.

However, as we will show in Chapter 2, there are important differences in the dimensions of exclusion according to the level of development and the nature of the political system. In particular, the issues of exclusion and poverty will be more closely intertwined in developing countries than in industrialized countries where relational aspects are more important.

CONCLUSION

Our objective in this monograph is not to analyse exclusion *per se,* but the specific forms that the processes of exclusion have taken since the late 1970s as a result of globalization, the evolution of the labour market towards flexibility, the crisis of the welfare state and the rise of individualism. Indeed, if the term exclusion in sociology is relatively new, its meaning can be seen in various forms according to the different socioeconomic contexts in many ancient societies – as, for example, in the case of ancient Athenian ostracism, the condition of the pariah in the Hindu civilization, the banishment from ancient Roma or the ghetto in the middle ages (Freund, 1993).

We will develop an analytical framework that does not focus on social exclusion as a final stage characterizing social and economic deprivation, but instead, on the dynamic processes that create those states and push individuals from a zone of integration to a zone of precariousness, vulnerability and finally, exclusion. As Castel (1995a) notes, the intermediate zone of vulnerability, which has rapidly increased in the 1980s and 1990s is crucial (see Chapter 4 below). Our objective is to point to the different paths leading to precariousness and exclusion.

The rise in long-term unemployment and precarious jobs is at the core of the approach to social exclusion used in this monograph. As we will show in Chapter 3, these phenomena are at the heart of the process through which individuals or groups are wholly or partially excluded from full participation in society within which they live. Indeed, the strength of the links between the employment situation and other dimensions of economic and social life (family, income, living conditions and social contacts) suggests that those people in situations of occupational precariousness – whether they are in an insecure job or are unemployed – have a great risk of becoming excluded from society.

2 Towards an Analytical and Operational Framework

Having defined the concept of exclusion in economic, social and political terms, our next task is to examine whether these three dimensions can be integrated into a coherent analytical, conceptual and operational framework. This is the chief concern of this chapter. We examine the three dimensions in respect of two chief aspects, namely, the *distributional* (economic) and the *relational* (social and political) for this purpose. We also explore whether suitable indicators of social exclusion can be found to make the concept testable and operational. The framework presented in this chapter is then tested in Chapters 3 to 6.

We showed in Chapter 1 that while the notion of social exclusion was related to that of poverty, it clearly concerned much broader issues. Even the concept of poverty has more recently been broadened to cover not only its economic or distributional dimension but also the social relations underlying its economic causes. The concept has also been redefined in terms of popular participation of the poor in decisions of a social, economic and political nature, so that the poor are now *included* in some sense rather than being entirely *excluded* from society.

While the broader and redefined notions of poverty bring it closer to that of social exclusion, we argued in Chapter 1 that the latter nevertheless has some novel and special connotations for an analysis of social issues that distinguish it from poverty. Our thesis is that the concept of social exclusion pertains to the interaction of distributional and relational problems of human relations, and is thus more comprehensive than the concept of poverty. We turn to this issue below.

DISTRIBUTIONAL AND RELATIONAL PROBLEMS

If *distribution* and *relations* are fundamental to the concept of social exclusion, it is essential to explore the relationships between these two variables. Some writers (Room, 1994, 1995a) have adopted the rather simplistic view that poverty is primarily focused on *distributional* issues (the lack of resources) while social exclusion is concerned mainly with *relational* issues (the lack of social ties to the family, friends, local community, state services and institutions or more generally to the society to which an individual belongs). The fact is that social problems associated with exclusion (namely, infant mortality, education, literacy, and so on) are partly income-determined. In a market economy, the abundance of basic needs goods is not much consolation to those who do not have the means to buy them. Thus, a distributional dimension also reflects the opportunities to achieve valuable 'functionings' and should not be regarded as unidimensional. Adequate levels of income are a *necessary* though not a *sufficient* means of ensuring the access of people to education, health and other basic human needs.

Furthermore, the notions of ownership, control and access involve social relations embodying property rights. These social relations and the structure of property rights determine the distribution of wealth and income in a given society. But social relations are also in turn influenced by economic factors such as income inequalities. Relations between the state and individuals or social groups are influenced by the economic muscle that the latter enjoy *vis-à-vis* the state or governmental authority. By virtue of their incomes and assets, the rich are much more powerful and influential than the poor, who, for lack of economic means, education, and so on, are badly organized. Thus, economic might enables the rich to extract civil and political rights and liberties from the state. One may, therefore, argue that economic resources enable access not only to economic goods and services but also to political goods like freedom and the ability to influence economic policies.

In discussing the *relational* aspects of exclusion, it is necessary to bear in mind that the situation may vary between industrialized and developing countries regarding the nature and extent of social relations and their influence on exclusion. These *relational* issues have been treated in both societies, although the focus of relations has been different. For example, relationships between individuals within families and extended households are far more important and stronger in developing countries. Such factors as caste, social class and gender determine social standing and relations among individuals in and out of the labour market. The relationships between the state and the citizen or civil society and the state have been relatively neglected. This dimension of civil and political rights is a distinguishing feature of the notion of exclusion which sets it apart from that of poverty.

Social relations between individuals and between individuals and the state are regulated by moral rules, social norms and organizations and institutions. Coleman (1988, 1990) and Putnam (1993a, 1993b) defined these norms as 'social' capital as distinct from physical and human capital. Three elements of 'social' capital are crucial: (i) the level of trustworthiness and the social environment that determine social obligations and expectations arising from relations between individuals; (ii) the channels of information and (iii) social norms. All three notions of social capital are relevant to the analysis of social exclusion and social integration and may grow out of such attributes as family and religion, and networks and institutions (Zucker, 1986).

Social relations have been defined by sociologists in terms of social norms, mechanisms and institutions that generate or sustain trust, or what Lyons and Mehta (1997) call 'socially oriented trust (SOT)'. But there may also be 'self-interested trust (SIT)', incentives for which 'are intentionally, in direct response to the presence of behaviourial risk' (p. 243). Such risk arises out of uncertainty about the behaviour of others. Coleman's thesis discussed above provides a bridge between the social norms and sanctions and self-interested behaviour. However, the following discussion and that in Chapters 3 to 5 is confined mainly to social norms of obligation and cooperation which are essential components of social cohesion.

Social obligations and expectations provide security or insurance against risk that may be particularly strong among families, friends and kinship networks. Information channels, both formal and informal, reduce transaction costs. As we will discuss in Chapter 3, these channels also facilitate job search and occupational mobility. Finally, social norms, particularly in developing societies, regulate modes of human behaviour and interaction. They promote collective action and group behaviour. In industrial societies, more formal laws and regulations take the place of these norms.

While 'social' capital has properties and characteristics similar to those of human and physical capital – it can depreciate over time for lack of renewal or maintenance of relations – it also has others that differ in many respects. For example, it is more of a public good than human and physical capital which is privately owned or embodied. Human or physical capital is not a full substitute for 'social' capital, because the former is less likely to act as insurance against risk and is more unevenly distributed (see Coleman, 1990, p. 653). Social exclusion adversely affects social capital formation by leading to vulnerability in the labour market, the tearing of family bonds and social deprivation (see Chapters 3 and 4).

Family, Community and the State

Three institutions and organizations which provide support and sustain individuals and social groups are the family, the community and the state. These institutions also help build the social capital of a society. However, while the institutions of the family and the state are quite straightforward, that of the community has different connotations which need some elaboration. The concept of the community is open-ended, and in common language embraces neighbourhoods, villages, ethnic groups, business and academia and so on. Taylor (1982, pp. 25–32) distinguished between three main characteristics of the concept: (a) common beliefs and values, (b) direct and many-faceted relations among members, and (c) reciprocity, that is, forms of cooperation and sharing based on some notion of social goodwill and altruism. Individual communities will differ in respect of the above characteristics depending on their size, motivation and the nature of commitment and values. Commitment to beliefs, relations among individual members and mutual goodwill are likely to be stronger, *ceteris paribus*, among a small community than a large one because 'in a large and changing mass of people, few relations between individuals can be direct or many-sided, and reciprocity cannot flourish on a wide scale' (Taylor, 1982, p. 32).

In order to examine the growth or decline of social capital, one needs to analyse different types of human relations that prevail in both industrialized and developing countries. Three main types of such relations are discussed below:

1. Relationships Within Families and Extended Households

We noted above that community is a multifaceted concept. The basic attributes of a community, namely, relations among members, common values and beliefs and reciprocity, may also apply to the family, which is a smaller unit than the community. There is evidence of this in the family businesses of China or Korea, for example (Fukuyama, 1995a, 1995b). The economic role of the family in employment placement, education, social insurance against risk and so on has been analysed by some economists. Becker (1974, 1976) shows how the head of the family takes account of the utility of the family members in his own utility function (he cares about the welfare of the family).

Both family and community provide social insurance against risk and uncertainty. In many developing societies, management systems are still based on the trust and loyalty of family members, who are hired in preference to outsiders (for example, the Birla family of leading Indian industrialists is known to prefer family members). The family contract creates collective identity among members, which facilitates transactions with the outside world (see Ben-Porath, 1980). But even within families, trust and loyalty may not be guaranteed; preferences, love and hate prevail among family members, and the possibility of conflict and emotional blackmail cannot be excluded. In this context, some cultures emphasize family relations to the exclusion of others which may limit the economic contribution of the family. On the other hand, when family bonds and non-kinship bonds reinforce each other, family-based enterprises may be more productive (Fukuyama, 1995b).

In industrialized countries, the state provides a safety net against risk and uncertainty through social welfare services and unemployment benefits. The welfare state in Europe provides risk insurance and security which, in developing countries, is provided by the family, kinship networks and the community. (For details of these informal mechanisms of social support, see Chapter 5.) There is a notable exception, however, in the case of industrialized countries such as Japan, where, in addition to social welfare provided by the state, employers make a long-term commitment to labour, which in turn offers loyalty to the employer.

Family relations are still important in many developing countries but families themselves have been reduced to nuclear or single-parent entities in many industrialized countries. One can argue that at higher stages of development with growth of affluence and the provision of welfare services, these family ties and kinship relations tend to weaken or break down altogether.

2. *Communal Relationships*

Communal relations are more prevalent in developing countries and in such socialist countries as China than in industrialized countries. They are governed by social norms as well as by modes of property rights and ownership. Some property, even if it is privately owned, may have its use restricted in some ways. For example, ownership of a house does not entitle its owner to make extensions to it without permission from the local authority. In pastoral societies, property is generally owned collectively. In industrialized countries such as Japan, communal relations are governed largely by cultural and religious factors. For example, the paternalistic system in industry and social cohesion between labour and management in Japan mentioned above, is determined largely by culture, group loyalty and ethics. The Japanese group-oriented society is based on relational contracts in business and caring and benevolence as moral obligations or duty in private and social life (see Dore, 1986).

In Western industrialized societies, even when the notion of community in terms of mutuality of interests of social groups and the sharing of costs and benefits is a reality, it may have negative effects in the form of social polarization rather than the intended benefits of keeping exclusion under control. The community may consist of antagonistic social groups (crime gangs, for example) organized to promote conflict (see Jordan, 1996, p. 164). The emergence of the *mafia*, for example, as a major form of social organization in Italy and the US, may reflect weak community bonds. For community to promote social welfare and alleviate exclusion, it is essential that the principle of moral duty to share and aim at collective good overrides considerations of private self-interest.

With the growth of individualism, social interaction tends to be weakened in both developing and industrialized societies (see Chapter 4). However, even in industrialized societies where individualism tends to be stronger, self-interest and social goodwill (or benevolence to others in society) may exist side by side.

Thus, it follows from the above that individualism erodes relational contracts and trust relationships, whereas social groups and community-based systems strengthen them. One can argue that a sense of common purpose and social commitment and obligations are stronger in homogeneous than heterogeneous societies, and among poor as opposed to affluent societies. An increase in exclusion, besides poverty, must imply that reciprocity relations, common beliefs and values and sense of purpose decline over time.

3. Relationships Between the State and the Citizen

Relationships between the state and the citizen may exist in several areas: the socioeconomic, the legal, and that of political rights and liberties. Socioeconomic rights of citizens may not be accompanied by any political rights. Also, they may not be backed by any legal sanctions.

The emergence of 'new poverty', precariousness in the labour market and social deprivation – these phenomena exclude an increasing number of individuals from full citizenship. As noted in Chapter 1, within a Marshallian framework citizenship can be defined as full and equal participation in the community, and welfare seen as a fundamental citizenship right. In particular, Marshall and Bottomore (1992, p. 18) argued that 'citizenship is a status bestowed on those who are fully members of a community. All who possess the status are equal with respects to the rights and duties with which the status is endowed'. Thus social exclusion can be seen from this perspective as incomplete citizenship. The present trend towards exclusion of a growing part of the population constitutes a serious challenge to social cohesion, because citizenship is the basis of social integration in capitalist societies where conflicts are endemic.

The loss of social citizenship right guaranteed by the welfare state and the regulatory authorities highlight a crisis of the relationship between the state and its citizens. Indeed, for Marshall only a welfare state could reduce inequalities and enforce citizenship rights to preserve social cohesion. The irrelevance of the traditional welfare mechanisms to alleviate social exclusion explained the failure of the state regarding these two objectives. Therefore, for a large part of society the nature of the link between the individual and the state is changing fundamentally, from a full exercise of citizenship – at least theoretically – to an increasing dependence on the institution of social assistance and to the weakening of the political representation of a growing proportion of the population which is associated with material and social deprivation.

However, if the welfare state has not been able to protect citizenship rights, at the same time there is a trend towards passive citizenship which implies an active participation in democratic life and a deep involvement in the future of society. This trend results from the rise of individualism and the development of the welfare state, which have deeply affected *horizontal* solidarity networks among individuals. There is a strong tendency among citizens to believe that the social problems will be solved by the state (through the *vertical* mechanism of state–individual solidarity), so that they do not have to get involved, despite the fact that tearing of the social fabric adversely affects the whole society.

While relations (1) and (2) are governed by social norms, religious guidelines or cultural factors, relation (3) requires state action and enforcement. Relation (1) need not call for any state action, while (2) may be deliberately promoted through such action (the so-called Hobbesian solution of coercive state action to generate cooperation). Furthermore, while (1) and (2) have become less important in industrialized countries, (3) is common in both developing and industrialized countries, although even in the latter the decline in the welfare state has weakened this relationship.

It is only the first and, to a lesser extent, the second type of relations that may decline with growth of individualism and self-interest. The third type of relation is unlikely to be adversely affected. In such industrialized societies as the Japanese, the cultural factors noted above explain why individualism has not grown as much as might have been expected.

Relations, Growth and Distribution

How do relations and trust summed up in 'social' capital interact with economic and distributional patterns and physical and human capital? Do social cohesion and solidarity promote faster growth and a more equitable distribution?

Coleman and Putnam argue that social capital enhances returns on investment in physical and human capital, and that this contributes to economic growth. Social capital is the foundation for good economic performance, because it enables the mobilization of resources and energy of the population. Since economic performance is embedded in the existing social structures, a decline in social capital is likely to slow down growth.

Furthermore, lack of social interaction and cohesion (lower social capital) can raise transaction costs and lead to suboptimal resource allocation. There is abundant literature on transaction costs (Ben-Porath, 1980; North, 1990) which examines such causal factors as costs of searching and acquiring information and costs involved in protecting rights and enforcing laws and regulations. Wallis and North (1986) have made quantitative estimates of these costs for the US economy during the century 1870–1970 showing that as a percentage of GDP they nearly doubled in 100 years, rising from 25 per cent to 45 per cent. This increase in transaction costs is explained in terms of the increased role of government, the shift from nonmarket to market activities, growing urbanization and technological change.

Transaction costs are likely to be higher in societies with high inequalities than those with low inequalities. Inequalities not only generate (economic) exclusion, but they also entail higher social expenditure on health care, crime control or law and order, public security and so on. This expenditure may be at the expense of capital accumulation and may thus slow economic growth and employment generation, thereby reinforcing exclusion. Alesina and Perotti (1994, p. 362) also highlight this unstable link between income distribution and growth by noting that the enforcement costs of inequality may take the form of high levels of expenditure on work supervision, security personnel, police, prison guards and the like, crowding out productive investment and other productivity-enhancing policies. Bowles and Gintis (1995, p. 409) note: 'Inequality fosters conflicts ranging from lack of trust in exchange relationships and incentive problems in the workplace to class warfare and regional clashes. These conflicts are costly to police.' Lack of trust and reciprocity between federal and provincial governments in Canada is noted to raise transaction costs by 'consuming huge amounts of time and energy' while it 'prevents effective problem solving on issues like the social safety nets which are of great consequence for the well-being of citizens' (see Maxwell, 1996).[1]

Transaction costs can be both measurable and non-measurable. The costs associated with low social capital or cohesion, high level of exclusion, social disintegration, lack of trust and so on may not be easily measurable, but they remain important. As we show in Chapter 3, the social costs of long-term unemployment (particularly in Western Europe) occur not only in terms of output forgone, but also in terms of depreciation of human and social capital, loss of human dignity, greater violence, crime and precariousness of employment.

In international comparisons, the more market-oriented industrial relations are not necessarily the more successful ones (Boyer, 1991). Indeed, Boyer shows that coordinating mechanisms implementing more cooperative values between managers, workers, subcontractors and banks – as represented by the German model – are more efficient in international markets than conflict-prone societies which rely on markets to monitor relations between capital and labour. The building of trust, loyalty and quality is the engine of competitiveness, and consequently of growth. Equally suggestive of a positive relationship between egalitarian institutions and policies, on the one hand, and economic performance, on the other, is the fact that the advanced capitalist countries, taken as a whole, have grown faster under the golden age of the post-Second-World War welfare state than during any other period for which relevant data exist. Bowles and Gintis (1995, p. 414) note that 'In historical retrospect, the epoch of the welfare state of social democracy was also the Golden Age of capitalism.'

Fukuyama (1995a) contrasts countries with healthy and abundant endowments of social capital (Germany, Japan and the United States) with countries and regions characterized by low trust (Hong Kong, Taiwan, Italy and France). He argues that a high degree of social cooperation is required for launching economic activities by organizations (instead of individuals) as is the case in both Japan and the United states. Rather than being asymmetrical, the experiences of both societies were similar in pioneering 'the development first of the corporate form of business organization and later the smaller, decentralized network' (p. 90).

We argue that the *distributional* and *relational* aspects of exclusion discussed above are interrelated, irrespective of the stage of economic development of a country. This relationship is depicted in Figure 2.1, which measures on the vertical axis the level of economic development, and on the horizontal axis the ratio of the two aspects. The lower part of the curve (representing a situation in developing countries) shows that at the lowest stage of development, far greater

Figure 2.1 Relationship between distributional/relational ratio and levels of economic development

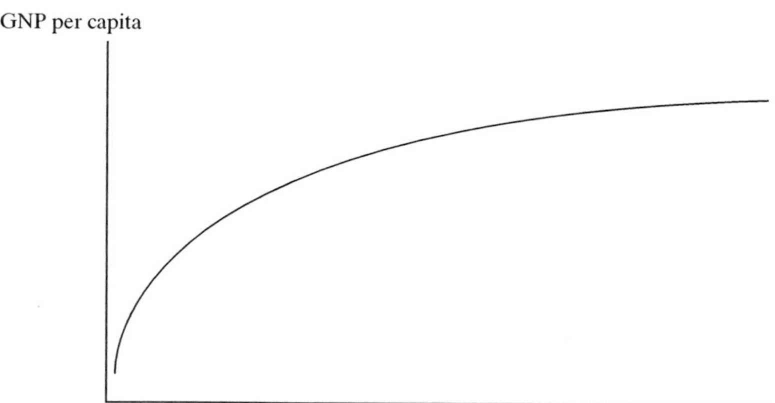

weight is given to the *distributional* than to the *relational* aspects. The upper part of the curve, which is flat, depicts the situation in industrialized countries. It shows almost equal weights to distributional and relational aspects. In general, a combination of the two aspects of exclusion may be present in differing mixes depending on economic and technological factors. In the context of scarce resources, overcoming material deprivation is perceived to be the main objective of low-income countries and receives priority over that of preserving social interactions. The following statement by Dasgupta (1993, pp. 46–7) seems to suggest a similar argument:

> *We may view the state of economic development as a parameter of the social contract. It is possible that political and civil rights would not be awarded priority over socioeconomic rights in a hypothetical social contract written by citizens of a poor society. It would be a mistake to conclude from this that political liberties would not, or do not, matter to the poor… They matter very much. Nevertheless, the relative weights on various categories of rights in a social contract may well depend on the state of economic development.*

Figure 2.1 depicts mainly the *distributional* and *relational* aspects in respect of category (3) above. As we noted above, family and communal relationships are important at low levels of income. This is because in low-income developing countries the state does not take care of problems arising out of income inequalities. There are no social welfare or formal security mechanisms as redistributive devices.[2] As poverty and low incomes are also associated with higher risk, uncertainty and vulnerability (see Chapter 3), the family and kinship relationships and religious groups act as social insurance and redistributive mechanisms. They also serve to promote interpersonal relations and the social identity of individual members. Social security is generally provided through control over land, through employment and through public provision of basic needs (see Osmani, 1991). Since the implementation of structural adjustment programmes began in developing countries several years ago, the state has been increasingly deprived of resources for the implementation of social policies and programmes. Therefore, specific solidarity networks, extended families and social groups (which had almost disappeared in industrialized countries but are being revived) have become much more important as social safety nets.

In industrialized countries on the other hand, since the Second World War the welfare state has provided a special institutional framework for an economic therapy for social ills. In most developing countries, this welfare system does not exist. Fighting social exclusion, when a welfare state is operating to provide a minimum social safety net for individuals and their families, is not the same thing as fighting it in situations when no such social safety net exists and when a majority of the population is excluded from adequate livelihoods. In the latter case, the *distributional* aspect becomes the most important because one of the most fundamental rights of an individual is not to die of starvation (see Sen, 1990).

The *relational* aspect may be more important in the case of industrialized countries because people already enjoy access to a minimum of survival income. Here the *quality* of the relationship between the individual and society is at the heart of the phenomenon of social exclusion. Sen's recognition aspect (mentioned earlier) in this case is more important than the income aspect, even though the two are closely linked. Indeed, in Europe exclusion is resulting less from political or human rights restrictions or from limited access to basic needs goods than it is from criteria of personal achievement that are socially determined (Brown and Crompton, 1994, and Chapter 4). The latter reflects the symbolic recognition of the individual in society. In a recent European survey, 70 per cent of the people interviewed considered that 'in order to have a decent life, it is absolutely necessary to be useful to others and to be recognized by society' (Eurobarometer, 1994, p. 7).

NEED FOR AN OPERATIONAL FRAMEWORK

To operationalize the concept of exclusion, one needs a yardstick against which progress can be measured and monitored. The impact of government policies, measures and programmes can be examined over time only if improvements can be measured and shortfalls identified and corrected. Moreover, policies and practical action to overcome exclusion and to promote social integration are much more likely to occur and succeed if indicators can show shortfalls that may be embarrassing to governments. As Streeten (1994, p. 236) notes, 'there is considerable political appeal in a simple indicator that identifies important objectives and contrasts them with other indicators'.

The measurement and monitoring of exclusion calls for different weights for its economic, social and political components. It also requires a choice of indicators and their measurement or quantification. While the economic component is more easily quantifiable, the other two pose difficult problems of measurement. Nevertheless, even short of measurement, an identification of indicators, however rough and approximate, can be operationally useful. While 'measures' represent a strong empirical basis of analysis, 'indicators' reflect a rather weak one. Both are useful for obtaining some indication of the magnitude of exclusion and its control and mitigation through appropriate policy measures.

Choice of Indicators

The origins of the concept of exclusion are quite recent. It is, therefore, not surprising that no systematic attempts have yet been made to measure or quantify social exclusion among social groups, countries or regions. But there have been several well-known attempts to measure poverty and well-being (see Dasgupta, 1993; Kanbur, 1994; Sen, 1973, 1976; UNDP, 1990, 1992). Efforts have also been made in the past to study and analyse quantitatively the relationships between economic, social and political variables (see Adelman and Morris, 1965, 1972). It is not our intention to review this literature. Our main interest is to examine the feasibility of building on existing data and indices to measure different components of exclusion.

In many cases, social indicators may be more helpful than the GNP per capita or income distribution in offering some information, even though indirectly, about the exclusion of people from access to basic goods and services. Indeed, the social indicators (for example, life expectancy, infant mortality rate, adult literacy rate, nutritional status, calories per adult equivalent) highlight the *distribution* of well-being in a society in a better way than do the aggregate economic indicators based on income and consumption. Sen (1998, p. 1) argues how, besides influencing life and death, 'mortality information can throw light also on the nature of social inequalities, including gender bias and racial disparities'.

Thus, a new operational framework for social exclusion needs indicators that will assess 'social-relations deprivation' (Penz, 1986) as well as the permanence of and intergenerational nature of the structural (rather than cyclical) aspects of exclusion.

There is a strong tendency to build indexes where several factors are weighted together (see the intense debate on the Human Development Index constructed by UNDP). In the case of social exclusion, the preparation of a composite index calls for a choice of appropriate weights for economic, social and political components. The main questions to be posed are: Would it be useful to develop an operational tool which would depict the net combined effect of economic, social and political dimensions of exclusion? In other words, can a composite index capture all the detail and richness of information? As Sen (1992a) has pointed out, while discussing the merits of a single social progress index,

> it is useful to distinguish between the demands of *comprehension* and those of *emphasis*. If one index is selected among a class of relevant indicators, the intention cannot reasonably be to supplant the entire class altogether by that one index.

We argue that the usefulness of a composite index is problematic: it may not make sense to aggregate economic, social and political indicators, especially when they are not moving in the same direction. Moreover, the weights attached to different indicators will vary according to the different stages of development in different countries.

For guiding policy-makers in their fight against exclusion, a set of separate economic and social indicators would be more useful than a single composite index. Apart from the policy-makers, citizens could also evaluate whether policies implemented by their governments correspond to the priorities resulting from a consensus reached on a 'social project'.

Below we define a set of indicators that may give relevant information on the economic, social and political aspects of exclusion:

1. Economic Aspects

On these, the GNP per capita is not an adequate indicator for evaluating the exclusion of individuals or social groups. Such aggregative measures do not reveal large inequalities in income distribution and extreme poverty, which are major manifestations of exclusion. As Sen (1983b) argues, the inhabitants of Harlem are much richer, in terms of income per capita, than people from Bangladesh but the probability of a black living in Harlem to reach forty years of age is lower than that of a starved Bangladeshi. Thus, to estimate the economic aspects of exclusion it may be more appropriate to give greater weight to the depth of poverty and income inequality. The Sen (1976) index or the Foster *et al.* (1984) index can be useful in that case, because they (i) identify different degrees of poverty and (ii) identify distribution of households according to different degrees of poverty. The Gini index or household income shares per decile are also attractive as indicators, since they give information about the unevenness in the distribution of economic assets. Individuals or groups at the bottom of an income pyramid are usually excluded from benefits of growth and access to education and health, decent livelihood, and so on. In the absence of proactive state policies to overcome unequal income distribution, improvements in the well-being of the most disadvantaged groups is generally only weakly correlated with growth performance.

2. *Social Aspects*

Here, three types of indicators may be considered which represent: (i) *access to public goods and services* (access to education and health can be evaluated through life expectancy at birth, infant mortality rate, adult literacy rate or secondary school enrolment, for example), (ii) *access to the labour market* and especially to the 'good' segment of it (rate of unemployment and long-term unemployment, vulnerability or precariousness of employment measured by some yardstick of insecurity and risk, for example, rates of job turnover, proportion of second jobs, assessment of people working in the informal sector, household income trends, and so on), and (iii) *social participation* defined in terms of say, rates of trade union membership and local associations engaged in activities designed to integrate the marginalized groups into the mainstream of civil society. Such indicators would also reflect the declining social fabric or fragmentation of society (for example, crime and delinquency rates). We need to examine whether appropriate indicators are available or can be easily quantified with the existing data bases because too often the available data sources are inadequate for assessing these social aspects (see Chapters 3 to 5 for a discussion of some of the above indicators).

A specific indicator need not necessarily be universally applicable; it may be more or less relevant depending on the stage of development and the socioeconomic system of the country studied. As Anand and Sen (1993) have suggested, we could divide all the countries into different groups corresponding to different levels of development. In the low-income group we would have a set of basic indicators focusing principally on the distributional aspects, whereas, in the high-income group, more complex indicators (pertaining to relational aspects) could be considered for evaluating the breakdown of the social fabric of society (homelessness, crimes rates, drug addiction, and so on). For example, increasing crime rates (especially in big cities) could be measured by an increase in the hiring of security guards to protect life and property. Reich (1991) shows that the number of private security guards in the United States doubled between 1979 and 1990, to reach 2.6 per cent of the country's workforce, outnumbering public police officers. Jordan (1996) notes that in the UK also there are more private security guards than employees of the police force. Taking another example of the declining social fabric, the prison population of the United States doubled between 1960 and 1980 and between 1980 and 1990. The American Correctional Association (1990) forecast another doubling by 1995. In Eastern Europe and Russia the number of crimes also considerably increased during the present phase of transition. If we take 1989 as a base year (1989=100), the total number of crimes in 1992 reached 285.8 in the Czech Republic, 198.4 in Hungary, 178.1 in Poland and 169.4 in Russia (UNICEF, 1993; see also this volume, Chapter 5).

3. Political Aspects

On these, either the political freedom index of Dasgupta (1990, 1993) or that of UNDP (1992), which is very similar, can be used. For the first time, in 1992 UNDP estimated a political freedom index besides a human development index and discussed the relationships between the two indices. A composite index of political freedom is based on five ingredients, namely personal security, rule of law, freedom of expression, political participation and equality of opportunity. UNDP data suggest a positive correlation between (i) the human development index and the political development index, (ii) income levels and political freedoms.[3]

An integration of the UNDP human development index (HDI) and the political freedom index (PFI) would seem to come quite close to a composite index of economic, social and political aspects of exclusion. However, UNDP (1992) preferred to keep the two indices separate because of differences in time scales (the HDI is based on much less volatile factors than the PFI). There is a further problem in combining the two, since the HDI is based on economic opportunities whereas the PFI is independent of them.

Estimation of political indices of the type developed by Dasgupta and UNDP is not new. Several earlier authors (namely, Adelman and Morris, 1965; Banks, 1989; Humana, 1983, 1986; Taylor and Jodice, 1983) have attempted to estimate political rights and civil liberties on the basis of a scoring system for different degrees of political freedom and freedom of expression. These attempts have led either to an ordinal ranking of countries as good, bad or worst, or to a partially ordered clustering of countries (see Banks, 1989). The difficulty with most of these quantitative attempts is that they are subjective and impressionistic, since they are based on normative judgments. While economic indicators are fairly universal, social and political indicators tend to be particularly culture-specific. We noted above that individualism is stronger in some cultures than in others. In countries where it is weak and community action and behaviour is strong, one may well expect relatively limited importance of individual liberties and rights. The notion of human freedom in these societies is likely to be different from that prevailing in Western industrial societies. There may, therefore, be room for controversy and disagreements regarding the values which may influence the choice of particular political indicators. These different perceptions, by countries and researchers and investigators, further complicate quantification of political indicators of exclusion and inclusion.

Notwithstanding, one can safely say that authoritarian and repressive regimes without any elections would be associated with a higher degree of political exclusion of individuals and groups than multi-party and open democratic systems. However, definition of an open democratic system and its elements is not so clearcut. Equally fraught with conceptual and measurement problems is the definition of what constitutes abuse of human rights (see McNitt, 1988).

Finally, the economic, social and political indicators of exclusion may often be correlated. The levels of human rights and their enforcement may be associated with the standards of living, average incomes, literacy rates and ethnic and religious diversity. For example, an illiterate person is much more likely to be politically excluded than an educated one who is conscious of rights and enjoys greater access to institutions designed to enforce these rights. One may argue that political rights are more likely to be observed at higher stages of economic development of a country than at lower stages. Similarly, indicators of economic inequalities are likely to be positively correlated with those of social and political conflict. High levels of discrimination (for example, against non-citizens, immigrant workers and religious minorities) will be associated with political unrest and internal conflict (see Taylor and Jodice, 1983).

A MATRIX APPROACH TO EXCLUSION

The above discussion on *relational* and *distributional* issues and on indicators can be presented in the form of a matrix (see Table 2.1).

The horizontal axis measures the elements of exclusion, and the vertical axis different categories, namely, individuals, social groups, countries (including regions within countries) and regions (groups of

Table 2.1 An illustrative matrix of economic, social and political aspects of exclusion

Elements / *Categories*	*Economic* (1)	*Social* (2)	*Political* (3)	*Patterns of development (distributional/ relational outcome)* (4)
I. *Individuals*	–	–	+	Balanced
	–	–	+	Unbalanced
II. *Social groups* – women, youth, the aged – minorities – ethnic groups				
III. *Countries/societies* – regions within countries				
IV. *Regions* – groups of countries (for example, Africa)	+	+	±	Unbalanced

\+ = increase in exclusion
– = decrease in exclusion

countries) for which the degree of exclusion and its outcome and impact may be considered. Disadvantage, be it economic, social or political, can affect individuals, particular social and ethnic groups and whole societies. Individuals may be poor and socially disadvantaged, or they may at least perceive that they are (the notion of exclusion can be subjective, especially as the degree of social interaction is more intangible than material deprivation). The social disadvantage of particular social groups and their nature and identity as well as composition will vary from society to society. For example, in the United States sociologists and economists have been concerned with the underclass and racial discrimination against blacks, minorities and illegal immigrants and others (see Chapter 4). In Western Europe (particularly, France) on the other hand, excluded social groups consist of members of broken families, abused children, single parents, drug addicts, delinquents, the mentally and physically handicapped, women and the long-term unemployed. In contrast, in developing countries, the poorest persons from the lowest social classes and castes, and those disadvantaged on account of gender and religion, would qualify as the excluded.

At higher levels of aggregation, societies and regions within nations may be disadvantaged or alienated. Societies where institutions, laws and social norms are biased against equality of opportunity and access to public goods and services would be particularly strong candidates for the study of social exclusion. Institutions influence both social participation and the means and processes of income acquisition. By affecting access to livelihoods and assets, they can influence income distribution. They may thus be inimical to egalitarian growth.

In such large countries as France, the United States and Brazil, the incidence of poverty and exclusion is likely to vary a great deal within the national boundaries and across regions and states. It is well known that the poor blacks in the US are concentrated in the South, whereas the North in general is more prosperous. Similarly, in Brazil, the Northeast region has been traditionally much poorer than the South (see Chapter 5).

In the literature on social exclusion, mainly the first three categories, namely, individuals, particular social groups and national society, are studied. One can, however, extend the analysis of exclusion to particular groups of countries in the same way as the debates on marginalization and North–South gaps have done.

We now illustrate the different components of social exclusion, taking the specific case of Category I, that is, individuals. An individual's perception of exclusion can be expressed in terms of three types of disadvantage: economic (low income), social (lack of social ties to the family or community) and political (lack of legal or political rights). In the case of Europe, as we noted in Chapter 1, economic and social disadvantage is expressed in terms of individuals who are without a job for prolonged periods (long-term unemployed). Category II, or social groups, may include specific categories that will vary from country to country.

With the emerging global economy, wide disparities in global integration of national economies has been observed (see Holm and Sorenson, 1995; World Bank, 1996a). From a regional perspective, globalization can be seen as a dialectic process increasing integration of OECD countries and NICs as well as the marginalization of a large part of the African continent (see Chapter 6). ILO (1995b) discusses the processes of the marginalization of Africa in terms of the total inflow of foreign direct investment (FDI), participation in world trade or percentage share of global GNP (also see Collier, 1995). Thus, matrix Table 2.1 shows that economic exclusion has increased in Africa. During the 1980s, social exclusion in the form of human insecurity has also increased, considering the process of deindustrialization in many countries, the withdrawal of the public sector and drastic cuts in public expenditure on social services as part of the structural adjustment programmes. However, the case of political exclusion is more complex. While most African countries are democratizing, the spread of liberal-democratic political forms in Africa has not been associated with a real empowerment of the people. In most cases, democracy has been interpreted as free elections without changes in power relations which are at the heart of the concept of democracy.

Table 2.1 shows that the different components – economic, social and political – need not move in the same direction. For example, the socialist state, before its breakdown in the USSR and Eastern and Central Europe, provided a safety net and social rights to the population despite the non-democratic political systems. Under that system, individuals were entitled to social rights without citizenship. In such a situation, the development pattern is unbalanced, and the outcome is indeterminate, as is shown in column (4) of the table, which illustrates the pattern of development according to the nature of the processes of exclusion. Dudley Seers (1969) notes that for development to take place, poverty, unemployment and inequality should all become less severe. He states: 'If one or two of these central problems have been growing worse, especially if all three have, it would be strange to call the result 'Development' even if per capita income doubled.' (p. 3). A determinate situation is the one when exclusion decreases in terms of all three aspects and balanced development *à la* Seers (noted above) takes place.

According to the above matrix, a country/society that is rich in terms of conventional economic indicators can have a low realization of well-being and social cohesion. Thus social change seems to be highly dependent on the pattern of development chosen (information could be given by column (4)). At an aggregative level of a country or society, social exclusion and marginalization are reflected in the nature or state of institutions rather than individuals.

In Chapter 3, we discuss precariousness of employment, which is a particularly useful indicator as it reflects both the distributional and relational aspects of exclusion. Indeed, we will argue that it is a better indicator than 'long-term unemployment', which is generally used in Western Europe.

3 Unemployment, Precarious Jobs and Exclusion

Having presented an analytical framework and a set of indicators of the economic, social and political dimensions of exclusion in Chapter 2, in this chapter we examine the merits and limitations of two specific indicators of social exclusion, namely, long-term unemployment and job precariousness.

While long-term unemployment can generally reflect social exclusion, a low rate of long-term unemployment does not tell us anything about the dynamics of social exclusion. It refers to exclusion *from* the labour market, but there is also exclusion *within* the labour market. In addition to the unemployed, and in particular long-term unemployed, there is a considerable number of people who are underemployed, that is, involuntarily working part-time or on stop-gap training courses or who left the labour market because they considered further job search futile and/or they were encouraged or forced to do so by early retirement schemes. Discouraged workers and those in involuntary part-time employment are estimated at around 13 million in the OECD area (OECD, 1996). They could well be a persistent feature in the future (Stevens and Michalski, 1994, p. 9).

Therefore, it would be more relevant in evaluating the dynamics of exclusion to consider both the rates of long-term unemployment and such other indicators as the proportion of the population (i) working in the informal sector or (ii) trapped in the precarious segment of the labour market (short time horizon, bad working conditions, low earnings, partial or full exclusion from access to social security). The growth of precarious jobs and the rise in inequality among those in employment are also crucial in explaining the transition from integration into the labour market to material and social deprivation (Heady, 1997). This *qualitative* dimension is provided by the precariousness of jobs in which people, even when in employment, suffer from serious social disadvantage, risk and uncertainty. Thus long-term unemployment and precarious forms of work, which are both at the core of the social exclusion approach, are discussed below.

LONG-TERM UNEMPLOYMENT

In Western Europe, consistently rising unemployment and the rapidly swelling numbers of long-term unemployed have become a serious social problem. Unemployment is no longer a purely short-term, cyclical phenomenon; it has structural characteristics. Unemployment, in particular long-term unemployment, remains the major economic and social problem confronting the European Union. In 1995, 50 per cent of those unemployed in the Union were out of work for a year or longer and more than 30 per cent of these for two years or more. This represents a net increase as compared with 1994, when the figures were respectively 48 per cent and 27 per cent. Moreover, 9 per cent of unemployed men and 10 per cent of unemployed women were out of work for at least four years (European Commission, 1996). The implication of this is that, for the Union as a whole, one out of two persons who were out of work for a year are likely to remain unemployed for at least another year and often longer (especially men in Ireland, Italy, the UK and the Netherlands and women in Belgium, Italy and the Netherlands).

Long-term unemployment and the 'new unemployed' in Western Europe are considered to be a symptom of increasing social exclusion from the labour market, which has wider implications for social cohesion in industrialized societies in general. Social polarization is growing between those who have jobs and those who do not. In industrialized countries, employment offers social recognition and is central to social integration, because it involves participation in production and consumption. In the case of France, Paugam (1991) and CERC (1993) show a strong relationship between labour market conditions, poverty and social deprivation (see Chapter 4). Focusing on the dynamics of poverty, Jarvis and Jenkins (1996) established that in the UK about 40 per cent of people entering poverty had experienced a change in their employment condition.

After a long duration of unemployment, unable to find jobs, the unemployed often become unemployable. Out-of-date or lost skills of the unemployed over time make them unfit for employment unless massive and costly training programmes are introduced for their reabsorption. The long-term unemployed (particularly youth) may end up as criminals and delinquents and sometimes they may turn to drug trafficking and petty crimes. Thus, social and human capital is depreciated, and alienation and loss of human dignity is the consequence.

The longer the duration of unemployment, the greater is likely to be the disadvantages from which the unemployed suffer. Women and older people tend to be in this category. Generally, countries with high total unemployment rates also show a high incidence of long-term unemployment (for example, Belgium, Italy and Spain) (see Table 3.1). However, there are exceptions such as Canada, where a high total unemployment rate is associated with a relatively low incidence of long-term unemployment (particularly for more than one year). Generally, the incidence of long-term unemployment is higher among women and young people. This was the case in both France and Germany during the 1980s and early 1990s, especially among women. However, in the case of the UK, long-term unemployment was higher among men. For the OECD as a whole, the incidence for women was slightly higher than for men (OECD, 1996).

Looking at trends, long-term unemployment (12 months and over) increased in Australia, Western Europe (France, Germany and the UK) and North America (US and Canada) since 1990 (see Figure 3.1).

In the welfare states of Western Europe, the permanent or long-term unemployed may be supported by welfare payments. Generous unemployment benefits in many countries account for the relatively high incidence of long-term unemployment by age and gender (OECD, 1994a). It is higher than in those developed countries, such as the United States, where social protection systems are relatively weak. In fact, Western Europe and the United States present a contrasting picture: in the former (with the exception of the UK), unemployment rates have risen over time and wage differentials have remained compressed, whereas in the US the long-term unemployment rate declined between 1982 and 1991 (see Figure 3.1) while wage differentials widened. Indeed, in the US labour market flexibility and a weak welfare system to support long-term unemployed led to the development of low-paid, precarious forms of work and the stagnation or decrease in real wages of a large part of the workers. In Europe, labour market regulation and the welfare state assistance have contributed to preserve standards of living, but unemployment rates have risen sharply.

The lack of safety nets implies that individuals are forced to look for survival through precarious jobs in both the formal and informal sectors. In most developing countries, where social security and other welfare systems are either weak or non-existent, people (except those who are rich) cannot afford to remain unemployed for long periods.

Table 3.1 Unemployment in industrial countries

	Total unemployment rate (%)	*Rates for*		*Incidence of long-term unemployment (%)*				*Involuntary part-time workers*
		Males	*Females*	*More than 6 months*		*More than 12 months*		*(% of total labour force)*
				Male	*Female*	*Male*	*Female*	
	1995	*1993*	*1993*	*1995*	*1995*	*1995*	*1995*	*1993*
North America								
Canada	9.5	11.8	10.6	29	25	14	16	5.5
USA	5.5	7.1	6.5	19	16	14	9	5.0
Japan	3.1	2.4	2.6	44	28	21	13	1.9
Australasia								
Australia	8.5	11.5	10.1	54	47	34	26	6.9
New Zealand	6.3	10.0	8.9	57	45	38	26	6.3
Western and Southern Europe								
Austria	6.7	6.7	6.9	29	32	17	17	–
Belgium	9.7	9.7	17.4	76	79	61	63	3.8
Denmark	11.3	11.3	13.7	52	42	32	25	4.8
Finland	17.1	19.5	15.7	49	45	35	29	2.9
France	11.6	10.0	13.7	67	71	45	47	4.8
Germany	8.2	8.0	8.4	63	68	46	51	1.5
Greece	9.7[a]	6.4	15.2	64	78	42	57	3.1
Ireland	12.9	18.8	19.5	80[a]	72[a]	63[a]	53[a]	3.3

Table 3.1 (Continued)

	Total unemployment rate (%)	*Rates for*		*Incidence of long-term unemployment (%)*				*Involuntary part-time workers*
		Males	*Females*	*More than 6 months*		*More than 12 months*		*(% of total labour force)*
				Male 1995	*Female 1995*	*Male 1995*	*Female 1995*	
	1995	*1993*	*1993*					*1993*
Italy	12.2	8.1	17.3	78	81	62	64	2.3
Luxembourg	2.1[a]	1.5	1.9	48	47	25	21	–
Netherlands	6.5	6.0	7.3	73	75	49	38	5.6
Norway	4.9	6.6	5.2	44	31	29	17	–
Portugal	7.1	4.6	6.5	60	64	46	51	1.8
Spain	22.7	9.9	23.8	67	77	51	62	1.0
Sweden	9.2	–	–	37	32	17	14	6.2
Switzerland	4.5[a]	4.4	4.7	48	54	32	35	–
United Kingdom	8.7	12.4	7.5	66	51	50	32	3.2
Central and Eastern Europe								
Czech Republic	2.9	3.1	4.6	52	53	30	31	–
Slovakia	13.1	12.7	11.7	–	–	–	–	–
Hungary	10.4	14.2	10.1	–	–	–	–	–
Latvia	6.6	5.2	6.4	–	–	–	–	–
Poland	14.9	15.0	17.9	–	–	–	–	–

Table 3.1 (Continued)

	Total unemployment rate (%)	*Rates for*		*Incidence of long-term unemployment (%)*				*Involuntary part-time workers*
		Males	*Females*	*More than 6 months*		*More than 12 months*		*(% of total labour force)*
	1995	*1993*	*1993*	*Male 1995*	*Female 1995*	*Male 1995*	*Female 1995*	*1993*
Russian Federation	3.2	0.4	1.1	–	–	–	–	–
Estonia	4.9	1.7	2.1	–	–	–	–	–
Romania	8.9	8.1	12.6	–	–	–	–	–
Lithuania	7.3	3.8	3.3	–	–	–	–	–
Industrial Countries	6.6	7.0	8.2	–	–	–	–	–
North America	5.9	7.6	6.9	20	17	12	9	5.1
OECD	7.5	7.6	8.9	43	40	28	25	3.8
European Union	11.1	9.4	12.8	66	66	48	47	2.9
Nordic countries	10.2	12.6	11.8	44	37	26	20	5.0
Western and Southern Europe	11.6	8.6	13.5	65	68	47	49	2.8

[a] 1993.
– = not available
Source: UNDP (1996, 1997).

Figure 3.1 Trends in long-term unemployment in selected OECD countries (1982–96)

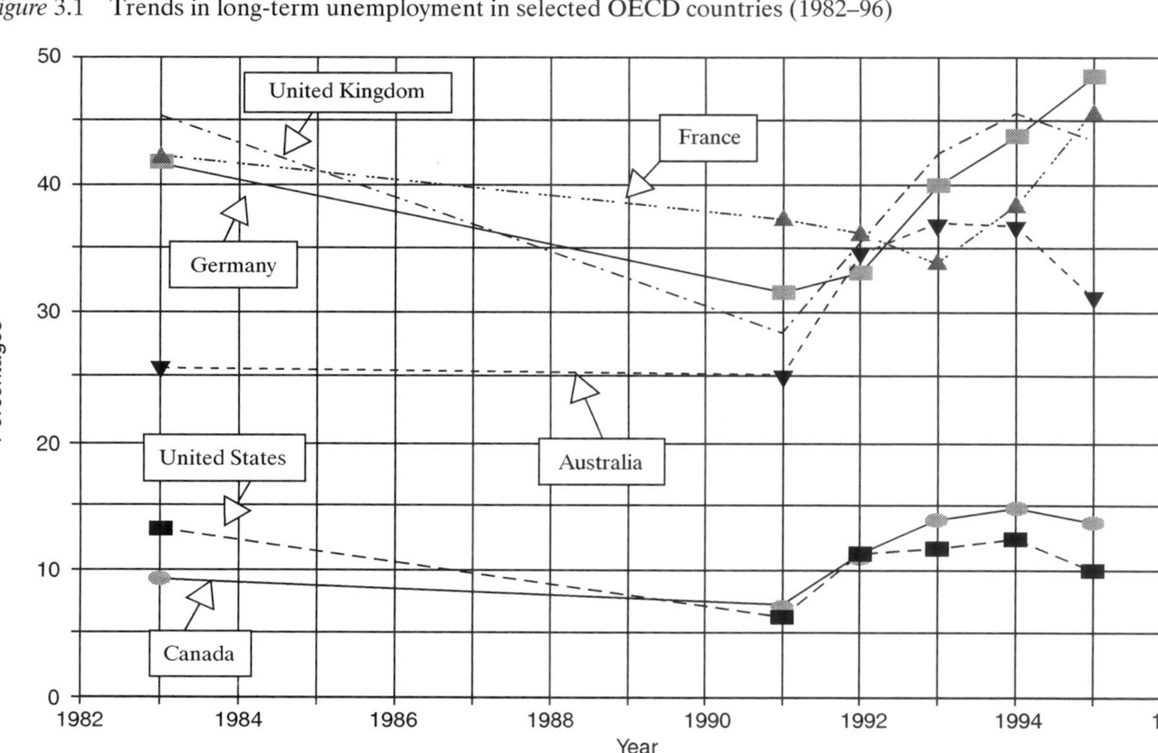

Note: Long-term unemployment (12 months and over) as percentage of total employment.
Source: Based on data from OECD (1996), p. 202.

Citing the National Household Sample Survey for 1983 (the worst year of the recession), Humphrey (1994, pp. 730–1) notes that only 1.5 to 2.6 per cent of active household heads in the metropolitan region of São Paulo (Brazil) were unemployed for more than six months. More recent data for São Paulo show that in 1994 on an average people remained unemployed for only 25 weeks (little over six months); half of them looked for jobs for only 13 weeks (SEADE, 1995). In Chile in 1986, 20 per cent of workers spent 45 weeks or more seeking work, compared with only 7.9 per cent in 1995 (personal communication).

Vulnerability and risk and uncertainty associated with it are the main indicators of exclusion and 'social disaffiliation'. Therefore, an aggregate indicator of long-term unemployment may be less appropriate than a more disaggregated one, for example, long-term unemployment by age, sex and family status. Older people, single parents and long-term unemployed without families (not living with any family members with or without employment) are likely to be more vulnerable than those with families having a bread winner. It would also be more relevant to consider such other indicators as the proportion of the population (i) working in non-standard (part-time and temporary) employment in the formal and informal sectors, (ii) trapped in the 'precarious' segment of the labour market (short time horizon, bad working conditions, low earnings, partial or full exclusion from access to social security) or (iii) occupying a second job.

We argue below that while long-term unemployment is one of the factors causing social exclusion, precarious employment and an increasing number of the 'working poor' are also at the heart of the dynamics of social exclusion. The notion of precarious employment may be of great value in explaining social exclusion, because it reflects vulnerability and insecurity of jobs. It stresses both *relational* and *distributional* dimensions of employment, as well as shifts in the labour market structure that contribute to such insecurity, namely, (i) the development of atypical and precarious forms of work in industrialized countries and (ii) the process of informalization of employment in developing countries.

PRECARIOUS EMPLOYMENT

One of the most important contributions of research on the segmentation of the labour market is the evidence that some groups are trapped in segments where jobs are insecure, ill-paid, and low-skilled. The underlying issue here is the dualization process, with on the one hand, 'bad' jobs with easier access but where poverty is concentrated (the new working poor), and, on the other hand, 'good' jobs with restricted access and which provide a degree of security and acceptable working conditions. This implies that there are different levels of exclusion, so that it is possible to be included in the labour market and at the same time excluded from the 'good' labour market. Thus, for an increasing number of people the emergence of precarious forms of work is associated with an increase in vulnerability.

The concept of precariousness is multidimensional and involves a combination of different factors: instability, lack of protection, insecurity and social and economic vulnerability (Rodgers, 1989). Paugam (1995) shows that several indicators of economic and social precariousness, namely, precarious employment, marital instability, economic poverty, inadequate family life, inadequate support networks and low level of social participation, are correlated so that there is a cumulation of handicaps and disadvantages (also see Chapter 4 for situation prevailing in France). Burchell (1989) notes that a short time horizon or a high risk of job loss leads to inability to plan for the future which is one of the principal causes of the worsening in *psychological* health and mental stress. This provides an additional dimension to the notion of vulnerability and precariousness.

However, precariousness and vulnerability is a complex phenomenon, whose incidence may vary from country to country. But vulnerability arises from an element of risk and uncertainty as well as job insecurity. The threat of losing jobs during a period of economic restructuring in response to globalization (see Chapter 6) may occur in both industrialized and developing countries. Workers may suffer from precariousness in employment on account of several factors: job insecurity resulting from a very short tenure of employment, low wages and incomes which may depend on a particular economic sector, labour status of the workers and gender and caste stratification. But the sources and origins of vulnerability may be different. For example, in industrialized countries vulnerability may be due more to structural characteristics of households (for example, low levels of education or single heads of households) than to factors outside the households. On the other hand, in the case of developing countries uncertainty and risk may be attributed more to factors outside the households; for example, to such exogenous factors as vagaries of weather that characterize agriculture in many parts of the developing world and weak institutions for welfare, credit or social insurance (see Morduch, 1994). Weather can also affect employment in industrialized countries particularly in the construction industry (the high unemployment figures for Germany in the period December 1996 to January 1997 were due largely to the severe winter and drop in building work).

Labour Market Transition: Decline in Stable Employment

The 'lifelong full-time' work pattern which characterized the so-called 'golden age of Fordism' until the late 1970s is progressively disappearing as a result of priority now given to flexibility in both production and labour organization in order to meet the challenge of economic globalization. Labour flexibility is the most frequently discussed form of flexibility. Compared with the long post-war era of full employment and labour security, the 1980s witnessed labour fragmentation and insecurity. A rise in unemployment, and in the number of part-time and temporary jobs, has led to an erosion of employment security.

The highly competitive environment of the emerging global economy has compelled firms to implement technological and organizational innovations that promote flexibility in the production process. Such flexible production often calls for greater labour market flexibility, which may conflict with the notion of 'secure' or 'good' jobs. The notion of 'good' and 'bad' jobs is associated mainly with industrialized countries. It became fashionable since divergence began in the labour market structures and employment conditions between North America and Western Europe. In North America, employment is growing but real wages are declining, whereas in Europe unemployment is growing (with the exception of the UK) but wages are relatively high. Betcherman (1995) notes that in Canada non-standard forms of employment (generally associated with the notion of 'bad' jobs), job insecurity and polarization are the direct result of employers' need for labour flexibility and low labour costs. The new flexible firm-level employment systems are based on low levels of commitment between employers and workers, short job tenures and limited investment in human capital. Firms invest less in training programmes, which generally helped employees climb the corporate ladder in the past.

Organizational innovations and new forms of labour management – within the general framework of flexibility strategies by the firms – have led to the growth of temporary and part-time employment. The advantages of these nonstandard working patterns to employers include:

(i) an increase in the operating time of machinery and equipment, (ii) a reduction in absenteeism, (iii) greater flexibility in adjusting staffing levels to demand fluctuations and (iv) lower labour costs.

In the Fordist regime, work offered a career path and a reasonably predictable and stable income, which formed the basis for durable consumption and investment decisions. This feature of the labour market is related to the central role played by the manufacturing sector. But since the late 1980s there has been a marked decrease in the number of manufacturing jobs in the capitalist advanced countries, whereas a large number of new jobs in the services sector are badly paid, insecure and unstable (Crompton *et al.*, 1996). The forecast regarding job creation is more gloomy than the idealistic vision of Reich (1991) about the rapid growth of knowledge-intensive jobs – the 'symbolic analysts' (managers, lawyers, academics, international consultants) – in the global economy. These new job categories – as systems analysts, computer engineers and other jobs that look like 'symbolic analysts' – will account for a small part of the total employment growth in the future – as compared with the growth of guards, cashiers, janitors and cleaners, care workers, waiters and so on. Thus it is hard to see how the working and living conditions of the working class as a whole will improve or even be maintained.

This change is reflected not only in job statistics but also in the evolution of the working conditions and wage levels. Deindustrialization and labour market deregulation may have contributed to the deterioration in the conditions of the working class (Standing, 1995). As the economy shifts away from its traditional manufacturing base to high technology and services industries, the share of jobs providing a middle-class standard of living is shrinking. Indeed, service industries that are the driving economic force in the 1990s are characterized by higher earnings and occupational dispersion, weak unions and a growing share of unsheltered jobs in lower echelons (Sassen, 1996; Mingione, 1991 and 1996b). In Europe, the resurgence of poverty in the 1980s was due primarily to the growth and persistence of unemployment, underemployment and precarious and low-paid employment.

To conclude, as Castells (1996, p. 268) argues: 'The traditional form of work, based on full-time employment, clearcut occupational assignments, and a career pattern over the life cycle is being slowly but surely eroded away.' If the present trend continues, 'atypical' work (short-term contracts, part-time employment and self-employment) will increasingly become the new standard form of employment (Allen and Henry, 1996). This raises a crucial question concerning the quality and quantity of citizenship rights, which workers will enjoy because full citizenship in industrial or 'post-industrial societies' continues to be realized through work as a source of income, recognition and social status. Thus, there is a serious risk of the emergence of a 'two-thirds society', with a shrinking majority more and less able to cope with and take advantage of future developments, and a growing minority without much of a prospect of decent life.

Today, the labour market is characterized by a dichotomy of groups included within the global economy and others excluded from the best working conditions. New occupations are inevitably polarized between highly professional work and jobs with a high skill content in the advanced technology sectors on the one hand, and casual, temporary, part-time and badly paid employment. Then, there is a deepening split between those who are able to cope with and take advantage of the changes in their environment and others who are not – which creates problems of social cohesion. In many countries, evidence exists of polarization between long-term or recurrent unemployed and low-qualification, low-paid jobs and high-qualification, high-income jobs. This phenomenon is reflected in the widening earnings differentials (Dore, 1997). If there is an increasing gap between incomes of those in and out of work, wage dispersion also increases sharply among those in work as a result of the labour market transition towards 'atypical jobs'. Estimating the changes between 1975 and 1990 in the distribution of income in the UK for all full-time workers, Atkinson (1995, p. 36) found that in 1988 a person at the top decile earned about 3.36 times what the person at the bottom decile earned, whereas this ratio was about 3.0 in 1975.

Conceptual and Methodological Problems

The notion of precarious jobs raises several conceptual and methodological problems. It is poorly defined in statistical, legal or economic terms (Rubery, 1989). It lumps together very heterogeneous types of skilled and unskilled workers and jobs that may be in both the formal and the informal sector. Thus, vulnerability may conceal diversity in labour markets that it is necessary to recognize before making appropriate policy interventions (see Scoville, 1989). Secondly, the boundaries between precarious employment and 'non-standard' or 'atypical' employment (for example, temporary and short-term work and self-employment, part-time work, irregular work in the black economy) are not clear. Equating non-standard employment with precariousness may be confusing, considering that precariousness can occur in both standard and non-standard forms of work. For example, full-time and standard forms of work in small firms (excluded from legal protection) and low-paid jobs in retail trades and personal services are indicative of precariousness in standard full-time jobs (see Büchtemann and Quack, 1990, p. 328).

Atypical jobs are not necessarily precarious jobs, because they also include an element of *voluntary* employment, particularly in the case of self-employment and part-time work. The identification of part-time employment with precarious employment is by no means straightforward. Indeed, part-time employment, which is the best studied of the atypical employment practices, by itself, is not a good indicator of precariousness, because in some cases part-time jobs can be regarded as indicating more options or personal preferences for child care, adult education and household activities and so on, as in the case of women's employment. The growth of part-time employment in Western Europe is associated largely with an increase in part-time employment of women (for a European comparison of the role of women in part-time employment, see Bruegel and Hegewisch, 1994). A positive situation of personal preferences and convenience needs to be distinguished from a negative situation of involuntary part-time work as a 'survival' strategy. Thus, the two categories of precarious jobs and atypical employment do not fully overlap, and can cover situations that have little or nothing in common with an analysis of the processes of social exclusion.

Furthermore, a distinction between 'voluntary' and 'involuntary' non-standard employment can be fuzzy. For example, those who report that they are involuntarily employed may have done only a limited job search. On the other hand, those who report being in 'voluntary' employment may take non-standard jobs only because they do not have a free choice. This may particularly be the case of female workers who cannot find child care facilities that alone could have enabled them to seek full-time employment (see Betcherman, 1995, pp. 90–1; Blank, 1990, pp. 153–4).[1]

One easier way to assess precariousness is to analyse the evolution of atypical employment in which the probability of precarious forms of work is high – although, as we noted above, the links between atypical jobs and precarious jobs can be ambiguous. At the heart of this approach is the basic idea that the development of atypical forms of employment is strongly correlated with an increasing share of precarious jobs. As Rodgers (1989, pp. 5–6) explains, 'the development of trends in the incidence and characteristics of atypical work are clearly major determinants of trends in precariousness overall.'

Having discussed some general issues related to precarious employment, we now provide some empirical evidence separately for industrialized and developing countries. The conceptual and methodological problems discussed above need to be borne in mind while interpreting such evidence.

Industrialized Countries

Generally, in industrialized countries, precarious jobs are defined in four different ways: (i) temporary work which involves a temporary work agency, (ii) temporary work which involves a fixed-term employment contract offered by a firm,[2] (iii) period of probation and training involved, and (iv) fixed-term contracts offered within the framework of public policy to fight exclusion from the labour market. For example, fixed-term workers tend to be excluded from many social security benefits (such as pension schemes) which depend largely on the total duration of employment. A temporary worker must have worked for the same employer for a minimum length of time to claim paid sick leave, paid leave or salary for the thirteenth month.

If precariousness is associated with the nature of the labour contract (short-term contracts with relatively low wages and few social benefits), it may also pose a threat or risk related to the probability of being laid off by the firm for economic reasons. Thus it is important to distinguish between secure and insecure jobs. The latter may be considered as precarious despite the fact that they represent regular full-time employment.

In the case of Western Europe, the rise in unemployment and the changing employment structure is a main source of uncertainty about the future of European citizenship which has been at the heart of the European Social Model in the past. Growing unemployment and an increasing spread of 'atypical' jobs are the two phenomena which clearly explain the new social question.

1. Job Insecurity and Non-Standard Employment

Nowadays, firms are no longer interested in providing job stability through regular full-time employment. Although stable employment is still the most usual pattern of work in terms of stock, it may not necessarily be so in terms of flow. For example, we note in Chapter 4 that in France the largest proportion of new labour contracts refer to atypical forms of work. Standard jobs have become rare, and the proportion between this form of work and atypical jobs is being reversed progressively. The two main forms of non-standard working are: (a) part-time employment and (b) self-employment. In particular, the proportion of part-time jobs relative to standard jobs increased considerably in the 1980s, and part-time employment is likely to grow in the future (see Table 3.2).

Part-time and temporary workers are offered lower hourly pay than comparable full-time workers and non-wage costs are lower because employers generally do not have an obligation to contribute to social security schemes. Length and regularity of employment are the main conditions for social insurance, which does not adequately provide for part-time and self-employed workers. All these elements explain why in the 1990s, long-term unemployment did not decrease whereas precarious forms of work increased in many OECD countries, especially during periods of rapid growth. For example, as we shall discuss in Chapter 4, in France the proportion of the labour force belonging to a standard working pattern declined during the 1970s and 1980s (INSEE, 1994).

Extreme job insecurity has been defined in terms of a job tenure of less than one year. Figure 3.2 indicates distribution of employment by relative degree of job insecurity (job tenure of less than 1 year, between

Table 3.2 Relative importance of part-time employment in industrial countries

Country	*Part-time employment as a proportion of total employment (%)*		*Change in the number of full-time and part-time employees 1983–8 (%)*	
	1979	*1990*	*Full-time*	*Part-time*
Belgium	6.0	10.2	–0.5	+ 36.1
France	8.2	12.0	–1.6	+ 36.6
Germany	11.4	13.2	+ 4.6	+ 11.4
Ireland	5.1	8.1	– 4.8	+ 39.2
Italy	5.3	5.7	+ 0.2	+ 45.5
Netherlands	16.6	33.2	+ 6.5	+ 68.4
United Kingdom	16.4	21.8	+ 3.8	+ 26.1

Source: ILO (1993a).

Figure 3.2 Distribution of employment by job tenure in selected OECD countries (1991)

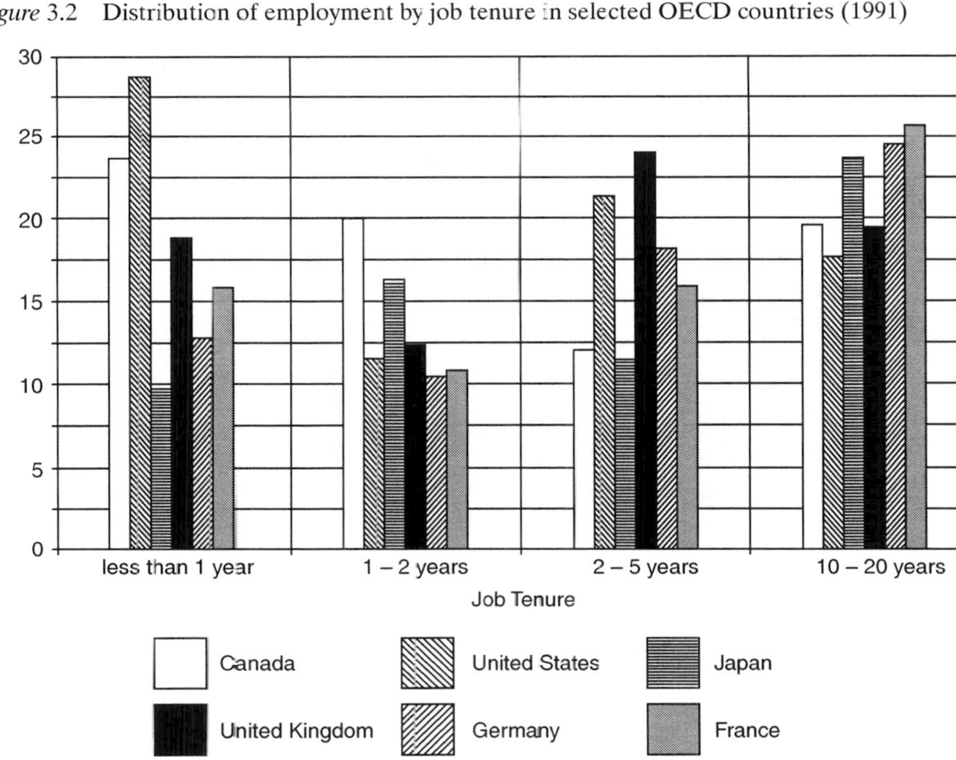

Source: Based on data from OECD (1993).

1 and 2 years, 2 and 5 years, and 10 and 20 years) in 1991 for Canada, France, Germany, Japan, UK and the United States. The bulk of wage and salaried employees had job tenures of two years or less. In North America (Canada and the US), the percentage employed with less than one-year tenure was much higher. Figure 3.3 compares over time the situation between Western Europe and North America on the basis of data on those employed with less than a one-year tenure. Unfortunately, since data are available for only a few years, the figure is only illustrative, and no definite trend can be observed. Job security and tenure of employment vary a great deal across countries. However, it is much greater in Western European countries (for example, France, Germany and the United Kingdom) than in Australia, Canada and the United States. As may be expected, Japan shows the lowest job insecurity of all the OECD countries. It also shows remarkable stability in terms of low job insecurity between 1979 and 1991 (in contrast, the US shows stability at a high level). It is somewhat puzzling, however, that in all other countries, job insecurity uniformly declined (except in France and Japan) between 1989 and 1991 (see Figure 3.2). Changes in job tenure are generally influenced by fluctuations in employment growth, which was low or negative in most countries during this period. Despite economic recession in the early 1990s a decline occurred in the proportion of workers with short tenure jobs. In difficult economic times, hiring is reduced and employers tend to lay off workers who are hired last (OECD, 1993, p. 122). In general, job insecurity among the unskilled in Europe and North America may arise from increasing global competition in the world economy. High unemployment rates among the unskilled are attributed largely to the relocation of production to developing countries. From the 1970s onwards, there has been a gradual shift of routine production jobs from industrialized to developing countries (as well as among developing countries) to take advantage, *inter alia*, of lower labour costs (for more details on globalization of production and the effects of trade on employment and wage inequalities in the North, see Chapter 6).[3]

During the early 1980s in the United States, one-third of the 2.8 million manufacturing workers who lost their jobs through plant closures and lay offs were rehired in service jobs paying at least 20 per cent less (United States Department of Labor, 1986). More generally, in high-income countries precarious employment (casual and low-paid jobs) increased considerably during the 1980s and 1990s.

OECD (1997, p. 134) notes that 'perceived employment insecurity has become more widespread in the 1990s in all OECD countries'.

Figure 3.3 Trends in job insecurity in selected OECD countries (1978–92)

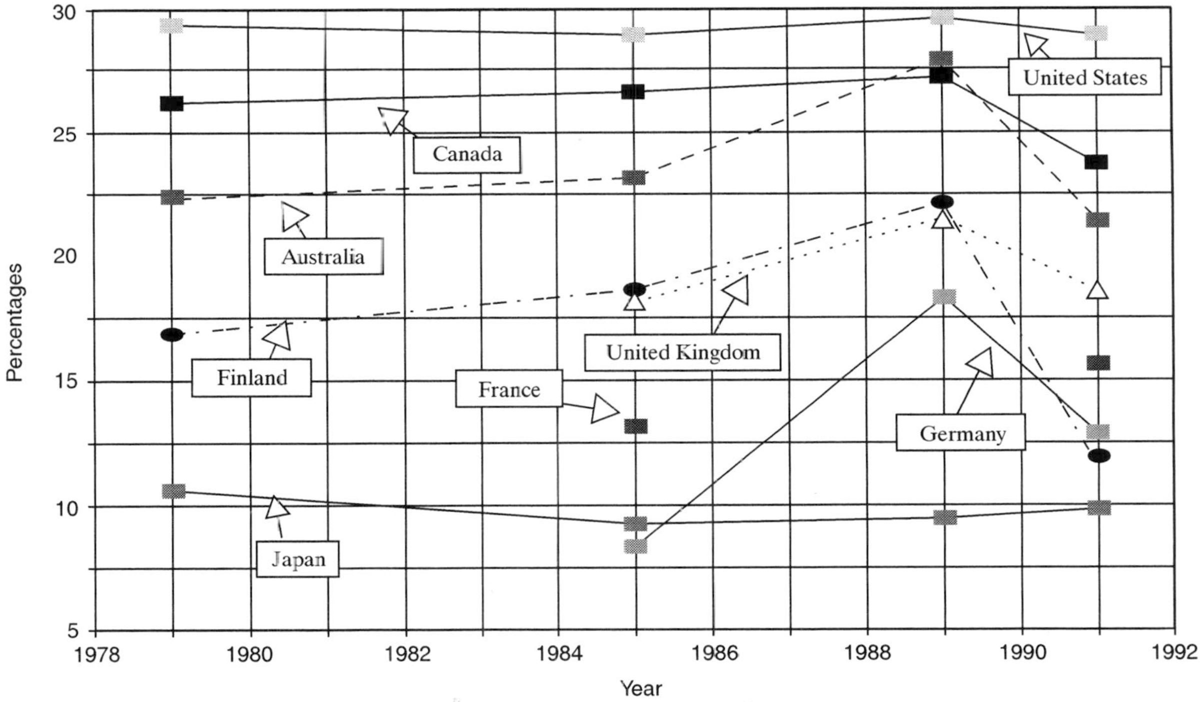

Source: Based on data from OECD (1993).

Table 3.3 shows such insecurity in the European Union countries in 1996 by age, sex, education, occupation and sector. The following tentative conclusions can be drawn from the table: perception of job insecurity is similar between men and women; it declines with age (except in Finland, the Netherlands and the United Kingdom) and education (with the exception of Denmark, France, Italy and the UK).

2. *Involuntary Employment*

As we noted earlier, growth of precariousness cannot be equated with the growth of non-standard jobs and, in particular, with the development of part-time working patterns. Indeed, the latter has coincided with a combination of different processes, namely: (i) a rise in women's labour force participation rates, (ii) an increasing share of employment in services and (iii) technological and organizational changes within the production process. As we show in Table 3.4, in many Western European countries a high proportion of employees expressed preference for part-time working arrangements. Therefore, to evaluate the incidence of precariousness in terms of atypical forms of work, we need a specific indicator that would give information on the proportion of (i) part-time workers who prefer to work full-time and (ii) temporary workers who cannot find permanent work. In its *1993 Employment Outlook*, the OECD developed and used such an indicator of *involuntary* part-time workers. The objective of the OECD study was to show that the labour market slack is even greater when discouraged and involuntary part-time workers are added to the conventional measure of open unemployment.[4]

Figure 3.4 gives a comparative picture of involuntary (part-time) employment for a selected number of OECD countries. During the 1980s, involuntary employment increased in Australia and Canada but declined in Japan and the United States. For example, 'reluctant' temporary workers are now more than half a million in the UK (*Independent*, 21 February 1997). The trend for involuntary employment may fluctuate with the labour market conditions. As the labour market conditions in both the UK and the US have improved the rate of involuntary employment has declined, but it has started rising again since 1990. A number of explanations may be given for this rise: non-standard workers' desire to seek standard jobs as a result of the rising incidence of single-parent families and growing polarization in the labour market, and employers' increasing preference for more flexible types of working arrangements noted above.

Table 3.3 Workers' perspectives on job insecurity by individual and job characteristics (1996) (percentage of employees not strongly agreeing that their job are secure)

	Australia	*Belgium*	*Denmark*	*Finland*	*France*	*Germany*	*Greece*	*Ireland*	*Italy*	*Luxembourg*	*Netherlands*	*Portugal*	*Spain*	*Sweden*	*United Kingdom*	*Weighted average*
Total	**62.8**	**71.5**	**43.9**	**68.7**	**78.7**	**71.8**	**66.0**	**66.5**	**69.6**	**61.5**	**60.3**	**75.2**	**71.2**	**73.3**	**66.9**	**70.2**
Men	63.4	70.9	43.8	66.4	75.2	71.9	70.6	68.3	70.9	68.0	63.3	76.7	65.2	73.4	66.9	69.6
Women	62.0	72.3	44.0	70.9	82.9	71.8	59.5	63.8	67.6	49.8	56.2	73.5	82.5	73.1	67.0	71.1
Age																
16–24 years old	62.5	56.7	42.3	61.9	91.1	77.6	85.5	71.1	83.7	55.0	61.5	84.0	97.1	77.9	58.7	74.1
25–44 years old	63.7	79.3	46.3	68.1	77.9	71.6	60.6	64.8	71.5	64.2	53.6	79.1	78.1	74.4	64.6	70.6
45 years old or older	61.0	57.9	41.0	71.5	76.3	70.0	66.1	67.2	59.5	57.8	74.0	66.4	45.2	70.6	75.4	67.9
Age first left full-time education																
16 years or younger	60.0	74.4	33.4	69.6	77.3	76.4	75.5	72.8	68.7	79.4	61.1	80.1	71.8	80.2	70.1	72.5
17–18 years old	60.2	71.9	40.3	83.1	73.1	76.3	75.4	60.3	63.4	69.8	59.9	80.7	76.8	73.0	59.2	69.2
19 years or older	69.3	70.1	46.5	61.9	82.9	63.7	47.6	67.4	73.2	44.7	60.2	61.6	67.8	69.7	66.6	68.5
Occupation:																
White-collar	58.9	74.0	43.7	65.7	78.4	60.8	43.2	63.4	65.6	45.9	65.2	63.1	65.6	65.0	62.3	65.3
Blue-collar	70.3	73.3	44.1	72.7	78.6	81.3	76.0	69.2	69.3	72.3	56.8	83.3	76.9	79.1	71.4	74.3
Sector																
Industry	65.7	82.5	43.6	71.0	80.8	73.3	82.1	72.5	80.2	78.6	55.5	83.2	73.5	70.2	64.8	72.7
Services	66.7	69.1	45.0	70.5	85.1	76.3	51.5	65.3	68.8	54.1	64.6	65.8	79.5	74.2	69.0	73.1
Public administration	42.4	45.2	40.7	63.7	44.7	46.4	26.7	43.9	24.2	31.8	50.1	75.2	28.6	85.2	59.4	44.7

Source: OECD (1997), p. 133.

Table 3.4 Individual employment preferences in European countries (1989)

Country	*Would you prefer a part-time job? (full-time workers) (%)*		*Would you prefer a full time job? (part-time workers) (%)*	
	Yes	*No*	*Yes*	*No*
Belgium	77	13	19	47
France	79	17	57	32
Germany	83	17	8	92
Greece	86	14	78	22
Ireland	90	7	–	–
Italy	68	32	49	51
Netherlands	86	12	18	78
Spain	73	24	63	35
United Kingdom	75	25	6	94

– = not available.
Source: OECD (1994b).

In the OECD area, on average, involuntary part-time work affects between 20 and 30 per cent of part-time workers – with the notable exceptions of France, Greece and Spain, where this rate is much higher. Indeed, according to a 1991 survey by the European Community, the rate of involuntary part-time employment is higher in the European Union area than in the OECD area. This survey found that 37 per cent of part-time workers would prefer to work full time. Thus only in the case of *involuntary* part-time employment can we consider part-time jobs as precarious jobs.

3. *Precarious Jobs and Social Exclusion*

Precariousness of jobs in terms of lower wages (*distributional* aspect) and instability of employment, risk of job loss and marital failure (*relational* aspects) may be correlated, as we noted above. A recent cross-country survey (Paugam, 1994) shows such a correlation in a selected number of Western European countries (see Table 3.5).To understand the relationship between precariousness and social vulnerability, it is necessary to analyse the patterns of integration and the nature of the society in which integration takes place. For example, in

Figure 3.4 Involuntary part-time employment in selected OECD countries, as percentage of labour force (1980–92)

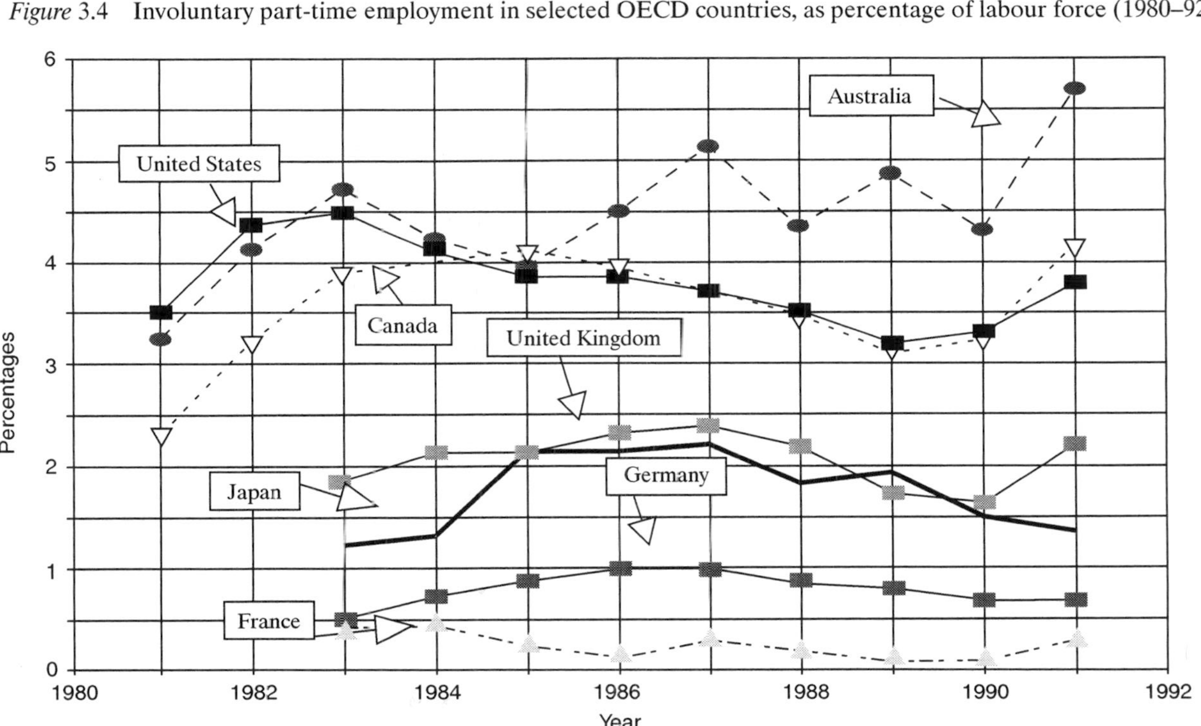

Source: Based on data from OECD (1993).

Table 3.5 Precariousness and social relations deprivation in selected European countries

Country	*Disintegration of conjugal ties (divorce, separation, etc.)*	*Weak relation within families*	*Low participation in associative activities*	*Weak network for private help (friends, neighbours)*
France	++	++	++	++
United Kingdom	++	+	++	++
Netherlands	++	0	++	0
Denmark	++	++	++	0
Italy	++	--	/	0
Spain	++	0	/	--

++ : high positive correlation;
+ : low positive correlation;
– : high negative correlation;
-- : low negative correlation;
0 : no correlation;
/ : indicator is missing.
Source: Paugam (1994).

France, Denmark and the United Kingdom, employment is the main mechanism for integrating individuals into society–employment provides access to income as well as social legitimacy. Therefore, long-term unemployment or precarious forms of work lead to deprivation of individuals with respect to material as well as non-material benefits and recognition.

The growth of exclusion highlights the crisis in the traditional pattern of solidarity, which leads to social disintegration. On the other hand, in Southern Europe societies are less individualistic. People excluded from the labour market are not particularly affected by social-relations deprivation, because the family provides mechanisms for social integration. For example, it is noted that in Italy many individuals suffer from economic or *distributional* exclusion, but not *relational* exclusion because the poor people maintain strong social ties and rely on family relations and a network of friends. Indeed, in Southern Europe, social integration is based mainly on the traditional role of the extended family. Therefore, in the Italian case it would be more relevant to speak of poverty rather than exclusion because the latter involves both *distributional* and *relational* problems. As we shall examine below, this situation resembles that of developing countries with social networks and kinship relationships as part of survival strategies of the poor.

As we shall examine in Chapter 4 with reference to France, quantifying precarious jobs is not a simple task because a precise definition of precarious employment does not exist. Data limitations also pose a problem, to overcome which Centre d'Etude des Revenus et des Coûts (CERC) undertook a survey based on Institut National de la Statistique et des Etudes Economiques (INSEE) data. This survey needed a complex questionnaire and a well-developed statistical apparatus. Moreover, a Europe-wide survey programme was started in 1994 in order to collect and process relevant and comparable data for analysing income, consumption, poverty, and exclusion on a cross-sectional basis. A large part of the individual questionnaire of this 'EUROPANEL' is devoted to the situation of individuals in the labour market. On the basis of this data it would be possible to evaluate and to compare precariousness in the countries of the European Union. However, in many low-income countries it is not possible to use the same methodology as it is too costly and difficult to implement.

Developing Countries

The nature and extent of precarious jobs in developing countries is different and more extensive than that in industrialized countries. In the absence of any well-developed welfare state, people in these countries have to eke out their living somehow through working on multiple types of economic activities. The only insurance the working poor and unemployed have is that of friends, and their social network of families and the community. But with growing urbanization and industrialization in these countries, these support networks and family ties are weakening, although they are still stronger than in industrial societies (see Chapter 5).

In developing countries, precariousness and vulnerability in jobs may occur by virtue of labour status (bonded labour, self-employed, subcontractee and so on), the type of productive activity and economic sector (agriculture, small-scale manufacturing, export-processing zones, petty trading) and ease of substitutability in conditions of labour surplus. Furthermore, there are social categories, such as migrants and women, who may suffer vulnerability on account of labour market segmentation and social stratification (see below). Intersectoral and interoccupational mobility tend to be very restricted in these countries. Surveys (see ILO, 1987) show that mobility by labour status (for example, from wage to own-account employment, or from casual to regular jobs) may vary a great deal in different developing countries, depending on the social groups and hierarchy to which workers belong. Insecurity of employment may also simply be explained by economic cycles. During periods of recession, large-scale urban enterprises may shed casual and part-time workers, relying mainly on the 'core' workforce.

1. Precariousness and Informalization of Labour

The absence of adequate safety nets noted above has led to a swelling of employment in the informal sector, which offers no social protection. In a case-study of non-standard employment in Argentina, Marshall (1992) shows that almost 50 per cent of temporary workers interviewed in 1989 did not receive any of the social benefits and were not covered by the social security system. Moreover, only 10 per cent received the three important legal benefits: holiday pay, wage for the thirteenth month and sick pay. To analyse the growth of precariousness and exclusion in low-income countries, it would therefore be essential to evaluate the size of the informal sector, particularly the marginal activities into which people are forced in order to earn a living. It is now well documented that in most developing countries, the informal sector accounts for a sizeable proportion of total output, employment, and incomes (see Psacharapolous *et al.*, 1993; Turnham *et al.*, 1990). According to rough estimates cited in the *ILO World Labour Report 1995* (ILO, 1995a), the informal sector now accounts for up to 40 per cent of total urban or non-agricultural employment in Latin American countries, 55 per cent in Asian and 70 per cent in African countries. For example, in Peru 60 per cent of the economically active population are engaged in the informal sector, which produces nearly 40 per cent of the country's GNP.

It is not always clear whether employment in this sector represents 'good' jobs or simply 'sweat' labour. All jobs in the informal sector are not necessarily precarious. Some can be more remunerative than employment in the formal and rural sectors. Indeed, the informal sector is very heterogeneous in terms of activities and incomes. Informal activities can range from street vending, shoe shining, hawking and other marginal activities relying on and exploiting family labour, to those that have shown a capacity for sustained growth and generation of high incomes (Swaminathan, 1991). Informal trading is known to be a high-risk activity, 'manifesting not only easy entry but also quick exits due to a high probability of failure' (Evers and Mehmet, 1994). Therefore, the extent to which informal activities can enable a decent income with adequate working conditions is a crucial factor in determining whether these activities are precarious or not.[5]

There is sufficient evidence to support the proposition that the incidence of poverty in the informal sector is high. As Jatoba (1989) argued, 'the mechanisms at work behind labour force allocation tend to place the majority of the poor workers in non-organized labour markets'. Indeed, the majority of the urban poor working in informal activities are threatened by insecurity of access to income and resources. Psacharopoulos *et al.* (1993) estimated the percentage of persons engaged in the informal sector by different income quintiles. For example in Brazil, people working in the informal sector were 27.9 per cent for the top income quintiles and 72.8 per cent for the bottom; Venezuela, as in many other Latin American countries, has the same type of distribution, with respectively 29.8 per cent and 62.5 per cent. Guatemala is an extreme case, with over 96 per cent of the labour force in the bottom income quintiles working in the informal sector. Therefore, the tendency for the poor to be clustered in the informal sector is very high. Individuals in the top quintiles who are engaged in the informal sector generally own small-scale profitable enterprises and at the same time work in the formal sector, whereas individuals in the bottom quintiles participate in precarious informal activities that are very vulnerable from an economic (income) point of view.

In the 1980s and early 1990s, almost all developing countries were forced to apply stabilization and structural adjustment measures in response to the debt crisis, changes in international terms of trade, rising interest rates and falling demand for their main export items. Drastic budget cuts, devaluation, privatization, credit squeeze and wage restraint, implemented within the framework of stabilization programmes, led to deindustrialization and the diminished role and downsizing of the state. Measures to restrain domestic demand and reduction of import capacity brought about a severe fall in production and capital accumulation. At the same time, these programmes typically included measures to improve the government's financial position through massive reductions in public-sector expenditure and employment. Therefore, at least in some cases, implementation of the programmes led to a reduction in formal-sector employment. The industrial labour force and the salaried middle-management employees were particularly affected by this trend because they were formerly engaged in a segment of the labour market characterized by secure and well-paid jobs. Thus the 'newly excluded', who previously participated in the development process, have joined the 'hitherto excluded' (Wolfe, 1995).

The crisis in the modern sector is confirmed by the rapid decline of employment in large public enterprises and the expansion of the informal sector as a response to limited employment opportunities in the formal sector. Indeed, in many developing countries the employment crisis was translated into forms other than unemployment. Latin America and Africa witnessed a shift from formal-sector to informal-sector employment (see Horton *et al.*, 1991).

Moreover, one of the major conclusions that can be drawn from data on wage trends is that real wages in the formal sector declined rapidly during periods of structural adjustment. During the 1980s, in many developing countries the number of better-paid and secure workers decreased both absolutely and as a percentage of the labour force. Therefore, the incidence of poverty among wageearners increased widely because more and more workers from the formal sector lost their privileges in terms of income and social protection.

2. Labour Market Heterogeneity, Precariousness and Exclusion

Informalization of urban labour, considered above in terms of the formal-informal dichotomy, rests on the foundations of the conventional analysis of labour market segmentation. In the literature in labour economics, this segmentation is generally considered in terms of a 'dual labour market', consisting of a 'core' workforce with relatively high wages, decent working conditions and security of employment on the one hand, and a non-standard workforce with low wages, poor working conditions and unstable employment. As we noted above, employment in the urban informal sector represents this latter segment of a dual labour market. Access to the high-wage sector is limited; the bulk of the labour force finds employment in the low-wage informal sector where entry is generally easier. However, empirical research has shown that such a labour-market dichotomy does not correspond to reality in developing countries with much greater heterogeneity and multiplicity of sources of income earning and work activity (see Harriss, 1989; Kannappan, 1985, 1988; Scoville, 1989, 1991). Even within the informal sector, there may be different labour markets for different types of labour with varying degrees of restrictions on access or entry. Focusing on persistent intersectoral earnings differences in Khartoum (Sudan), Cohen and House (1996) assume five different categories of employees in the urban labour market: public segment, private–large-segment, private–small-segment, unprotected workers and self-employed. Their empirical analysis confirms the importance of informal social networks and ethnic ties in determining job search and allocation in urban markets in developing countries.

Migrant workers from rural areas of developing countries are generally a very important source of supply of non-standard urban labour. These workers tend to be in precarious and short-term employment. But the extent of their precariousness is reduced by the existence of kinship networks. These networks are an important source of information which reduces the cost of job search and risk associated with migration to an unknown territory. Tight-knit family ties with the village where the migrants originated provide security and insurance against risk. Thus migrant workers coming from farming households with some land will be less vulnerable than those who have no physical and social assets (like land and family connections) (see Jagannathan, 1987).

In societies such as the Indian, the caste factor and social hierarchy play an important role in allocating jobs in the labour market and in segmenting labour into mutually exclusive groups. Thus, access to 'good jobs' would be restricted to members of the higher castes, whereas those from the lowest caste (the untouchables) will enjoy access only to casual, low-paid and insecure jobs.[6] The hereditary nature of these occupations and the lack of interoccupational mobility gives these jobs a permanent character. In many developing societies, social structures are such that gender accounts for low social status. Thus women as a social group may suffer greater vulnerability or precariousness than their men folk. Many migrant workers in several developing countries are women who, on account of poverty and destitution of their families, are forced to search for any jobs (including prostitution) however precarious they may be.[7] Casual employment and 'outworking' are the two main types of womens' precarious employment.

Besides low incomes and wages and risk and uncertainty, the exploitation of one social group by another may also characterize vulnerable or precarious employment. This control and subordination can explain much of the force of social structure, status, caste and gender in regulating the functioning of imperfect labour markets in developing societies. Thus, bonded labour and tenancies may be considered as some of the most oppressive forms of exploitation. On the other hand, social relationship between the landlord and the attached labour provides a sense of security and stability of economic livelihood that is not found among casual or seasonal labour.

CONCLUDING REMARKS

In this chapter, we have shown that although vulnerable or precarious employment suffers from ambiguity, it offers a good indicator (which is common to both industrial and developing countries) additional to

Figure 3.5 Long-term unemployment, precariousness and the dynamics of social exclusion

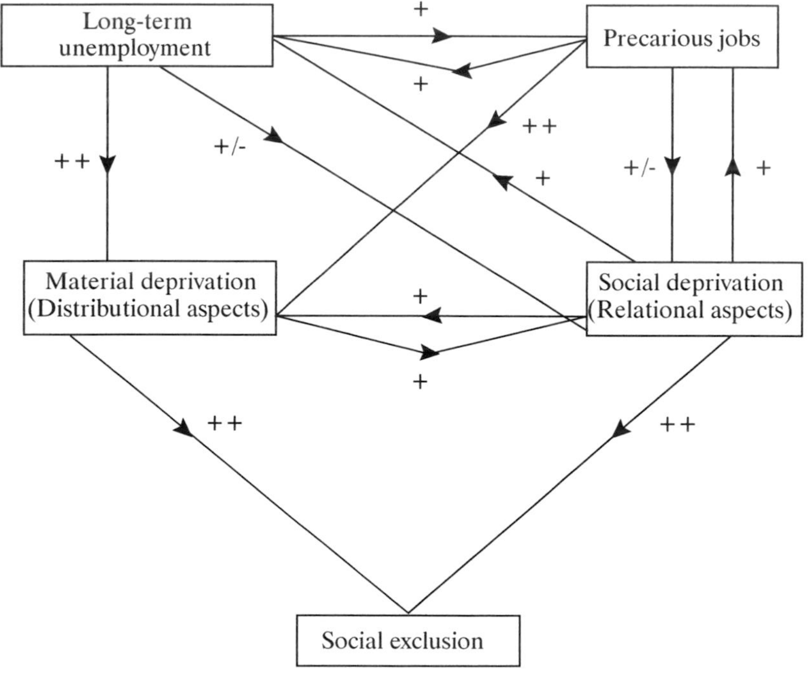

Note: + denotes a positive correlation; ++ denotes a highly positive correlation; +/– denotes the intensity of the relation depending on the social system.

that of long-term unemployment for a better understanding of the dynamics of social exclusion. Figure 3.5 illustrates the relationship between long-term unemployment, precariousness and social exclusion, which summarizes and brings together our arguments in the first three chapters. Under different socioeconomic systems, these indicators will be more or less relevant in explaining the processes of social exclusion (in the case of the United States, precariousness and the rise of the 'working poor' are key indicators, whereas in France, where the labour market is regulated, long-term unemployment gives a good picture of the growing category of the excluded). Moreover, in the European societies a strong link exists between these two labour market situations. Unskilled workers who are trapped in precarious jobs have a higher probability of being unemployed and, in particular, being long-term unemployed. On the other hand, the long-term unemployed generally tend to move into low-skill precarious jobs; for example, in the UK, data show that half of all claimants who leave the unemployment register for a job are back on the dole within a year (*Independent*, 21 February 1997). Thus, we need to underline the importance of the relationship between long-term unemployment and precariousness and material and social deprivation because the former reflects both *distributional* and *relational* aspects in societies where work is central for ensuring access to income and social recognition. Social deprivation leads to the loss of solidarity networks (which are crucial in particular for job-seeking). Material deprivation can produce a sense of social inferiority, which leads to social isolation and alienation. Finally, the acccumulation of disadvantages aggravates social exclusion.

We found that in developing countries, in the absence of any public-funded welfare services, most people (except the wealthy few) cannot afford to remain unemployed for long periods. In these countries, social and family ties and kinship networks substitute for welfare services as risk insurance. The situation differs between developing and industrial countries in some other respects also. For example, in the latter, affluence and the welfare system account for the existence of long-term unemployed, and the decline in such social institutions as family and marriage and social support networks. On the other hand, in developing countries, despite urbanization and industrialization, social networks continue to prevail and society is much less individualistic. In these countries, poverty and destitution forces people to find informal institutional mechanisms to substitute the formal ones (for example, informal credit associations, village gangs screening labour in the absence of educational certificates). Economic exclusion forces people to look for strategies to cope with poverty and destitution through a network of social relations. Thus, in general, one would find *distributional* problems (or the economic dimension) more predominant in developing countries, and *relational* problems (the social dimension) more predominant in industrial ones.

In Chapters 4 to 6 we will examine the validity of the above hypotheses by undertaking case studies of France, Poland and Hungary (Chapter 4), Brazil (Chapter 5) and by examining the implications of globalization for industrialized and developing countries (Chapter 6).

4 Exclusion in Developed Countries

In Chapters 2 and 3 we developed an analytical and operational framework for the study of social exclusion. This and the following chapter are concerned with the testing of this framework in both developed and developing countries. In this chapter we examine the experiences of North America with regard to what is termed there as the underclass, Western Europe and the Central and East European countries' approach to social exclusion. In order to place the discussion in a concrete country setting, we undertake case studies of France, Hungary and Poland (in this chapter) and of Brazil (in the following chapter). Our discussion covers the following three related sets of main issues: (a) economic, social and political aspects of exclusion, (b) *distributional* issues (the lack of resources) and *relational* issues (the lack of social ties with family, friends, local communities, state services and institutions, and more generally, with the societies to which an individual belongs) and (c) indicators of job precariousness.

THE GOLDEN AGE OF FORDISM IN THE WESTERN WORLD

In the 1950s and 1960s, the Western world experienced what is generally described as the golden age. Between 1960 and 1973, the OECD countries achieved an annual rate of growth of real GNP of nearly 5 per cent. During this period, conflicts were kept in check (by a set of institutions sometimes described in terms of a structure of accumulation or mode of regulation) by maintaining appropriate levels of production, savings, investment, social cohesion and economic growth (Aglietta, 1982; Boyer, 1990; Boyer and Saillard, 1995; Kotz, McDonough and Reich, 1994; Tickell and Peck, 1995). The structure of accumulation was characterized by (a) Fordist methods of production which separated organization of the production process and the execution of standardized and formally prescribed tasks, (b) guaranteed distribution of productivity gains to workers in the form of higher wages, and (c) growth in domestic demand, credit and oligopolistic competition.

Furthermore, Fordism implied that gains in productivity would be distributed between an increase in investment from profits and an increase in workers' purchasing power. As a system of rules and regulations, it implied a long-term contractual relationship between capital and labour under which wage and salary increases were indexed to prices and the general productivity level (Lipietz, 1997). Wage formation was more administered than market-determined. Industrial relations were characterized by collective bargaining and institutionalized trade unions. These arrangements governing relations between capital and labour minimized conflict. The French Regulation School has demonstrated that (i) 'growth-centred Fordism created an institutional setting which proved extremely efficient in enhancing innovation, productivity and continuous increases in standards of living' and (ii) the success of the Fordist growth regime lay in 'its impressive synchronization between mass production and mass consumption' (Boyer and Drache, 1997, p. 5).

After 1945, a vast socialization of revenue through the welfare state assured permanent income for wage labour. Thus wage earners were freed from risks related to illness, unemployment, retirement and so on. About this welfare state or the golden age, Esping-Andersen (1994, p. 3) notes that:

> economically it departed from the orthodoxy of the pure market nexus and required the extension of income and employment security as a right of citizenship. Morally, it sought to defend the ideas of social justice, solidarity and universalism.

We can argue that a virtuous circle resulted from a social compromise between capital and labour, and between the development of Fordist methods of production and the distribution of productivity gains (the growth in real wages being proportional to increase in labour productivity). Wage earners had access to mass consumption through rises in direct wages as well as indirect wages associated with the welfare state. This arrangement generated growth in demand for consumer goods, which led to the development of mass production. Under a favourable environment, this allowed systematic exploitation of economies of scale and optimal investment planning.

Thus, the post-war accord between capital and labour institutionalized continuous increases in real wages as well as rising benefits from social welfare programmes. Stability of employment and social insurance provided by the welfare state, along with a high growth rate and expanding welfare expenditures, kept under control workers' risks and vulnerability.

THE CRISIS OF FORDISM

The crisis of the welfare state in the 1970s exposed the declining effectiveness of the mechanisms introduced in the 1940s and 1950s to ensure achievement of the basic goals of the capitalist economy (Aglietta, 1982; Boyer, 1990). The indicators of a major crisis included: a crisis in profitability, slowing down of high levels of accumulation; the destruction of the social arrangements that hitherto sustained the accumulation process; and a rise in social and political conflicts at national and international levels. The crisis appeared on the demand side as: the search for economies of scale-induced internationalization (and to some extent, globalization) of the productive processes. On the supply side, a slowdown of productivity growth, an increase in labour costs and a decline in profitability were witnessed (Lipietz, 1997). In the 1960s, the rate of productivity growth started to slow down while the strong union bargaining power maintained wages, thus causing a crisis in profitability.

During the 1980s, in the OECD countries a neoliberal form of capitalism gained ascendancy, spreading from the United States and the United Kingdom to much of the Western world and developing countries. It involved the strengthening of the private sector at the expense of state intervention, and market rules replacing planning. The principal new criteria were flexibility, competitiveness, deregulation, privatization and the withdrawal of the state from economic activity. The new model of capitalism that emerged in the 1980s was characterized by (i) the appropriation by capital of a significantly higher share of surplus from the production process through the decentralization of production, the weakening of trade unions and the deregulation of the labour market; (ii) the decline in state intervention, with a shift from a redistribution policy to that of capital accumulation, and (iii) the accelerated internationalization of the economic processes in order to increase profitability and open up markets (Castells, 1989).

Increasing pressure of competition and increased capital mobility explained both the shift in domestic macroeconomic policy towards fiscal austerity and tight money and an end to social compromise within firms, through deregulation of the labour market and the weakening of industrial relations (so-called 'labour flexibility'). In the name of flexibility and competitiveness, the private sector has increased pressure on workers' rights. Competition for capital and markets increases pressures on firms to adopt a low-wage strategy, including a reduction in social benefits and a weakening of labour standards. As Boyer and Drache (1997, p. 16) argue, 'The stiff competition, by leading firms to increase their market share by any means possible, coupled with the drastic effects of monetary policies, has significantly weakened the collective bargaining position of labour in all industrial countries.' It is estimated that more and more European workers were in non-regular and part-time wage employment, a significant proportion of whom were excluded from such contributory national insurance schemes as unemployment and sickness benefits (Kennett, 1994, p. 20). An increase in the relative importance of the service sector and a decline in 'good' and 'secure' jobs associated with the manufacturing sector have further weakened the trade unions in the OECD countries.

Globalization of capitalism (see Chapter 6) implies that firms are no longer an important means of social integration at the national level (Aglietta, 1997). There is an increasing contradiction between national regulatory systems and global capital accumulation. The changing nature of power relations between employers and organized labour, and the introduction of flexible working practices, have weakened social cohesion. In the OECD countries, social disintegration is partly the result of firms going global. Moreover, conservative macroeconomic policies implemented in the 1980s have failed to improve overall economic performance. In fact they sharply raised economic inequality. The widening incomes gap in most of these countries during the 1980s is seen as an additional source of strain on the social fabric. No institutional structure has been developed to replace the arrangements that fostered economic growth in the post-war period.

THE NEW SOCIAL QUESTION IN WESTERN EUROPE

From a historical perspective, the debate on social exclusion in Europe is related to the emergence of new forms of poverty and marginalization in the late 1970s. The social transformation of the last few decades has revived serious questions concerning impoverishment in practically all major cities in the industrialized world, particularly Western Europe (Mingione, 1996a). The controversy regarding the notion of the 'new poor' was a reflection of changed thinking and a growing belief in the structural nature of the emerging socioeconomic situation. Thus, towards the end of the 1980s a conceptual shift occurred from poverty to social exclusion. It became obvious that the emerging problems were related not only to a lack of material wealth, but also to various phenomena characterized by a declining access to the labour market, a weakening of family ties, a growth of informal networks, the growing violation of human rights and a decline in social participation.

Indeed, since the late 1970s European societies have been facing deep socioeconomic transformations. The foundations of the European social model are being eroded due to the difficulties that all States are facing in financing existing social protection schemes. Fissures in social cohesion have emerged, and social exclusion is now affecting an increasing number and variety of individuals, groups and geographical areas. The number of people estimated as poor in the 12 member states of the European Union increased from 38 million in 1975 to 44 million ten years later; they were estimated at 53 million in 1992. There are an estimated 3 million homeless. It is also important to bear in mind that in 1995 in the European Union about 17.8 million were unemployed out of a total population of 372 million people or 10.7 per cent of the total labour force (European Commission, 1996). More than half of the unemployed have been out of work for at least one year, and approximately one-third have been jobless for at least two years (a phenomenon defined as long-term unemployment).

In the particular case of the UK, Buck (1996, pp. 287–88) showed that the proportion of households in poverty – below 50 per cent of the median equivalent income – doubled in the 1980s, from 9.4 per cent of all working age households to 19.0 per cent. Moreover, a growing number of households in the UK (around 10 per cent) appeared to be only marginally attached to the labour market during the last two decades (Buck, 1996, p. 290). In the UK in the 1980s, unemployment and precarious labour market conditions contributed to a sharp decline in income from work; in 1975, 80.6 per cent of families had an adult at work, and income from work accounted for more than 80 per cent of the total; ten years later, the figures were respectively 69 per cent and approximately 70 per cent (Atkinson, 1995, pp. 28, 30).

A Eurostat survey on the living conditions of Europeans gave an alarming picture of the professional and social situation in Europe. According to that survey, based on a sample of 12,800 Europeans: (i) 11.4 per cent were unemployed at the time of the interview, (ii) about one-third of the working population was unemployed at least once over the past five years, and half of them were unemployed for more than one year, (iii) one wage-earning worker out of five had no work contract whatsoever, (iv) 5.5 per cent of Europeans interviewed considered themselves as 'poor', (v) about 12.1 per cent considered themselves to be partially excluded from society, and 0.8 per cent completely excluded (Eurobarometer, 1994).

Poverty represents a major challenge not only for the individual member states but also for the European Union as a whole. Urban crises, the resurgence of homelessness, interracial tensions, the increase in long-term unemployment (see Chapter 3), the marginalization of young people who have never been able to gain access to the labour market, the persistence of poverty in certain rural areas or regions seriously affected by industrial decline and the slide into poverty of households in debt are all phenomena that have led to a serious debate on the fight against poverty and social exclusion in Europe. For this reason, the European Commission adopted in 1992 a communication, *Towards a Europe of Solidarity – Intensifying the Fight against Social Exclusion, Fostering Integration*, which included a very compehensive analysis of the forms and processes of social exclusion as well as policies to overcome it (Room *et al.*, 1991, 1992, 1993).

'New poverty' is increasingly affecting people ready and able to work, but unable to find a job or having lost it as a result of economic restructuring and greater competitiveness. Major changes in the employment structure, growing tensions in the labour market, the threat of loss of jobs slowly extending from the less qualified towards those in management, are developments that have radically changed the approach towards the social question in Europe. By excluding a growing number of individuals from full citizenship, the spread of 'new poverty' constitutes a serious threat to social cohesion. Considering the pressure of globalization on the European social model, the European Commission's White Paper on *Growth, Competitiveness, Employment – The Challenge and Ways Forward into the 21st Century* (1994a) attempted to promote 'a synthesis of the aims pursued by society (equality of opportunity and work as a factor of social integration) and the requirement of the economy (competitiveness and job creation)'.

As the European Commission notes:

> Poverty can today no longer be regarded as a residual state of affairs, a mere heritage of the past which will disappear with economic progress and growth. Moreover, it can no longer be regarded as merely an absence or insufficiency of financial resources affecting individuals. On the contrary, we must recognize the structural character of poverty and mechanisms which led to it and the multidimensional character of the processes by which persons, groups, and sometimes urban and rural areas, are excluded from the social exchanges, practices and rights which are an intrinsic part of social and economic integration. (European Commission, 1994a, p. 43)

A picture of an 'hour-glass' society is emerging where the low-middle part is falling into precariousness and exclusion. This crisis in the upward social mobility of the Fordist period is at the heart of the social fissure. Hutton (1995) speaks provocatively of a 'two-tier' society: 30 per cent excluded, 30 per cent precarious, and 40 per cent in a secure and stable situation.

THE UNDERCLASS DEBATE IN THE UK AND THE US

The intellectual debate in the United Kingdom and the United States has hitherto referred more to the underclass than to social exclusion which is central to the debate in France. But increasingly the term 'social exclusion' is also being used in the other Western European countries within the framework of European Union programmes such as Poverty III. For example, in the UK academics and policy-makers now use the term more frequently to address social issues (Room, 1995a; Jordan, 1996; Nolan and Whelan, 1996; Dahrendorf *et al.*, 1995). In the UK, a Social Exclusion Unit reporting directly to the Prime Minister was established in December 1997 in the Cabinet Office to tackle such interrelated and interdepartmental problems as unemployment, poor skills, low incomes, poor housing, high crime environments, bad health and family breakdown.[1] Below we assess the different interpretations of the underclass debate and compare them with the social exclusion approach defined earlier (see Chapters 1 and 2).

A Controversial Concept

The term 'underclass' was coined by Myrdal (1963, p. 10) to refer to the emerging structural unemployment and to those 'who are more and more hopelessly set apart from the nation at large and do not share in its life, its ambition and its achievements'. Myrdal's emphasis was on structural factors leading to the creation of economic victims. However, in the 1980s the term 'underclass' became the mainstream framework for an analysis of the contemporary social problems in the United States. The debate has so far been dominated by the conservative view, which focuses on individual behaviour and cultural obstacles – so-called 'individual-as-cause thesis' (Aponte, 1990, pp. 132–3). This debate bears a striking resemblance to the nineteenth-century Victorian debate on pauperism and the dangerous classes. Indeed, it blames the victims for deviant behaviour and psychological deficiencies including a sense of resignation, passiveness, low aspirations and so on, which marginalizes them in terms of social values and goals (Auletta, 1982). Thus, the underclass is seen as 'a certain type of poor person defined not by his condition ... but by his deplorable behaviour in response to that condition' (Murray, 1990, p. 68). Its key characteristic is not economic deprivation but behavioural deficiencies. From this perspective, the emergence of the American underclass is not a result of structural socioeconomic changes but of a distinct underclass culture shared by the passive poor, street criminals, hustlers or the traumatized (Auletta, 1982).

The conservative arguments concerning the importance of culture versus environment to explain the underclass are partly built on the Lewis thesis (1965, p. 188) on the 'culture of poverty' as 'both an adaptation and a reaction of the poor to their marginal position in a class-stratified highly individuated, capitalistic society'. According to Murray (1984), the growing underclass in the United States can be seen as a pathological manifestation of a culture of dependency that devalues work and social responsibility. This culture results from social assistance policies that encourage deviant or anti-social behaviour and a decline in work ethic. Murray's book, *Losing Ground*, was preoccupied with the American welfare system, in particular, on the programme on Aid to Families with Dependant Children (AFDC). Arguments concerning the withdrawal of the welfare state are based on the fact that welfare is a non-contributory system of social assistance, which must be distinguished from the social security system (that is, a mutual insurance system). The idea is that people who are long-term claimants of public assistance suffer from deviant behaviour compared with the mass of the population.

Murray's provocative book was based on the notion of the perverse effects of welfare policy, which allegedly raised the rate of joblessness, crime, single motherhood, or welfare dependency. The non-workers and the permanent poor, who are on welfare for a long time, were suspected to be personally responsible for their situation (Morris, 1994). However, Murray's arguments came under strong attack in the late 1980s; critics pointed out that a sharp increase in the number of single mothers in the 1970s occurred when the real value of the AFDC was falling. This showed that the welfare mechanism was not the underlying cause of the changes in the family structure in the 1970s and 1980s. Moreover, there is no empirical evidence to support the conservative view concerning the lack of work ethic of welfare recipients.

In the United States, apart from the conservative approach whereby the underclass is explained in terms of individual behaviour, the liberal approach explains it in terms of structure. In *The Truly Disadvantaged*, Wilson (1987) emphasizes the need to strengthen the position of liberals against conservatives in the controversy concerning the underclass. Wilson's underclass thesis emphasizes structural economic changes, especially deindustrialization and the rise of the service sector, as the main factors explaining the underclass. He links individual characteristics of the underclass to the broader social problems of social dislocation (economic, societal, demographic and spatial) in the inner city. The cultural argument concerning deviant individual behaviour of the underclass in Wilson's thesis (1987, pp. 7–8) is seen as 'a response to social structural constraints and opportunities' (Wilson, 1987, p. 61) rather than as a cause (as in the conservative view).

Wilson emphasizes the impact of structural economic changes affecting particularly the urban poor characterized by low educational levels, deindustrialization of the urban centres and the development of skilled labour in skill-intensive service activities. As the Afro-Americans are heavily concentrated in inner cities, they are particularly hard hit by the polarization of the labour market into low-wage and high-wage segments. Wilson further argues that contemporary discrimination contributes to, or aggravates, social and economic deprivation of the ghetto poor, that is, the underclass.

Wilson's theory is spatial, as it deals with the problems of inner-city dislocation. What he later called the 'ghetto poor' (his notion of the underclass) are found almost exclusively in a specific urban area, 'the inner city'. The term 'ghetto underclass' refers to the 'heterogeneous group of families and individuals who inhabit the core of the nation's central cities' (Wilson, 1987, p. 143). The exodus of the working- and middle-class Afro-Americans out of the ghetto led both to social isolation of the most disadvantaged segments of the Afro-American urban community in the ghetto and to the tearing of the community structure. Indeed, the Afro-American middle class no longer lives in ghetto neighbourhoods. Thus what Wilson calls the 'role models' have disappeared from the black ghetto.

Finally, another approach to the underclass is related to the preoccupation of British intellectuals with social class (Silver, 1994). The underclass is defined as consisting of those unable to participate in the labour market. As Smith (1992a, p. 4) stated: 'If the social classes are viewed as a hierarchical array, then the underclass lies outside the schema, and beneath the bottom class.' Indeed, according to Smith, 'The underclass are those who fall outside this class schema, because they belong to family units having no stable relationship at all with "the mode of production" – with legitimate gainful employment.' It is thus defined by a more or less permanent inability to participate in the labour market (Buck, 1992, p. 9).

The debate on the development of an underclass in the United Kingdom is linked to the Thatcher era, when both the process of economic restructuring and income inequalities were more severe than in most of the rest of Western Europe. In a British Gallup poll on social problems, nearly 85 per cent of the respondents answered 'yes' to the question: Do you think an underclass is appearing in this country or not?' (Gallup, 1995). The rise of the underclass in the UK – from 4.2 per cent of the total population in working-age households in 1979 to 9.9 per cent in 1986 – is strongly related to the growth of long-term unemployment arising from major structural economic changes (Buck, 1992).

Dahrendorf (1992, p. 55) argued that these groups are not classes in any technical sense, because classes are necessary 'social forces'. The underclass or the category of people who are classified in it are those who are either unable, or unwilling, or both, to participate fully in the economic, political and social life of the communities in which they live. This definition emphasizes the Marshallian concept of citizenship based on political, social and civil rights. In this respect, it is close to the European Observatory's definition of social exclusion (see Chapter 1).

Social Exclusion vs. Underclass

It is paradoxical that the underclass debate has strongly influenced the poverty debate in the United States, considering that it is, by definition, not the poor as a whole but a specific group of those concentrated in the inner cities, who are characterized by cumulative disadvantages and deviant behaviour. Jargowsky and Bane (1991) show that in 1980, for example, only 1 per cent of the American population lived in urban ghettos where at least 40 per cent of the population were below the poverty line. Indeed, the underclass covers only a narrow segment of the poor and socially disadvantaged, spatially concentrated in the inner cities. It can be seen as a stable group of the extremely poor who have very few prospects of improvement in their living conditions and intergenerational social mobility.

As Silver (1996, p. 130) notes, 'The urban dimension of underclass discourse spatially fixes social disadvantage, racial difference and deviance.' But poverty is not concentrated in the urban ghetto in Europe so that the underclass cannot be defined as poor people living in specific 'ghetto' areas. Neither is the analytical framework developed in the United States relevant to European countries. The differences between American and European cities are quite important, and the race issue in the latter manifests itself very differently. Few of the neighbourhoods in European cities contain any significant proportion of ethnic minorities or immigrants. Moreover, a large majority of the unemployed are not concentrated there. Indeed, the urban neighbourhoods constitute heterogeneous cultural, social and economic spaces. In the case of Ireland, for example, studies show no evidence of concentration of marginals in the main urban centres (Breen *et al.*, 1990). The problem with the underclass concept is that it covers individuals hit by structural economic and social changes who are expected to form a homogeneous group in terms of spatial distribution (concentration effect), status in the labour market (long-term unemployed), culture (deviant behaviour) or family structure (over-representation of single persons and single-parent households). In Europe, even if certain neighbourhoods possess cumulative negative characteristics, they cannot be seen as mirror images of the American ghettos (see Table 4.1 on France).

Table 4.1 Living conditions in disadvantaged areas in France (%)

	Disadvantaged urban areas	*France (Metropolitan)*[a]
Unemployment rate (active population > 15 years)	24.2	13.6
Bad housing conditions	17.7	6.7
Low living conditions (2500 FF per consumption unit)	11.7	6.1

[a] Excluding overseas territories.
Source: INSEE (cited in *Le Monde*, 1998b).

In France, the state implements multidimensional policies to overcome the marginalization of disadvantaged areas. The Republican tradition (based on the concept of solidarity – see Chapter 1), is a key element in explaining why the French State intervenes significantly (within the framework of '*la politique de la ville*') to fight exclusion in the neighbourhoods. This situation differs fundamentally from that in the US (Avenel, 1997). French urban policy is designed to fight the marginalization of the neighbourhoods through local investment, transport, education and housing. Within its framework, local projects are developed with consultation and participation of local residents.

Even if concentration does not lead to social exclusion in France, it could still provide a key argument for the nationalist right. During a recent French election campaign President Jacques Chirac spoke about '*un seuil de tolérance*', referring to the growing problems in the *banlieues*, or suburbs, where there is a concentration of migrants and children of migrants. In particular, following an increase in the incidence of urban violence – as in Strasbourg on New Year's Day in 1997, or an increase in violent behaviour in public transport – the *banlieues* are increasingly seen as dangerous areas where the disadvantaged and juvenile delinquents are concentrated. This trend has stimulated the debate on urban issues. The notion of '*quartiers défavorisés*' or '*zones sensibles*' is symptomatic of some neighbourhoods that could increasingly resemble the American images of 'inner cities' or ghettos.

We pointed out above that the underclass is an ambiguous and controversial concept, loaded with numerous ideological connotations.

The cultural bias of that concept has led to blaming the victim, and presenting a negative image of the poor. Thus the underclass is seen as a crude synonym for the undeserving poor (Katz, 1989).

It becomes clear from the above that the conservative approach to the underclass (based on behavioural arguments and a critique of the welfare state) has nothing in common with a social exclusion approach. Neither can an underclass approach for Europe be defined in racial terms or of spatial concentration, since most of the large European urban areas are not characterized by a homogeneous population of the long-term unemployed displaying anti-social behaviour.

Nevertheless, a structural notion of the underclass presented above is closer to the notion of social exclusion, since it emphasizes major economic and social transformations. Indeed, a structural definition – as developed initially by Myrdal – conveys the present maginalization or exclusion of workers from production through the development of precarious forms of work and unemployment (Gans, 1996). In this respect, the 'underclass' concept is very similar to that of the 'social excluded', as currently understood in France and the European Commission – that is, individuals who have experienced a progressive breakdown in the relationship between themselves and society resulting from major changes in the economic and social structures. Buck (1996, pp. 278–9) emphasizes a structural approach to the underclass when he writes that 'by focusing on the underclass, the marginal, the (new) urban poor, we need to ensure that we do not lose sight of the fact that their experience is a part of a social and economic process affecting the whole society'. As a process of cumulative disadvantages, social exclusion is close to the Nolan and Whelan approach (1996, p. 156), which 'restricts the application of the term 'underclass' to those situations where evidence exists of the effects of a kind that, through their impact on factors such as feelings of self-efficacy, contribute to 'vicious circles' in terms of detachment from the labour market'.

The structural interpretation of the underclass and social exclusion emphasizes new social issues associated with major socioeconomic changes. The two approaches converge on the question of the emergence of a dual society, characterized by people 'in' or 'out' (in a social exclusion approach) or those beneath the bottom class (the underclass approach) (Fassin, 1996a, p. 68). Both approaches emphasize social breakdown and its causal mechanisms. Besides identifying the processes of marginalization and exclusion, the two approaches also focus on how the interrelationships between changes in productive structure and social institutions affect those within the emerging global economy who are becoming permanently superfluous or irrelevant to its functioning. As Robin Marris (1996, p. 14) has noted about the underclass:

> That is a problem for the whole community: It is a problem not only on account of crime or social breakdown – grave though these may be – but also because a society with an excessively disadvantaged underclass is a society with low economic welfare.

The term 'underclass' is rarely used in French academic and political debates. The French Republican paradigm (discussed in Chapter 1) rejects the cultural or racial aspects of this debate. It views the whole society as bearing responsibility for the existence of social exclusion. Therefore, it would not be appropriate to equate the French '*exclus*' (the excluded) with the 'underclass'. The excluded are not those with deviant behaviour (criminals, hustlers, single mothers, welfare dependants, and so on) but those who hitherto shared the mainstream social values but have become redundant in the productive system. Strong emphasis is placed on the process of cumulative disadvantages, on the intermediate zone of vulnerability and on the factors leading to vulnerabilty and exclusion, factors that do not figure prominently in the notion of the underclass. As Smith (1992b, p. 5) notes, for example, there are good reasons for not including in the underclass people trapped in the secondary labour market, which offers poor security, low pay and atypical forms of work.

To conclude, the relevance of the term 'underclass' in discussions on new social issues is facing strong criticism. Although in the United States it was widely used in the past, it is progressively disappearing from academic debates; Wilson (1996b), for example, dropped it in favour of the 'ghetto poor'. Based on the Irish situation, Nolan and Whelan (1996, p. 179) argue against the underclass framework by showing that 'the search for an underclass, and a focus on a category of the population that is nominally separated from other groups, proves less fruitful than a concentration on the larger-scale processes affecting all class groups'. In contrast, the term 'social exclusion' is gaining popularity in Europe, where it has been introduced in social debates and research programmes. The growing use of the concept of social exclusion is, for the large part, due to its comprehensiveness (Berghman, 1995). A social exclusion approach has to do both with multidimensional processes leading to material and social deprivation and the cumulative disadvantages (regarding health, education, employment or housing situation, for example). Xiberras (1993, p. 22) highlights the two main risks related to exclusion: on the one hand, at the individual level, there is the risk related to the tearing of the social bond that links each individual to society, and on the other hand, there is the risk to the whole society associated with social breakdown and the loss of collective values.

A CASE STUDY OF FRANCE

In a front-page newspaper article about a demonstration by the unemployed in January 1998, it was noted that 78 per cent of the French have or had an unemployed member in their family or amongst their friends, 38 per cent are or have been unemployed and 33 per cent are afraid of losing their jobs soon (*Libération*, 19 January 1998). This return of mass vulnerability after a historic period of improvement in working and living conditions is fundamental to the study of the new social question.

Several key works have contributed to the spread of the concept of social exclusion in the French debate; in particular the report of Father Wrésinski (1987) to the Social and Economic Committee, the publications of the *Commissariat Général au Plan* (1992, 1993) and CERC (1993). Father Wrésinski, who launched the ATD-Quart Monde movement, has played an important role in the widespread use of the term as part of political vocabulary. In his report, he emphasized the importance of socioeconomic restructuring in driving some people into a state of permanent exclusion. In this respect, social exclusion is both a *process* and a *state*. Wrésinski stresses cultural aspects in the context of material and non-material aspects of 'New Poverty'. He notes the violation of the fundamental rights that guarantee the freedom to live with dignity and to participate in the future of society.

The Commissariat Général au Plan (1992) highlights the macrosocial dimension of social exclusion and notes that redistributive social policies are, by themselves, not adequate to fight exclusion; prevention rather than cure is considered crucial. Unemployment, and in particular long-term unemployment, is explicitly noted as a fundamental causal process.

An important step forward in the conceptualization of exclusion was reached with the development by CERC (1993) of a multidimensional and dynamic framework for a better understanding of economic and social precariousness and 'social disqualification' leading to fragility and then to exclusion from the labour market. The labour market status is viewed as a key element in the understanding of the processes of social disqualification. The CERC methodology is an interesting attempt to operationalize the notions of cumulative material and nonmaterial disadvantages. This is done by establishing links between unemployment and precariousness on the one hand and social deprivation on the other. CERC (1993) estimates that approximately 27 per cent of the total active population are in a situation of social and economic integration with the risk of being pushed to fragility whereas approximately 7 per cent are facing the risk of being excluded from the labour market. A large majority of those excluded from the labour market are very close to suffering from serious material and relational deprivations (see Table 4.2). Finally,

Table 4.2 Distribution of the working population 18 to 64 years in France (1986–7)

	Million	*%*
Population in a situation of socioeconomic integration (secure jobs without and with a risk in the future)	20.1	80.3
– no risks of fragility	13.3	53.1
– risks of fragility	6.8	27.1
(very high risk)	(0.7)	(2.7)
Population in a situation of fragility (precarious forms of work or unemployment for less than two years)	3.6	14.5
– no risk of exclusion from the labour market	1.8	7.1
– risk of exclusion from the labour market	1.8	7.4
(very high risk)	(0.4)	(1.5)
Population excluded from the labour market (unemployment for more than two years)	1.3	5.2
– no risk of marginality	0.4	1.8
– risk of marginality	0.9	3.4
(very high risk)	(0.3)	(1.2)
TOTAL	25	100

Source: INSEE (1988); CERC (1993).

1 per cent of the working-age population (for example, the homeless) are completely excluded. However, the CERC data are rather outdated and exclusion and precariousness are most likely to have increased during the 1990s. During the recent debate on social exclusion, approximately 12 million individuals were reported to suffer from precariousness (*Le Monde*, 1998a). According to the High Committee for Public Health (1998) between 400,000 to 600,000 children aged less than 6 years live in households with incomes below the poverty line (cited in *Le Monde*, 1998c).

Distributional and Relational Aspects

The dynamics of social exclusion can be understood only if we consider the continuum of social situations and the processes of 'social disaffiliation' (Castel, 1995a) or 'social disqualification' (Paugam, 1991; see also this volume, Chapter 3, Figure 3.5). Our objective in this case study of France is to illustrate the complex relationships between *relational* and *distributional* aspects of this process and to operationalize our analytical framework developed in Chapter 2.

Paugam (1995) emphasizes the idea of a 'spiral of precariousness' and studies the correlation between several economic and social indicators. He shows that economic vulnerability, social-relations deprivation, bad housing, health conditions and weak social participation are highly correlated with employment status. For example, a high risk of job loss leads to an inability to plan for the future. These results are consistent with the analysis in Chapter 3, where precariousness is presented as a composite index providing, *albeit* indirectly, information on the different forms and processes of social exclusion. As Mingione (1996, pp. 27–8) notes: 'The loss of self-confidence, physical and psychological illness, stigma of failure, alcohol or drug abuses, the difficulty in forming or maintaining a 'normal' family life and 'proper' housing arrangements, are all interconnected elements that appear in the life history of the socially excluded. A climate of high work instability and unemployment lies at the origins of these exclusion syndromes.'

In societies based on work, precariousness and lack of integration in the labour market are the main elements that influence *relational* and *distributional* dimensions of social exclusion. These elements, which underlie our approach, are identified as: (i) participation in the good segment of the labour market and good social relationships, (ii) social vulnerability characterized by precarious forms of work and uncertain social relationships, and (iii) exclusion from the labour market and social breakdown. Castel's approach (1995a, p. 21) emphasizes the origin of the social trajectory leading to exclusion. His dynamic concept of 'social disaffiliation' refers to a progressive tearing of the social bond rather than a sudden social breakdown.

Paugam (1991) developed a similar approach based on the notion of 'social disqualification', which emphasizes the relationship between society and its poor. He defines three groups based on the situation of individuals *vis-à-vis* social assistance institutions:

- *Those at risk* face a precarious situation in the labour market. They experience a decline in their living standards but are reluctant to seek social services as this would reinforce their feeling of 'social inferiority' (p. 53). This is the first step to 'social disqualification'.
- *Those dependent on social assistance institutions* are generally excluded from the labour market or are trapped in a vicious circle characterized by successive phases of unemployment and precarious jobs. Nevertheless, they keep social bonds intact through their contacts with social workers. In this case we see a particular mode of integration through individuals' dependence on social service institutions.
- *Those at the end of the process of social disqualification* have accumulated disadvantages and are no longer protected by social assistance (the homeless, alcoholics and so on). They are economically and socially excluded.

The CERC methodology discussed above is an interesting attempt to operationalize social exclusion in terms of material and non-material disadvantages and gauge the intensity of the link between unemployment and precariousness on the one hand, and social deprivation on the other.

In the following section we show that the French Revenue Minimum d'Insertion (RMI) Programme constitutes an original attempt to overcome both *distributional* (through guaranteeing of minimum income) and *relational* (through provision of social and occupational integration) problems associated with exclusion.

Revenu Minimum d'Insertion (RMI) Programme

RMI (established in 1988 and revised in 1992) is certainly one of the most illustrative examples of the French approach to social exclusion.

In the term 'RMI', the most important element is not the minimum income, which is similar to the guaranteed income mechanism implemented in many European countries. The French innovation is the notion of *'insertion'* (integration), which implies a contract linking the individual responsibility of the recipient and the collective responsibility of the whole society (Lafore, 1992). The originality of the RMI lies in its objective to reach a portion of the disadvantaged population which had no access to social assistance before. The term 'integration' emphasizes the new social question. It goes beyond a minimum income and other *redistributional* policies, which, by themselves, are unable to overcome exclusion, and seeks recognition of the right of an individual to an occupation which gives social status.

Within the RMI framework, an integration contract is complementary to that of the minimum income allowance. Integration implies two things: on the one hand, a recipient must be engaged in 'integration' or 'reintegration' activities developed for him or her. On the other hand, society or the state must break the vicious circle by implementing a set of policies and institutions to overcome exclusion, particularly from the labour market, housing and health. It is an integration contract implying both rights and obligations of recipients. The collective responsibility of the state involves two categories of activities: first, the implementation of integration programmes aimed at offering work experience or training to the recipients (for example, the '*Contrat-Emploi-Solidarité*' or the '*Actions d'Insertion et de Formation*'); second, the social worker support to the RMI recipient to fight social isolation and promote occupational (re)integration.

1. Scope and Content

The RMI programme is a response to socioeconomic changes resulting in the exclusion from production of a growing number of people who also suffered from lack of adequate safety nets. Indeed, a large proportion of the population is not shielded by the conventional mechanisms of social protection. A CERC study (Euvrard and Paugam, 1991, p. 11) shows that 23 per cent of RMI recipients were not protected by the social security system prior to receiving support. Moreover, a large majority of single persons were new recipients; 55 per cent of them were unknown to social assistance services (Viveret, 1992, p. 52).

The RMI aims to: (i) guarantee a minimum income, (ii) ensure such complementary social rights as free access to health services and housing assistance, and (iii) establish a contract between the recipient and a state civil servant to facilitate social and economic integration of the recipient. To enjoy access to the RMI programme, an applicant must have an income below a certain poverty line (if the applicant is not single his wife's or husband's income is included for assessment) and should be more than 25 years of age (except if the applicant has a child). Resident foreigners must have lived in France for a minimum number of years in order to qualify for RMI support.

The RMI programme has the clear social objective of mitigating hardship caused by exclusion. It legally entitles each excluded person to enjoy access to resources from public funds to maintain a minimum living standard. It is designed to fight exclusion from education, labour market, training, health or housing. The minimum income allocated within the framework of the RMI is not the same for all recipients. It is a supplementary income over and above a recipient's own resources, which is intended to guarantee a minimum level of income. Thus an RMI allowance depends on household composition and its income level before receiving RMI support.[2] Indeed, RMI support is additional to the housing and family allowances of a household. Four recipients out of 10 in 1995 were receiving both the RMI and an income from an occupation. Only a part of the latter is taken into account in calculating the RMI in order to encourage occupational integration during the transition period (Afsa, 1997, p. 30). In 1996 half of the recipients were also receiving housing allocation, whereas 14 per cent of the recipients were receiving only the RMI support. The RMI share in the total income of the recipient is lower for a household with several children, which usually has entitlement to other types of social allowances at the same time (du Boullay, 1997, p. 82).

According to the CERC-Association (formerly CERC, which was split by Prime Minister Balladur in 1994 for political reasons), 3.3 million households (approximately 6 million persons) received one or more of the different allowances aimed at preserving a minimum income (quoted in *Le Monde*, 1998a). The Association highlights the degradation in living conditions since 1983 of the households dependent on these minimum income allowances. Indeed, resources allocated to the RMI programme as a proportion of GNP have remained constant since 1982, whereas the number of recipients has sharply increased. This trend has adversely affected the purchasing power of the minimum income allowances.

Table 4.3 Total number of RMI recipients in France

	1992	*1993*	*1994*	*1995*	*June 1996*
Total	671,200	792,900	908,300	946,000	994,000

Source: du Boullay (1997).

In mid-1996, there were 994,000 RMI recipients (see Table 4.3). Considering the households to which the recipients belonged, 1,920,000 persons benefited from RMI (du Boullay, 1997, p. 76); in 1989, there were respectively 400,000 and 870,000 such recipients. A majority of the RMI recipients were young: 30 per cent were under 30 and approximately 65 per cent were under 40 (du Boullay, 1997, p. 78). In 1996, 19.8 per cent were couples, 21 per cent single-parent families and 59.2 per cent were single persons (du Boullay, 1997, p. 83)

A CREDOC-DIRMI study gives some interesting information on the new RMI recipients (Aldeghi, 1996). First, a majority of the newcomers have a lower level of education than the average for their generation (19 per cent of the French population between 25–29 years of age have no diplomas compared with 27 per cent of new RMI recipients). Secondly, most of the new recipients did not have a childhood characterized by material deprivation. Indeed, there is no evidence of a process of intergenerational reproduction of disadvantages. The newcomers apply for the RMI in response to their exclusion from the labour market. Thus, the conservative argument about the 'culture of poverty' is not relevant for explaining an increase in the number of recipients. Moreover, social workers noticed a strong demand from the RMI recipients for '*Contrats-Emploi-Solidarité*'. The fact that income earned under this type of contract is not very different from the RMI demonstrates a strong willingness to work (and to enjoy social recognition associated with an occupation) on the part of a large proportion of the RMI recipients. Finally, the study shows that if the newcomers suffer from material deprivation, they are not socially isolated. Instead, they continue to belong to a family solidarity network (during the first year of the RMI, three-quarters of the new recipients received material aid in the form of money, food, housing accommodation and so on). For that reason, there are very few homeless among the new recipients; more than a third of the newcomers are housed free of charge by family or friends.

From a labour market perspective, there are two main categories of people: on the one hand, those who have been pushed out from the labour market (the long-term unemployed), and who no longer qualify for unemployment benefits but apply for RMI support; and those (youth and women) who have never been fully integrated into the labour market. According to a preliminary analysis of RMI recipients, 77 per cent of the recipients had no labour market activity; 13.5 per cent were unemployed for less than a year, 20 per cent for one to three years and more than 50 per cent had never worked or were unemployed for more than three years (Castel and Laé, 1992, p. 18).[3]

2. *An Assessment*

The RMI is based on a paradoxical analysis. Indeed, on the one hand there is a strong belief in the lack of sufficient jobs for everybody as a consequence of socioeconomic structural changes. According to the law, the RMI is a right for those who cannot work because of their physical or mental deficiencies or because of the economic and labour market situation. Thus the RMI covers both handicapped people and those who are able to work but who are redundant in the new productive system. But on the other hand, integration in the spirit of RMI implies having secure and stable employment. If social and occupational integration are both emphasized, the latter objective is dominant in the sense that the final objective of integration policies is to ensure participation in the labour market. The state is expected to help a portion of the excluded population to become 'employable' (Thalineau, 1997, p. 72). However, the contractual provisions of RMI do not guarantee success of integration or reintegration. Individuals who are engaged in integration activities or who work for public bodies or associations, effectively exit from the RMI after two and a half years on average (Allain, 1993, p. 18).

An integration contract is a means of taking a portion of the population out of a 'social no man's land' where it suffers from a lack of recognition. The implementation of RMI has led to a sort of dualism between RMI recipients and the excluded who do not benefit from it. There is a real risk of creating a new category of people dependent on the RMI and trapped in the process of perpetual insertion. As the National Commission for Evaluation of the RMI notes, the integration activities implemented so far drag most of the recipients into a 'durable transitory' state (Valereyberghe, 1992, p. 332). Castel (1995a, p. 431) estimates that 15 per cent of the RMI

Table 4.4 Distribution of RMI recipients in France by duration of support

Length of time	*Number*	*%*
Less than 6 months	143,805	16.7
6 to 12 months	112,644	13.1
1 to 2 years	177,147	20.5
2 to 3 years	130,594	15.1
3 to 5 years	144,654	16.8
More than 5 years	153,842	17.8
Total	862,686	100

Source: du Boullay (1997).

recipients have found some employment, stable or precarious; another 15 per cent are engaged in training or collective utility programmes; and finally, 70 per cent are characterized by unemployment or inactivity. In fact, in mid-1996, approximately 30 per cent of the RMI recipients received support for less than a year. Table 4.4 shows the distribution of the recipients in France according to the length of time as RMI recipients.

Drawing on the results of the CERC studies, Paugam (1991) defined three different groups of recipients according to their situation in the labour market and the intensity of their social bonds. The first group consists of those who do not participate fully in the social and economic life but who are not too marginalized in the labour market. They (approximately 40 per cent of the recipients) still have an opportunity to find a secure job in the short or medium term. Most of them are under 35 years old. The second group (also 40 per cent of the recipients) comprises those who have a low probability of finding a secure job in the short term. Nevertheless, they do not suffer too much from social deprivation, because they are still integrated into social networks. For example, single mothers are classified in this group. Finally, the third group (approximately 20 per cent) consists of those characterized by social deprivation and cumulative social and professional disadvantages. For example, single men with health problems or the homeless belong to this category.

To conclude, integration policies implemented so far have failed to offer 'true jobs' to a significant portion of the recipients. Most of those who signed an integration contract are trapped in training and integration programmes or work for a public body or an association, activities which are badly paid or which do not offer positive social recognition. Indeed, the limitation of integration policies lies in the weak participation of enterprises in a collective effort to fight precariousness and exclusion. In fact, employment in the nonmarket sector is the main tool of occupational integration for RMI recipients. In the market sector, integration is encouraged through contracts of occupational reintegration ('*contrats de retour à l'emploi*'), for example, but this covers only a small portion of the recipients. In the case of contracts of '*emploi-solidarité*', which increased sharply from 34,050 recipients in 1990 to 50,240 in 1996, the employers are local governments, public sector and non-governmental associations. In 1993, 15 departments had more than 25 per cent of the RMI recipients with this kind of contract and 4 departments had more than 30 per cent (*Bulletin d'information de la délégation interministérielle du RMI*, 1993)

Legislation requires that an integration contract be signed within three months. However, in July 1990 only 30 per cent of the recipients had signed such a contract within this time limit. This percentage increased subsequently, but in 1996 only half the total recipients had signed a contract. In the new draft of the law against exclusion, to be voted on in 1998, one of the objectives is to boost the integration dimension of the RMI. Thus, there is a risk of the RMI becoming a reactive instrument, which aims to take care of those who have become redundant in the new productive process. By creating this intermediate social sphere (a sort of social no man's land noted above), the RMI is reducing the risk of social breakdown without addressing the processes that push more and more people out of production. In particular, insertion programmes can be seen as a mechanism created by the state to allow some time for the redefinition of the notion of citizenship in societies where a growing part of the population are excluded from full participation in the economic, political and social life of society. A similar critique has been made about exclusion. Some authors (Castel 1991, 1995a; Paugam 1991) underline confusion in the French debate between exclusion as a final *state* in which the excluded are trapped and exclusion as a *process* that excludes an increasing number of people who were hitherto integrated in society. Indeed, a targeting approach to exclusion may fail to analyse the factors creating what Castel (1995a) calls 'the *supernumeraries*' and Donzelot and Estèbe (1994) the '*useless normals*'. An emphasis on the processes and global social dynamics calls for a definion of a new type of *proactive* social policy rather than a *reactive* targeting policy.

Exclusion and Job Precariousness: The CERC Study

The objective of the CERC study was to analyse interactions between the different aspects of exclusion and to assess the risks involved. Its approach is based on a definition of different types of situations regarding employment, poverty and social vulnerability: (i) five types of *employment* situations: secure standard jobs, insecure standard jobs, precarious jobs, unemployment for less than two years, and unemployment for more than two years; (ii) three situations that refer to *distributional* aspects: non-poor, poor and very poor; and (iii) three degrees *of social vulnerability*: non-vulnerable, vulnerable and very vulnerable. According to the results of a statistical survey on the underprivileged, the CERC estimates the number of people in the five types of employment categories as follows:

- *Secure standard jobs*: 51.6 per cent of the 18 to 64 -year-olds.
- *Insecure standard jobs*: 28.5 per cent (people who have the same job for more than one year but whose probability of losing their jobs in the next two years is high).
- *Precarious jobs*: 7.8 per cent (people who faced unemployment or turnover a year before the survey or who recently found a job and who estimated a high probability of losing that job in the next two years).
- *Less than two years of unemployment*: 6.8 per cent.
- *More than two years of unemployment*: 5.3 per cent.

Table 4.5 indicates a massive decline in standard forms of work between 1982 and 1993, leading to changes in the labour market structure. Indeed, 779,000 standard jobs disappeared during this period,

Table 4.5 Evolution of standard and non-standard employment in France (1982–93) (000)

	1982	*1993*
Secure and full-time jobs	16,210	15,431
Total non-standard forms of work	516	1,249
– temporary jobs	441	805
– period of probation and training	75	444
Unemployment	2,059	3,172

Source: INSEE (1994).

Table 4.6 Decline in stable employment in France (1980–95) (per cent)

	1980	*1985*	*1990*	*1994*	*1995*
Unemployment rate	6.3	10.2	8.9	12.3	11.6
Share of long-term unemployment	32.6	46.8	38.0	38.2	45.6
Fixed-term contracts (as a percentage of dependent employment)	–	1.8	3.1	3.2	–
Part-time (as a percentage of total employment)	–	10.8	11.8	14.8	–

Source: OECD (1997b), p. 165.

whereas the number of non-standard jobs increased rapidly, and unemployment rose by more than 1 million. During the same period the share of the total labour force who were unemployed for more than one year increased from 21.4 per cent in 1980 to 43.8 per cent in 1995 (OECD, 1997b, p. 65). The unemployed, whose number sharply increased until the mid-1980s, suffer from a high risk of becoming more and more detached from the labour market. Table 4.6 gives a clear picture of the decline in stable employment in France during the last decade.

The poor are defined as the proportion of individuals living in a household with a disposable income between 40 and 60 per cent of the minimum income fixed by the state (SMIG);[4] the very poor correspond to less than 40 per cent of the SMIG. The indicator of vulnerability is based on a combination of three elements: (i) social relations within the family, (ii) participation in associative activities, (iii) relational 'support' (possibility of help from friends' and neighbours' networks). Data for these categories are collected on the basis of sample surveys and on individuals' responses regarding the quality of their social relations. Thus the quantification of the vulnerability index is highly subjective. *Non-vulnerable* people are defined as those who enjoy strong family ties and 'relational support' regardless of their participation in associative activities. *Vulnerable people* enjoy average family ties and 'relational support', regardless of their participation in the associative activities. Individuals with weak family ties and 'relational support' but who participate actively in associative activities belong to this category. *Very vulnerable people* are those who suffer from social-relations deprivation.

Table 4.7 Poverty, unemployment and social vulnerability in France

Category	*Non-poor*	*Poor and very poor*	*Total*	*Non-vulnerable*	*Vulnerable and very vulnerable*	*Total*
Secure standard jobs	94.4	5.6	100	74.2	25.8	100
Insecure standard jobs	87.6	12.4	100	63.6	36.4	100
Precarious jobs	80.6	19.4	100	61.5	38.5	100
Unemployment < two years	73.4	26.6	100	61.5	38.5	100
Unemployment > two years	59.8	40.2	100	50.7	49.3	100

Source: CERC (1993).

The CERC results show that precariousness and exclusion from the labour market are at the heart of economic poverty and social vulnerability (see Table 4.7).[5] We note that the worsening of the labour market situation since the mid-1970s has led to the pauperization of a part of the French population – approximately 12 per cent of the labour force have an income per capita equal to less than 60 per cent of SMIG. A correlation analysis shows that the higher the precariousness the greater is the probability of being poor. Moreover, in a 1993–4 survey on underprivileged households, INSEE shows that the number of household heads looking for a job was three times higher for low-income households than for the total number of households (17.2 per cent compared with 6 per cent) and 39 per cent of the heads of households belonging to the first deciles are part-time or temporary workers. On the other hand, the risk of being excluded from the labour market leads to a progressive disintegration of an individual's social ties with his or her family, friends or society. The CERC results also highlight a high probability (more than 50 per cent) that the population affected by precariousness and social relations deprivation with shift from a stage of vulnerability to a stage of marginalization is characterized by long-term unemployment and economic deprivation.

The above framework developed by the CERC is similar to the illustrative matrix Table 2.1 in Chapter 2. The matrix, which emphasizes economic, social and political dimensions of exclusion can be easily applied to the concrete case of France. Indeed, INSEE has collected and processed a vast amount of data on different aspects of exclusion. These data provide useful information on the *distributional* and *relational* outcomes (also stressed in Table 2.1) for individuals and different social groups. For example, it is found that youth, older workers and migrants are hit hardest by precariousness and unemployment, which underlie economic and social vulnerability. However, the political dimension is missing from the INSEE data. Such a dimension could be developed by focusing, in particular, on deficiencies in citizenship rights and unequal citizenship status. For example, migrants are excluded from political participation at the local and national levels even when they have lived in the same place for several years. Furthermore, thousands of homeless people are unable to exercise their political rights because they do not have a home base.

THE TRANSITION ECONOMIES OF EASTERN EUROPE: POLAND AND HUNGARY

After the fall of the Berlin wall in 1989, a neoliberal counterrevolution occurred within most of former Central and Eastern Europe, including the former Soviet Union. The governing élites in these countries rejected all hybrid forms of market socialism on the grounds that this so-called 'third way' had proved to be unworkable. Kornai (1986) played a major role in that radical shift of Eastern European élites on the efficiency and reformability of Socialist Systems. Sachs (1995) argued that 'the Capitalist Revolution of the 1990s is the unraveling of the tripartite world system that emerged after World War II. There is of course one overriding reason for the revolution: the alternatives preferred by the Second and Third World did not work'.

Neoliberalism has been implemented abruptly (as in Poland, see below) or through a more gradual economic transformation (as in the case of Hungary). This predominant ideology has been invoked to legitimize the privatization of the state-controlled economy, the liberalization of trade and external payments, and deregulation and stabilization policies. In the transition economies, the shock therapy model was defended as a means to ensure high rates of economic growth, to lock in economic reforms, to boost investor confidence and to protect the transition process from vested interests (Sachs, 1993, 1995). However, after an initial sharp increase during the stabilization period, unemployment and poverty appear to have become stagnant in Eastern Europe (with the exception of the

Czech Republic) where a stagnant pool of jobless and poor people has emerged (Cornia, 1996). Milanovic (1996) estimates that the total number of poor in Central and Eastern Europe increased from 4 million in 1987–8 to 19 million in 1993, out of a total population of approximately 100 million. During the same period, the poverty head-count ratio increased from 6 per cent to 26 per cent in Poland and from 2 per cent to 33 per cent in Bulgaria, while the increase was more modest in Hungary and the Czech Republic.

The Cases of Poland and Hungary

Both Poland and Hungary are considered as advanced reformers moving from planned to market economies. These two countries are, therefore, good cases for studying the impact of transition on economic growth and exclusion defined in terms of poverty as well as long-term and precarious employment. In both countries, the introduction of market-oriented reforms coincided with major traumatic shocks involving price increases, trade losses, unprecedented decline in GDP and deterioration in the standards of living. Open unemployment appeared on the scene and grew sharply as we shall examine below, employment rates fell and real wages declined.

The most remarkable event during the first phase of transition was a tremendous contraction of output experienced by both Hungary and Poland (Mundell, 1997). This output decline was caused by a combination of depressed aggregate demand, a credit squeeze, and a shift in the relative costs/prices. According to official statistics, in Poland shock therapy resulted in a steep recession between 1990 and 1992, including a fall of more than 30 per cent in industrial production in 1990 and 1991. The decline occurred exclusively in the public sector while private output rapidly increased. By late 1992, industrial production was still officially at about 70 per cent of its 1989 level. Since the collapse of the planned system, Hungary's recession mirrors the contraction in aggregate output observed in Poland. Between 1989 and 1993, its real GDP fell by an estimated 18 per cent and the cumulative decrease in industrial production was 31 per cent (Blanchard *et al.*, 1994).

The output decline has led to a substantial increase in open unemployment (Table 4.8). In both Hungary and Poland, state sector employees were the biggest component of flows into unemployment. The private sector and the pool of new entrants and re-entrants

Table 4.8 Rates of unemployment in Poland and Hungary (% of labour force)

	1989	*1990*	*1991*	*1992*	*1993*
I. Registered unemployment					
Poland	0.1	6.1	11.8	13.6	16.4
Hungary	0.3	2.5	8.0	12.3	12.1
II. Cumulative decline in employment					
Poland	–	7.5	11.5	13.8	14.9
Hungary	–	0.0	3.7	12.8	20.0

– = not available.
Sources: For registered unemployment, IMF (1997b), World Bank (1995, 1996b); for cumulative decline in employment, Rutkowski (1995).

each accounted for between a quarter and a third of flows into unemployment (World Bank, 1994).

Although open unemployment is the most visible impact of the shocks, the cumulative decline in employment was very high, and in the case of Hungary, it was even higher than the growth in unemployment in 1993 (Table 4.8). Employment reduction occurred as a consequence of attrition, a freeze in new hiring and induced retirement. A significant increase occurred in the number of beneficiaries through early retirement and invalidity pensions. In 1990, in Poland early retirement accounted for at least 70 per cent of the employment decline and in Hungary, it accounted for about 20 per cent between 1990 and 1992. After a ceiling in the number of recipients of early retirement benefits is reached, most of those losing jobs become unemployed. Thus one can see a clearer correspondence between job losses and the rise in unemployment (Boeri, 1994, p. 22). The nature of the employment decline has changed from voluntary departures to increasingly involuntary separations.

However, economic growth has recovered since the mid-1990s. The recovery of Poland and Hungary was based, to a very large extent, on the revival of industry and the development of the service sector. Between 1994 and 1996, industrial production rose by respectively 9.5 per cent, 4.6 per cent, and 3.3 per cent in Hungary and 11.9 per cent, 9.4 per cent and 9.1 per cent in Poland (UNECE, 1997, p. 60). The private sector is now responsible for more than half the GDP, providing a substantial and growing number of jobs. For instance, the share of the

Table 4.9 Annual change in real GDP in Poland and Hungary (%)

	1994	*1995*	*1996*	*1997*
Poland	+ 6.0	+ 6.5	+ 5.5	+ 5.2
Hungary	+ 2.9	+ 1.5	+ 1.0	+ 2.0

Sources: IMF (1997b); World Bank (1997).

private sector in total output doubled in Poland between 1989 and 1995, from 28 per cent to 55 per cent. The share of private-sector employment rose less, from 47 per cent in 1989 to 63 per cent in 1995 (OECD, 1997a, p. 59). Since 1990 Poland and Hungary have implemented a broad set of systemic reforms to promote full participation in the global economy and are now reaping the fruits of these reforms. They are experiencing relatively robust economic growth (5 per cent and 2 per cent for 1997 in Poland and Hungary respectively) (IMF, 1997b and Table 4.9). Both countries have succeeded in adapting their socio-economic structures to meet the requirements of integrated and competitive world markets. But the social exclusion approach defined above calls into question the hegemonic statement of the IMF (1997b, p. 4) that 'if policies are adapted to meet the requirements of the global economy, then all countries should be better able to develop their comparative advantages, enhance their long-term growth potential and share in an increasingly prosperous world economy'. Our objective below is to analyse what has been happening to unemployment and inequalities, and to assess the impact of these phenomena on social cohesion in these countries.

1. Unemployment and Long-term Unemployment

From being virtually non-existent at the end of the 1980s, by mid-1992 open unemployment in Hungary and Poland had risen above OECD levels. Both countries are now facing massive unemployment after six years of transition towards integration into the global economy. The nature of the unemployment problem in Hungary and Poland is similar to that in many Western European countries (see Table 4.10): (i) a two-digit unemployment rate, (ii) a rate of youth unemployment at double the average rate, (iii) rapid growth in long-term unemployment (without work for more than one year) despite growth in output and a decline in total unemployment. Increasingly, the new unemployed are

Table 4.10 Unemployment and long-term unemployment in Poland and Hungary (labour force surveys, 1994–96)[6]

	1993	*1994*	*1995*	*1996 (Q2)*
Poland				
Unemployment				
total / % total labour force	14.0	14.4	13.3	12.4
males / % male labour force	12.7	13.1	12.1	11.0
females / % female labour force	15.6	16.0	14.7	13.9
youth / % youth labour force	30.0	32.6	31.2	28.1
Long-term unemployment				
total / % total unemployment	37.7	40.2	40.0	38.8
males / % male unemployment	36.5	36.5	36.2	34.4
females / % female unemployment	38.9	43.7	43.7	42.9
youth / % youth unemployment	28.4	29.0	28.0	25.5
Hungary				
Unemployment				
total / % total labour force	12.1	10.8	10.3	10.0
males / % male labour force	13.5	12.1	11.6	10.8
females / % female labour force	10.4	9.4	8.7	9.0
youth / % youth labour force	22.9	20.9	20.2	19.4
Long-term unemployment				
total / % total unemployment	33.6	41.3	49.3	53.2
males / % male unemployment	33.0	43.7	51.0	56.4
females / % female unemployment	34.6	37.6	46.4	48.7
youth / % youth unemployment	21.7	30.3	37.1	40.8

Q2 – Second quarter.
Source: OECD (1997b).

people who have been forced to give up their jobs. In late 1992, 56.4 per cent of the unemployed were dismissed, while the rest had either entered the labour market for the first time (16.9 per cent), had re-entered (19.9 per cent) or had voluntarily given up their jobs (6.8 per cent) (Koltay, 1994, p. 297). In the overwhelming majority of cases, those forced to seek employment find themselves suffering from long periods of unemployment. For example, according to a Labour Force Survey, in Poland the share of long-term unemployed increased from 39.6 per cent in 1992 to 39.9 per cent in 1995, while the share of very long-term unemployed (over two years) increased from 12.9 per cent to 19.2 per cent (OECD, 1997a, p. 96). According to the OECD, the low rate of outflow from the unemployment pool is one of the key factors behind the growth of long-term unemployment in Poland and Hungary.[7] This low turnover also explains why unemployment has stabilized at high levels. As unemployment benefits are offered for a limited period only, many of the long-term unemployed drop out of the labour force.[8] The main explanation for the low turnover is that the majority of people employed by the growing private sector have come directly from the state sector without experiencing unemployment. Private employers have a tendency to recruit workers directly from the state sector because they see the unemployed as low-qualified workers. Thus an increase in the duration of unemployment (used as a screening device) exerts a strong negative effect on worker flows from unemployment to employment.

Unemployment threatens disproportionately some well-defined groups of the population such as youth and women (Table 4.11). We noted earlier that the youth unemployment rate is high; also, the female unemployment rate is higher than the male rate. The unskilled and underqualified are overrepresented among the unemployed. In the case of Hungary, the gypsy population suffers from the highest unemployment (50 per cent) (Nagy and Sik, 1993). The process of social marginalization (related to the evolution of the labour market)

Table 4.11 Unemployment and long-term unemployment among different groups in Poland and Hungary (percentages)

	Share in unemployment (1996)	*Share in long-term unemployment (1992)*
Poland		
Women	59.9	52.2
Youth	33.0	7.2
Primary/low education	30.8[a]	23.3
Hungary		
Women	44.7	39.7
Youth	26.0	20.3
Primary/low education	55.4[b]	51.8

[a] Primary school and basic vocational education.
[b] Primary school and apprenticeship school.
Source: OECD (1994a); UNECE (1997); Hungarian Labour Force Survey (Ministry of Labour, Budapest 1997).

is associated with that of spatial marginalization. The regions most threatened by unemployment in Hungary and Poland include those with a non-diversified economic structure concentrating mainly on such declining industries as textiles and electrical goods. This is also true of mining areas and certain agricultural regions. At the end of 1995 in Poland, disparities in regional unemployment rates ranged from 5.3 per cent in Warsaw to 38.6 per cent in Slupsk. Notwithstanding rapid economic growth, the geographical dispersion of the unemployment rates was extremely stable. In Hungary, the highest unemployment rates were recorded in the regions with heavy industry, in particular metallurgy and mining. The unemployment rate in the northeast, in Borsod-Abauj-Zemplen, Nograd and eastern Hungary bordering the former USSR (which is agricultural) is almost three times higher than in the region with the lowest rate (the capital). Since 1992, the geographical dispersion of unemployment rates has remained virtually unchanged.

To conclude, unemployment is an increasingly painful experience in the transition economies, since traditional safety nets have been weakened under pressures to reduce public expenditure and make labour markets more flexible. In particular, eligibility rules for unemployment benefits have been tightened and the period of entitlement and the ratio of benefits to average wages have been reduced. Future prospects of a significant reduction in unemployment rates are not very bright. As the experience of Western Europe suggests, the prospect of reducing the number of long-term unemployed is probably even worse (United Nations, 1997, p. 4). Indeed, output recovery has been accompanied by a rapid growth in productivity instead of an increase in total employment. This apparent anomaly results from the restructuring of production, investment in new equipment, recovery from low levels of capacity utilization and a drop in surplus labour reserves. The slow response of labour demand to the increase in output reflects the existence of large labour surpluses in all the former socialist economic systems. Given the already high levels of unemployment and sharp rise in income inequalities, another large dose of labour-shedding is likely to generate intolerable social tensions.

Unemployment rates tend to be higher in countries where output has recovered the most (de Melo *et al.*, 1997, p. 44). This trend may reflect the success of these countries in downsizing or closing loss-making firms and freeing resources for new activities. Output recovery will have to proceed faster before a significant net increase occurs in the number of new jobs.

2. *Poverty and Income Inequality*

The shifts in employment status discussed above have had profound effects on living standards and household welfare. Most formal-sector workers who lost their jobs or suffered steep cuts in real wages came from households that were not poor before the stabilization and reform programmes were introduced. In the 1990s, the rapid increase in unemployment and a decline in overall income associated with it contributed largely to an increase in poverty. Data from national accounts and household surveys show that the decline in household labour income during 1989–93 reflected rising unemployment and labour force inactivity more than any significant decline in real wages. The poverty rate in Poland (calculated on the basis of the real 1993 minimum pension), which fluctuated between 5 and 10 per cent of the population during the 1980s, jumped to 15 per cent in the 1990s (World Bank, 1995). Based on the poverty line (the minimum sustainable level of income per household) monitored by the Institute of Labour and Social Studies, the proportion of the poor in Poland roughly doubled between the late 1970s and the late 1980s, and roughly doubled again between the late 1980s and 1992 (OECD, 1997a, p. 91). The overall average real income declined by about 10 per cent in Poland (Milanovic, 1996). In Hungary the incidence of poverty (based on minimum pension) between 1989 and 1993 increased from less than 1.6 per cent of the population to over 8.6 per cent (World Bank, 1996b). The poverty line, based on households with an income at half of the mean household income, reflects a more marked increase in the incidence of poverty.

Estimates concerning poverty in Central Europe differ greatly from one author to another, depending upon the definition of the poverty line used. There is, however, a consensus as regards the importance of its increase in the 1990s. All countries in Central Europe have experienced a process of impoverishment during the transition, but the relative importance of the population affected and the extent have differed from one country to the next. Table 4.12 gives one picture of that process.

Labour market status is the most important determinant of poverty in both Poland and Hungary. Indeed, the incidence of poverty is much higher (35 per cent of all the poor in Poland) in households with an unemployed member. This incidence is higher if the household head is unemployed and if he is unemployed for more than a year. In Poland, the 'working poor' represent 60 per cent of all the poor.

Table 4.12 Incidence of poverty and low income among households, persons and children in Poland and Hungary (1989–94)

		Low income			Poverty		
		I	*II*	*III*	*I*	*II*	*III*
Poland LIL = 40% of average wage; PL = 60% of LIL	1989	22.3	30.6	24.1	4.8	8.4	5.8
	1992	29.6	52.6	36.3	7.2	19.9	10.9
Hungary LIL = 40% of average wage; PL = 60% of LIL	1989	8.5	15.8	10.1	0.8	1.8	1.1
	1993	17.3	36.1	22.5	2.4	7.4	4.0

Notes: LIL = Low Income Line; PL = Poverty Line; Column I = Households; Column II = Children; Column III = Population.
Source: data from UNICEF (1995), 'Poverty, Children and Policy: Responses for Brighter Future', *Regional Monitoring Report no. 2*, UNICEF–ICDC (International Child Development Centre), Florence.

In Hungary, the percentage change in the probability of being poor (that is, below minimum pension) is 8.6 per cent for a temporary employee and nearly 5 per cent for an unemployed household head (World Bank, 1996b).

To conclude, the labour market trends suggest three groups of workers. The first group consists of those who cope well with the new labour market conditions. The second group consists of those who may suffer a temporary wage decline or unemployment, but who are likely to regain a job when the economy recovers. The third group suffers permanent losses through long-term unemployment and precarious forms of work. Poorly educated, prime-age workers and unskilled or semi-skilled workers belong to this vulnerable group.

It is to be noted that the transition has resulted not only in a rise in poverty but also in a wider range of types of poverty and insecurity. An ever greater proportion of poor people are in work which reflects the fall in average wages to a level closer to the official poverty line. Numerous households cannot escape poverty when only one member of the household is in work. Thus during the transition, the rate of badly paid workers has increased considerably reaching almost 20 per cent in

Table 4.13 The incidence of low pay in Poland and Hungary

	1987	*1992*	*1995*
Percentage of workers earning less than half of median earnings			
Hungary	5.0	5.5	6.9*
Poland	2.9	3.1	4.6
Percentage of workers earning less than two-thirds of median earnings			
Hungary	17.5	18.9	20.0*
Poland	14.2	14.2	17.3

Note: * = 1994.
Source: Rutkowski (1997).

Hungary and 17.3 per cent in Poland when one takes as a reference point wages corresponding to less than two-thirds of the average wage (Table 4.13): in comparison in the OECD countries, this rate was on average 14 per cent, ranging from 5 per cent in Belgium to almost 20 per cent in the UK and Spain.

Income inequalities have also risen in Poland and Hungary. In the 1970s, historically low levels of the Gini coefficient (around 20 to 25 per cent) showed much more egalitarian income distribution than in the rest of the world. But Gini coefficients considerably increased during the 1990s (see Table 4.14), and are now comparable to those of many Western European countries. Indeed changes in wealth and income distribution are among the most dramatic in the transition countries in recent years. In Poland and Hungary, wages and incomes at the high end of the scale have increased substantially reflecting an increase in the number of highly-paid white collar workers (Rutkowski, 1995). The quintile ratio (ratio of top quintile's share of income to bottom quintile's share) rose from 3.6 to 4.8 between 1988 and 1995 in Poland, and from 3.3 to 3.9 in Hungary during the same period. The first wave of the panel surveys of household incomes in Hungary in May 1992 showed that between the spring of 1991 and that of 1992, 46 per cent of those interviewed experienced a decline in real per capita household income, whereas 16 per cent became considerably richer (cited in Andorka, 1994).

To a large extent, the widening of income inequalities is attributable to a greater dispersion of earnings caused by larger wage differentials, lower participation rates and an increase in unemployment. As a

Table 4.14 Income inequality in Poland and Hungary

	Poland			*Hungary*	
	1989	*1992*	*1993*	*1989*	*1993*
Gini index	24.9		33.1	21.4	32.2
Income share of lowest 20%	9.2	9.3		10.9	9.4
Income share of highest 20%	35.3	36.6		34.4	36.6

Sources: For Gini index, Deninger and Squire (1996); UNICEF (1993); for income shares, *Hungarian Household Income Survey* of the Central Statistical Office (1993), quoted by R. Andorka and Z. Speder (1994) *Poverty in Hungary: Some Results of the First Two Waves of the Hungarian Panel Survey in 1992 and 1993*, Tilburg, mimeo.; World Bank (1997).

result, there emerged in both countries a relatively small layer of wealthy individuals usually involved in entrepreneurial activities, and a growing number of poor and vulnerable people.

3. *Crime*

The fall of the communist regimes was accompanied by an explosion in crime in Eastern Europe. The reasons are multiple: anomie following the collapse of the socialist regimes and the loss of legitimacy of the former normative systems, the disappearance of state control over the population by means of a repressive police system, the period of uncertainty following the restructuring of the legal system, the opening of borders, and enormous opportunities for rapid gain linked to the economic changes initiated.

The collapse of the pillars of the welfare system of the socialist regimes and the decline or stagnation in real income and household earnings provoked phenomena of social disintegration and weakened the social fabric, thereby giving rise to greater insecurity and an increase in crime. Thus the major cities of Central Europe, which in the past had been safe, have found themselves having to confront rampant criminality (UNDP, 1996).

If, on the one hand, political freedom and human rights are now respected in Central Europe, on the other hand it is clear that there has been a deterioration in material and physical safety as a result of the increase in crime and delinquency (Matutinovic, 1998). These phenomena, which have a negative effect on the quality of life, can be explained by a combination of the increase in inequalities, unemployment and poverty and the loss of values that followed the collapse of the socialist systems.

4. The Socialist Legacy

In order to understand the changes of the post-socialist period, it is important to understand the communist system itself and its social roots. It is, above all, necessary to go beyond the ideological rhetoric on the oppressive nature and irrational economic logic of the socialist systems and to acknowledge that the systems operated for a long period and had, at least until the 1970s, a certain social legitimacy (Illner, 1996). When one assesses the results of the socialist systems, it is important to take into consideration the factors which compensated, at least to a certain extent, for the disadvantages in terms of the level and dynamics of consumption, the shortages and the weight of the bureaucracy in all areas of life (Brus and Laski, 1989, p. 31). Despite the eruptions of repression at certain periods, as in Budapest in 1956 and in Prague in 1968, the relative social stability (though not in Poland) which reigned for a long period cannot be explained simply by the existence of an authoritarian regime. This relative stability was also due to the existence of an implicit social compromise which guaranteed economic security and social rights to a wide range of social groups under the socialist systems. It can be said that once people accepted the explicit and implicit rules of the socialist regimes, they had the right to a vast range of social rights which provided them with basic economic and human security.

The three pillars of the socialist welfare state were full employment, price controls as part of a policy of subsidies for essential goods and services, and universal, free access to education, health services, day nurseries and childcare facilities as well as superannuation and sickness benefits, maternity leave and family allowances. Job security in a context of over-employment, a more equitable distribution of income and the absence of a wide gap in wealth and a specific form of the welfare state avoided the development of pockets of poverty and destitution.

Consequently, generations of workers in the socialist countries enjoyed job security in a context where unemployment was almost unknown. This sense of security was underpinned by the full employment situation and the paternalism that linked employers and employees. A large part of the social services and goods were distributed through the workplace. Sachs (1991, p. 2) notes that job security is one of the fundamental successes of the socialist systems which not only provided a certain degree of economic security. Indeed, it 'plays additionally a prominent part in inducing a sense of financial security, strengthening the workers' resolve and firmness toward their employers, and helping to bring about equal rights for women'.

Under the socialist regimes the state assumed the responsibility of the full cost of certain products and services which it made available free of cost in order to guarantee the economic security of the whole of the population. Free education and social and health services thus played a key role in increasing human security in society.

The socialist regimes in Central Europe had welfare budgets amongst the most generous in the world, with between 15 and 30 per cent of GNP being allocated to such expenditure, compared with 5 to 10 per cent in East Asia in countries with comparable income (Kornai, 1992, p. 210). At the end of the 1980s, the socialist countries of Central Europe had social security systems that provided safety nets against all types of social risks, except for unemployment which was almost non-existent. Those characteristics explain the low level of economic insecurity amongst the population.

Companies played a pivotal role in the social security system under the socialist regimes. Companies provided not only job security and a majority of social benefits and services, they also had a social budget which enabled them to provide goods and services to their employees. Thus the major companies were able to provide their employees with housing, hotels and holiday centres, day nurseries, canteens, clinics, training schools and other cultural and sports activities, for example. In addition employees had the possibility of obtaining at their place of work consumer goods that for some people were not available in the stores, given the shortages that existed. Taking into account the low level of real income, food expenditure was one of the most important items in the family budget and consequently any possibility to make savings on food expenditure considerably increased the family's overall standard of living.

This legacy has an important influence on the population's opinion regarding the current transition process. We have demonstrated the deep-seated world trend towards social disintegration in the framework of the current phase of globalization. We would once again emphasize at this point that the reactions to those regressive social phenomena depend very much on the population's previous experiences. Thus, as Boyer (1994) states: 'The expectations, values and behaviour, in short the habitus of Eastern Europeans, have been moulded by almost half a century of so-called 'socialist' institutions which continue to determine to a large extent their reactions to economic reforms'.

That is why the analysis of the socialist legacy in the social area is fundamental. The social impact of the changes under way cannot be fully grasped without analysing how such changes have destroyed the three fundamental pillars of the former socialist systems through the appearance of mass unemployment, privatization and measures to reduce social expenditure and/or increase the selectivity of such expenditure. The result is an alarming increase in poverty and social divisions. Another consequence of the current changes is the growth in crime and violence (UNICEF, 1993). In addition, as we shall see later, the brutal differences in wages and income since the start of the 1990s cannot be ignored.

For the great majority of the population, the advantages of the democratic process cannot offset the negative effects of economic insecurity. That is why the retreat of the state as regards its social and cultural responsibilities is highly unpopular. In his survey referred to above, Sagi (1993) showed that 96 per cent of the people questioned expected the state to provide health care for the whole population, 88 per cent were in favour of a system of universal, free education provided by the state and finally 89 per cent believed that the state should guarantee employment for all. As Illner (1996, p. 15) has shown for the Czech Republic, that seems relevant for all the countries in transition, 'in the period after November 1989, people actually asked for both market freedom and state guarantees at the same time'.

Thus the electoral success in Poland (in September 1993) and in Hungary (in May 1994) of the former communist parties only a few years after the transition can be attributed in part to the concerns of voters regarding the loss of the basic social rights which had been established universally by the socialist systems. However, even those parties are committed to the transition to a market economy and to reforming in part the social security system. In concluding an important study on the electoral behaviour of citizens from Central Europe during the systemic changes at the start of the 1990s, Mateju (1996, p. 75) writes: 'we can say that the results presented in this paper have shown that despite the vital role played by specific historical, political and economic circumstances in shaping political scenes in the post-communist countries, the social costs of the transformation constitute a very important common factor that may contribute to an understanding of voting behavior and the political future of the countries escaping socialism'.

The impact of the social changes in Poland and Hungary – notably as regards the increase in economic vulnerability and precariousness of employment – is strongly associated with the social rights that existed in the socialist systems taking into account the welfare institutions in place.

The socialist systems succeeded in offering the population extensive security through job security, universal social services and family allowances. That situation is very important in order to understand the acceptance of the system by the population. Moreover, taking into account the nature of the political systems and the relative economic security, there was a low level of crime and law and order was greater than in the developed capitalist countries. But the level of economic security under those systems was only achieved at the expense of, and serious constraints upon, individual freedom.

5. *The Increase in Economic and Social Vulnerability*

At the start of the 1990s the post-socialist systems in Central Europe underwent an historic process of social change which profoundly affected the lives of the population. The transition towards market economies led in fact to the liberalization of many spheres of society. But following the fall of the communist regimes, the priority of the reformers was the dismantling of the old system and the setting up of a market economy. In this framework, the 'social question' was overshadowed by the process of economic and institutional changes. At the start of the transition, the new political freedoms acquired and the population's very strong optimism regarding the consequences of the reforms implemented meant that the social and distributional aspects were not considered priority issues.

If an increase in unemployment and poverty was considered as inevitable in the first phase of the transition, the extent and the ongoing nature of the regressive social phenomena resulted in a radical change of opinion regarding the transition policies. The deterioration in living conditions had been accepted by the population as a temporary phenomenon linked to the changes necessary to re-establish 'healthy' growth, but the absence of a turning point has provoked growing discontent among the population and made people less tolerant of the reforms.

The disappearance or the transformation of the three traditional pillars of the former welfare state, combined with the impoverishment of a large part of the population, and unemployment, have weakened the basis of citizenship and popular support for the reforms. In all the countries in Central Europe, the legitimacy of the growing inequalities is being questioned and the population considers that it is the state's responsibility to combat poverty and unemployment in order to preserve social cohesion. It is interesting to note here that according to the survey on behaviour and economic expectations carried out in the Czech Republic, an ever-increasing number of people believe that it is society and not individual aptitudes that is responsible for poverty (40 per cent of those replying at the end of 1994) (Vecernik, 1995, p. 116). Against that background of increasing insecurity, the calling into question of the state's social security role arouses great fear amongst the population.

6. *Summary and Conclusions*

The phenomena of poverty and unemployment seem to be deep-seated and long-term, contrary to the initial forecasts which saw them as the short-term price to be paid during the changeover from the socialist systems to a market economy. The dominant thinking emphasized the fact that once the necessary basis had been established for strong, rational economic growth the severity of those phenomena would diminish. However, the considerable increase in long-term unemployment tends to produce a lasting fragmentation of society between those who, for various reasons, do not have access to the fruits of economic growth and those who have been able to take advantage of the opportunities created by such growth. The problem henceforth is to know whether the rigid divisions of the two-tier society that is emerging following the systemic changes will be perpetuated or whether over time the social structure will be less extreme.

A process of rapid economic convergence has indeed been launched in the case of Hungary and Poland and those countries are now starting to gather the fruits of their efforts to that end by way of reasonably strong growth. However, the convergence process has been accompanied by profound social consequences, for the transition put an end to the relative economic and social security and to the low level of social differentiation inherited from the socialist systems. These societies have experienced growing social fragmentation between those who have been able to profit from the new opportunities created by the liberalization process, those who in terms of income and employment have seen their situation become more precarious, and finally, those who have been excluded from the labour market and progressively have been excluded from participating fully in the society in which they live.

The initial phase of transition had been characterized by the mobilization and optimism of the populations, resulting in a large consensus in favour of the neoliberal policies designed to transform the existing systems. But this confidence in the reform process has progressively deteriorated as the social consequences of the transition have worsened. The consensus has thus collapsed and strong divisions have started to appear regarding the values and objectives pursued (Kolarska-Bobinska, 1992).

The growing social split has resulted in a breakdown in the social fabric. On the one side, those with their newly acquired wealth have taken advantage of the new opportunities created by the liberalization of the economy (in terms of income and consumer habits in particular), and others have become impoverished and believe there is no way of escaping from the degradation of their situation (Domanski, 1994; Zioklowski, 1994). Consequently, discontent and disillusion have increased in the Hungarian and Polish societies.

The danger is that impoverishment and the return of economic and social vulnerability will produce political apathy and will lead people to abstain from voting in local and national elections which would threaten the stability of the democratic system. There is a considerable lack of trust in the institutions on account of the awareness of the increase in inequalities and the declining social mobility. Anomie and social alienation in that context could turn into active hostility towards the economic and political system that the reforms have shaped. Even the advocates of the global economy are starting to become aware of that threat, for as Tanzi (1997, p. 325) points out: 'Although it will not be possible (nor perhaps desirable) to prevent inequitable income distribution entirely, too much inequity will create an environment that will lead to populist policies and will make the transition all the more difficult, thus reducing the prospects for growth for many years to come. This is why the objective of equity cannot be ignored even by a government set on creating a market economy'.

The loss of social cohesion and the growth of micro-conflicts that may result are a threat to the new conditions of accumulation. We have pointed here how exclusion processes and social fragmentation weaken the social consensus regarding the objective of growth paired with the globalization of the economy, just when the necessary changes as part of the ongoing process of adaptation to international standards (in terms of flexibility and competitiveness amongst others) require the support of a stable social basis. It is in fact difficult to believe that the losers in the transition can much longer support policies which have produced a hard core group of poor people and long-term unemployed people, and led to the return of great vulnerability for certain social categories which have seen their social status deteriorate during the 1990s (in particular unskilled workers, peasants, persons with a low level of education). Only a limited number of specific social categories have the feeling that henceforward their situation will improve thanks to the changes initiated and that they will be able to enjoy the opportunities of growth offered by the global economy.

CONCLUDING REMARKS

In this chapter, we have reviewed exclusion (in terms of long-term unemployment, poverty, inequality, and social alienation) in North America, Western Europe and Eastern Europe. On the basis of case studies on France, Hungary and Poland, we have shown that the dynamics of precariousness and labour market exclusion is at the heart of a process of social exclusion and disintegration affecting a growing part of the population. Where jobs do grow, they are generally 'bad' jobs associated with poverty. Indeed, the crisis of the wage-earning society – growth of long-term unemployment and precarious forms of work – is the crisis of the most important mode of social integration in advanced industrialized countries.

In the short term, active labour market policies and social safety nets can provide some temporary relief. But they do not offer a solution to social disintegration and exclusion. A new social question is emerging from the plight of a growing number of individuals who face economic and social deprivation throughout the industrialized world. These people are trapped in a kind of 'social no man's land' involving risks related to the development of a ghetto. People are dependent on social benefits without any positive recognition in the new social structure that is based on unregulated and unfettered economic globalization (see Chapter 6). Moreover, with the growth in long-term unemployment and of precarious forms of work, channels of upward social mobility are gradually being closed, a phenomenon with crucial consequences for the stability and dynamic evolution of society.

5 Exclusion in Developing Countries

We noted in Chapter 1 that in developing countries exclusion is studied mainly in terms of poverty, its characteristics, evolution and structure. Although in these countries the notion has not yet gained much currency, the process and its underlying causes are hotly debated. For example, in Latin America the debate on marginality and marginalization in the 1950s and 1960s provides a genesis of social exclusion there. This phenomenon is, therefore, briefly discussed below.

Our concern in this chapter is to examine in the context of developing countries, economic, social and political dimensions of exclusion and the interrelationships between its *distributional* and *relational* problems as defined in Chapter 2. We shall discuss the particular case of Brazil as a concrete country situation and examine the relevance of job precariousness as one of the indicators of social exclusion. Although we discuss below the economic and social dimensions of exclusion separately for ease of exposition, the two dimensions are closely interrelated. As we noted in Chapters 1 and 2, the state of economic exclusion is embedded in the prevailing social and political structures. Furthermore, it is empirically established that a more egalitarian income distribution can promote such social goals as an increase in aggregate school enrolments (see Birdsall and Sabot, 1993; Bourguignon, 1993).

MARGINALIZATION AND EXCLUSION

An important literature exists in Latin America on the *state* of marginality and the *process* of marginalization. In that region, the notion dominated the debate in social sciences during the 1960s and 1970s. Two main approaches – structuralist and individualistic – are used to explain the phenomenon. Both address problems of new urban poverty as a consequence of mass rural-to-urban migration and significant changes in the production structure. The structuralist approach (based on Marxist theory of exploitation) regarded marginality as the outcome of the capitalist system (Nun, 1969), whereas the individualistic approach focused on deviant individual behaviour and values in the modern urban society (Lewis, 1965; Becker, 1985). Both the above approaches were the subject of severe criticism in the 1970s (see Fassin, 1996a). The critics argued that marginalization was not so much a lack of integration due to the existence of a dual society but more a specific mode of insertion into the urban productive structure (Castells, 1971). Some Latin American scholars (for example, Faria, 1995) have argued that poverty and deprivation in the region is less a reflection of 'lack of integration' (as in Europe) than a phenomenon that is structurally related to the functioning of economies and societies.

Marginalization was defined in several different ways in Latin America. The early literature referred to such phenomena as urban poverty, rural–urban migration and shantytowns. The debate focused mainly on the urban population on the fringes of urban development in the bidonvilles and centred around economic, social and psychological aspects of urban squalor (Lomnitz, 1977, pp. 9–14). To sociologists, marginalization also encompassed the lack of political participation. Concentration of wealth and industrial organization, and increasing economic and social inequalities, create a dualistic society consisting of those who have economic and political power and others who are denied it for lack, *inter alia*, of access to incomes and assets.

The recent debate on social exclusion in the context of developing countries closely resembles that on marginality and marginalization in Latin America in the 1950s. As in industrialized countries discussed in Chapter 4, exclusion in developing countries is manifested in several forms. Although open unemployment and long-term unemployment are not common phenomena in developing countries, job insecurity, poverty and deprivation are. In these countries informalization of the labour market is reflected more in the growth of the urban informal sector than in the 'flexibilization' of organized labour through the emergence of casual and part-time employment.

Several factors, both national and international, were put forward to explain the process of marginalization. First, national factors included the process of industrialization and technological change, which led to the emergence of a new industrial proletariat. Second, at the global level, the notions of the 'centre–periphery' type of development (see Prebisch, 1950) of world capitalism and the 'dependency theory' in Latin America explain marginalization and exclusion in terms of the adverse terms of trade of developing countries in the export of primary commodities. The impact of declining commodity terms of trade has been particularly severe for some developing countries. Berry *et al.* (1997) note that the benefits of trade for the least developed countries were more than offset by a cumulative decline of 50 per cent in their terms of trade during the past 25 years. According to Sunkel (1973), limited access to the means of production and different types of discrimination (social, cultural, racial, and political) are the two important sources of marginalization. He noted that 'underdevelopment, marginality and dependence are manifestations ... and consequences of the general evolution of the international capitalist system' (p. 142). However, as Berry (1998) notes, despite the pessimism of the dependency school, the subsequent events were far less gloomy than predicted. The Latin American region recorded significant growth, employment generation and trickledown, leading to a decline in the incidence of poverty in the 1960s and 1970s.

Fassin (1996b, p. 263) describes the emergence of poverty giving rise to three phenomena: exclusion in France, *underclass* in the United States (both discussed above in Chapter 4) and marginalization in Latin America. He notes that these concepts reflect three configurations of social space: 'in/out', 'high/low' and 'centre/periphery' respectively. The debate on exclusion in Western Europe has led some scholars to speak about the Latin Americanization of Europe, thereby suggesting a similarity between exclusion and marginalization. The two phenomena are characterized by the informalization of the labour market and growth of casual employment. However, there are differences also. First, as we noted in Chapter 4 in the case of France, Western Europe and North America, a portion of the population described as 'new poor' were at one time part of the dominant capitalist system (they were 'in') but now have been excluded from it (they are 'out'). On the other hand, in Latin America and other developing countries, the urban poor are former rural migrants who were never integrated into the urban capitalist system in the first place. Thus it may not be appropriate to call them excluded. Second, in developing countries the urban poor may often represent the bulk of the urban population which is not the case in industrialized countries.

Thus marginalization encompasses the economic, social and political dimensions of poverty and exclusion. The phenomenon is not peculiar to Latin America, although it was the subject of a vigorous debate there in the 1950s. On the basis of literature survey, Gore (1994) shows that the relationship between social identity and entitlement to resources has been a central issue in sub-Saharan Africa, even though the term 'social exclusion' is not used explicitly. In the African literature, some studies focus on the Weberian notion of 'social closure' under which the rich and powerful seek to maximize rewards by restricting access to resources and opportunities (see below). The classic example is Arrighi's analysis of the exclusion from land resources by white European settlers in colonial Rhodesia (Arrighi, 1970). Other studies focus on the situation of the marginalized or weak groups.

Weber's theory of 'social closure', under which some groups with command over resources exploit others is one interpretation of exclusion in developing countries. In the Marxist tradition, much of the literature on social closure is concerned with antagonism between organized labour and capital. However, collective response to exclusionary practices can be generalized to include all types of social and economic groups and classes that are excluded or exploited. Street violence, increased crime and terrorism can be interpreted as manifestations of extreme poverty and exclusionary closure (see Table 5.2 for data on crimes and rape in selected Latin American countries). Although there are no consistent trends in all countries for which data are available, between 1979 and 1988 the number of homicides and drug offences increased in Chile, the Dominican Republic and Ecuador. In Venezuela, while homicides declined drug offences increased; Cartaya *et al.* (1997, p. 45) note that 'poverty and political exclusion of the majority have traditionally been recognized as latent forms of violence'. Prevention of access to social and political rights has led to violent reactions from the population in the form of different types of demonstrations. In the case of Brazil discussed below, we show that crime by the 'street' children may be linked as much to extreme poverty and destitution as to social delinquency.

At a more general level, marginalization can be defined in terms of the material (low levels of income), social (low levels of education, health, nutrition and poor housing) and political (limited citizenship rights and lack of political participation) aspects and the indicators of poverty discussed in Chapter 2. The material indicators of poverty for developing countries in different regions can be presented in terms of the income share of the lowest 40 per cent of the households, the ratio of the shares of the highest 20 per cent to the lowest 20 per cent of the population, and the number of people benefiting from social security in rural and urban areas (see Table 5.1). (As we noted in Chapter 3, exclusion from any social security benefits is one of the characteristics of the urban informal sector as defined in Latin America in particular.)

Table 5.1 Poverty and income inequality in developing countries

	Income share		People in poverty	Social security	
	Lowest 40% of households (%)	Ratio of highest 20% to lowest 20%	Urban Rural (%)	Social security benefits expenditure as % of GDP	
Region/Country	*1981–93*	*1981–93*	*1990*	*1990*	*1993*
I. Latin America and Caribbean					
Argentina	–	–	15	20	4.5
Brazil	7.0	32.1	38	66	–
Colombia	11.2	15.5	40	45	2.4
Chile	10.2	18.3	–	–	–
Costa Rica	13.1	12.7	24	30	–
Bolivia	15.3	8.6	–	86	1.6
Guatemala	7.9	30.0	60	80	–
Honduras	8.7	23.5	74	80	–
Peru	14.1	10.5	52	72	–
Panama	8.3	29.9	36	52	–
Venezuela	14.3	10.3	30	42	–
Uruguay	–	–	10	23	14.8
Jamaica	15.9	8.1	–	–	–
Nicaragua	12.2	13.2	–	–	–
Mexico	11.9	13.6	23	43	–

Table 5.1 (Continued)

	Income share		*People in poverty*	*Social security*	
	Lowest 40% of households (%)	*Ratio of highest 20% to lowest 20%*	*Urban Rural (%)*	*Social security benefits expenditure as % of GDP*	
Region/Country	*1981–93*	*1981–93*	*1990*	*1990*	*1993*
II. Asia					
Hong Kong	16.2	8.7	–	–	–
Singapore	15.0	9.6	–	–	7.2
Korea	19.7	5.7	5	4	2.3
Thailand	15.5	8.3	7	29	0.1
Malaysia	12.9	11.7	8	23	2.3
Sri Lanka	22.0	4.4	15	36	2.5
Philippines	16.6	7.4	40	54	1.2
Indonesia	20.8	4.9	20	16	–
China	17.4	6.5	–	12	–
India	21.3	4.7	38	49	0.3
Pakistan	21.3	4.7	20	31	–
Bangladesh	22.9	4.1	56	51	–
III. Africa					
Algeria	17.9	6.7	–	25	–
Tunisia	16.3	7.8	16	31	4.1
Botswana	10.5	16.4	30	64	–

Table 5.1 (Continued)

	Income share		*People in poverty*	*Social security*	
	Lowest 40% of households (%)	*Ratio of highest 20% to lowest 20%*	*Urban Rural (%)*	*Social security benefits expenditure as % of GDP*	
Region/Country	*1981–93*	*1981–93*	*1990*	*1990*	*1993*
South Africa	9.1	19.2	–	–	–
Morocco	17.1	7.0	28	32	1.8
Zimbabwe	10.3	15.6	–	–	–
Kenya	10.1	18.2	–	–	0.7
Ghana	18.3	6.3	59	54	0.1
Lesotho	9.3	20.7	–	–	–
Zambia	15.2	8.9	–	–	–
Nigeria	15.2	9.6	–	–	–
Tanzania	8.1	26.1	–	–	–
Côte d'Ivoire	18.0	6.5	–	–	–
Mauritania	14.2	13.2	–	–	0.9
Senegal	10.5	16.7	–	–	–
Uganda	20.6	4.9	25	33	–

– = not available.
Source: UNDP (1996), pp. 170–1.

Table 5.2 Violence and crime in selected Latin American countries

Country	*Homicides (per 100,000 inhabitants)*		*Drug offences (per 100,000 inhabitants)*		*Rapes (per 100,000 inhabitants)*		*Suicides (per 100,000 inhabitants)*	*Divorces (per 1000 inhabitants)*	
	(1979)	*(1988)*	*(1987)*	*(1992)*	*(1979)*	*(1988)*		*(1980)*	*(1990)*
Argentina	–	–	–	–	–	–	6.7[2]	–	–
Brazil	–	–	–	–	–	–	3.5[1]	0.23[7]	0.23[11]
Chile	6.27	6.54	13.48	15.50	11.44	10.33	4.9[1]	–	–
Costa Rica	5.72	4.05	4.81	6.57	9.25	8.84[10]	5.4[6]	0.77	0.87[11]
Dominican Republic	8.47[5]	11.93	7.35	14.77	3.59[6]	3.02	2.0[3]	2.10	1.22[8]
Ecuador	0.25[3]	5.06[9]	1.20	18.90	0.57[4]	4.84[9]	2.9[3]	0.34	0.43[11]
Honduras	–	–	–	–	–	–	0.23	–	
Mexico	–	–	–	–	–	–	1.6[5]	0.31	0.63
Peru	1.81	1.20[7]	9.55	8.50	7.69	3.40[7]	1.41	–	–
Uruguay							11.2[7]	1.55	1.51[10]
Venezuela	14.49	9.11	554	1 022	15.03	14.36	4.8[6]	0.31	1.14[12]

[1] 1978; [2] 1979; [3] 1980; [4] 1981; [5] 1982; [6] 1983; [7] 1984; [8] 1985; [9] 1986; [10] 1987; [11] 1988; [12] 1989.
– = not available.
Source: Wilkie (1995), vol. 31, pt. I.

Large economic and social disparities exist within the South. For example, per capita income in sub-Saharan Africa (in terms of purchasing power parity) is much lower than that of even South Asia, where the bulk of the world's poor are concentrated. Similarly, such social indicators as the human development index, including literacy rates and life expectancy, vary widely across regions and countries (Bhalla and Berry, 1998).

DISTRIBUTION, RELATIONS AND SOCIAL NETWORKS[1]

We noted in Chapter 2 that the *distributional* and *relational* aspects of exclusion are closely interrelated. We also noted that in developing countries family and community provide social insurance and protection in the absence of any state-protected welfare provisions. Family is the first mechanism through which protection and support is provided, especially to the very young and very old. The economic value of children in poor societies is now well known. It is reflected in the very high fertility rates in the very poor countries. ILO (1993b, p. 54) notes that 'between 1990 and 1995 the average number of children born to a woman in Europe is expected to be 1.7 and in North America 1.8, but in Latin America, the figure is likely to be 3.2, in South-East Asia 3.3, in South Asia 4.4 and in Africa 6.0.'

Family and community support systems continue to prevail in developing countries, although their strength may have weakened in some countries. For example, under India's *jajmani* system, higher castes employ lower caste people (invariably the untouchables) on their farms and pay fixed quantities of food regardless of the size of the harvest. Labour is bonded in the sense that it cannot move freely to earn higher wages elsewhere. In Java, Indonesia, the *bawon* is a communal system under which landowners invite anyone to help on their farms in exchange for a share of the crop. This system has been modified and restricted to people from the same village or those who are invited by the landowner. Jellinek (1991) reports how in a poor community of Jakarta, social ties are based more on the proximity of households than on kinship ties. Men are known to provide against insecurity and disaster through numerous loose marital relationships, whereas women rely on their children for social security. Communal lodging houses (*pondok*) and rotating credit societies (*arisan*) are two other forms of social networks in Indonesia which soften the severity of poverty.

Social ties are found to be strong among the very poor households.The poorer the household with very low incomes, the greater the need for social ties to provide income and social security. The richer households in Indonesia are known to gradually break away from the social network and become outsiders. This finding provides an empirical support to our hypothesis (see Chapter 2) that *distributional* and *relational* problems are interlinked, and that social relations tend to weaken at higher levels of development. As we show below with examples, the experience of Indonesia is likely to be shared by a large number of poor developing countries. In Sri Lanka the fishing communities, suffering from precariousness, have devised schemes to insure against risk, for example, a rota system allows everyone access to the sea during the season of good catches. In tribal societies of sub-Saharan Africa also, similar schemes based on kinship relations are known to exist. Each head of household with family to support is entitled to a piece of communally held land. For example, in the Sahel, farmers relying on flood-retreat irrigation are allocated widely dispersed plots of land at different heights above the river to reduce chances of flooding (similar custom prevails in the Andes).

In Africa, some literature (Berry, 1988; Gore, 1994, 1995) shows how distributional issues of poverty and access to resources are closely related to social identity and the rules of membership of various social networks. Drawing on the Nigerian data, Berry (1988) shows how agricultural surpluses are used not only for production but also for improving connections and social recognition.

The Latin American literature on marginalization describes how the 'marginals' organize their economic and social life in terms of networks of reciprocal exchange. These reciprocity networks are based on family and kinship relations; they consist of groups of neighbours cooperating in daily life in order to ensure economic survival. Lomnitz (1977, p. 209) notes: 'Family structures, residential patterns, occupational structures, household organization, leisure time activities, alcohol consumption, and the use of traditional institutions such as *compadrazgo* and *cuatismo* were all modified and directed toward protecting and furthering reciprocity relations among kin and neighbors.' In conditions of chronic economic insecurity, cooperation through social networks in developing countries is likely to survive more than competition under market exchange.

In Venezuela, neighbourhood associations are quite common among the inhabitants of localities. However, the activities of these associations are of a political rather than socioeconomic nature. They consist of lobbying local, regional and national government in order to defend the localities' or community's interests against encroachment and abuse by urban developers, industrialists, landowners and so on (Ying, 1993, cited in Cartaya *et al.*, 1997). The associations provide citizens with political information and training. In other developing countries like China, unlike the above voluntary mechanisms, the constitution specifies that children have an obligation to support their parents and grandparents. Local governments police observance of this law. Family support supplements the public system of social security. The latter is considered a last resort, since generally people feel ashamed to be on public support.

Social networks and local movements in developing countries received a boost as a consequence of recent democratization in most developing countries which is briefly discussed below.

DEMOCRATIZATION AND EXCLUSION

Democracy is becoming a universal phenomenon, particularly in developing countries. Yet it is understood differently in different places. The conventional notion of political democratization involves free elections, a multi-party system and constitutional guarantees of civil and human rights. One can also think of social democratization, which calls for freedom of speech and association, freedom to choose and form social groups and movements (so-called 'globalization from below', in contrast to 'globalization from above', which involves alliances of the state with transnational capital). With the emerging global economy, democracy is being redefined to include 'social and cultural practices' besides a positive relationship between the state and citizenship (see Dagnino, 1993).

In the 1980s, the process of democratization accompanied that of globalization (see Chapter 6). The forces of globalization and opening up of developing economies have contributed to the weakening of authoritarian regimes and dictatorships, particularly in the developing world. The weakening of the nation state partly weakens the national rulers and their autocratic hold on power. In developing countries, the democratization process has several important implications. First, it gave rise to new social movements championing the cause of minorities, women, youth and green groups (see below the case study on Brazil). These movements claim equality of rights and recognition of social and cultural differences. Dagnino (1993) notes that many social groups are fighting for the 'right to be different' and promoting the 'idea that difference shall not constitute a basis for inequality'. Second, democratization is leading to the emergence of new grassroots and non-governmental organizations. Thirdly, it is leading to the promotion of civil and human rights and the strengthening of civil society in general (see Sunkel, 1995).

All these manifestations of a new democratic order will exercise a favourable influence on poverty and exclusion, by granting civil rights to those who were formerly denied these rights, by enlarging the spread of primary and secondary education, and by providing free access to information. However, the processes of democratization and globalization may also lead to some negative social effects. For example, they are leading to the internationalization of crime, the drugs trade and terrorist incidents (see Table 5.3). The Latin American experience shows how guerrilla movements and the drugs trade in the Andean countries continue to support anti-democratic elements. Crime and violence associated with drug trafficking are likely to put brakes on the process of democratization by leading to the militarization of governments and civil society (see Sunkel, 1995).

In Latin America, while authoritarian and military regimes have been overthrown, democracy has not always taken root. The limited democracy implies that class alliances are wider in scope and strength, and the state is forced into making concessions to various pressure groups. However, as Mittelman (1996, pp. 8–9) notes, this process of modernizing the state 'leaves unchanged the basic structures of power and domination', which can change only through a reformulation of the social and political institutions, and through a bigger role for the community in the political process as opposed to the rights of individuals. Under an individualistic system, citizenship may not necessarily allow political and social participation in decision-making at different levels of social structures.

RECENT EMPIRICAL EVIDENCE

The most recent studies on social exclusion in developing countries were undertaken by the International Institute of Labour Studies (IILS) within the framework of a UNDP-financed research project. There were six main studies – India, Peru, Russia, Tanzania, Thailand, and Yemen (for detailed summaries, see Gore and Figueiredo, 1997, pp. 16–34) – and five other studies – Brazil, Cameroon, Mexico,

Table 5.3 International terrorist incidents

Region	*1988*		*1989*		*1990*		*1991*		*1992*		*1993*	
	No.	*(%)*	*No.*	*(%)*	*No.*	*(%)*	*No.*	*(%)*	*No.*	*(%)*	*No.*	*(%)*
Africa	53	8.2	50	12.3	53	11.6	3	0.5	10	2.7	6	1.4
Asia	178	27.6	42	10.3	92	20.2	48	8.5	13	3.6	37	8.7
Latin America	152	23.6	131	32.3	163	35.7	229	40.5	143	39.3	97	22.7
Western Europe	150	23.3	98	24.1	77	16.9	199	35.2	114	31.3	180	42.2
North America	1	0.2	4	1.0	0	0	2	0.4	2	0.5	1	0.2
Total	644	100	406	100	456	100	566	100.2[a]	364	99.9[a]	427	100.1[a]

[a] Percentages do not add up to 100 because of rounding.
Source: US Department of State, *Patterns of Global Terrorism*, cited in Wilkie (1995), vol. 31, pt 1.

Tunisia and Venezuela – released as working papers. The scope and coverage of these studies in developing countries are summarized in Table 5.4 for illustrative purposes according to our schema elaborated in Chapters 1 and 2. In some cases, it is difficult to specify whether the above studies dealt with economic, social and political aspects of exclusion. As the studies did not follow any common analytical framework, it is difficult to make any generalizations. They do not provide any basis for a comparative analysis of patterns and processes of social exclusion in developing countries. They were exploratory in nature giving wide discretion to local research teams. They are useful in so far as this approach allowed for the diversity of conditions and analyses between countries.

Table 5.4 Social exclusion in developing countries: summary of case studies

	Scope and coverage				
	Economic	*Social*	*Political*	*Target groups*	*Distribution/relations*
I. Africa/Middle East					
Cameroon	x				
Tanzania	x	x		Beggars, workers in urban informal sector, street vendors, the landless	
Tunisia	x				
Yemen	x	x	x	Urban day workers, rural people in remote villages, returning international migrant workers	
II. Asia					
India	x	x	x		
Thailand	x		x		
III. Latin America					
Brazil	x			Blacks, women	
Mexico	x				
Peru	x	x	x		x
Venezuela	x	x	x		

Sources: Appasamy *et al.* (1996); Bédoui and Ridha (1996); Cartaya *et al.* (1997); Figueroa *et al.* (1996); Gore and Figueiredo (1997); Hashem (1996); Inack (1997); Kaijage and Tibaijuka (1996); Phongpaichit *et al.* (1996); Singer (1997).

As Table 5.4 shows, studies of individual countries interpreted social exclusion differently. Thus, for example, the study of Thailand concentrated on the denial of citizenship rights, whereas those of India and Tanzania followed a more conventional approach in terms of poverty, relative deprivation and the lack of access to resources and goods and services. The Indian study also analysed the denial of basic welfare rights and freedom to participate in economic and social life. The Venezuelan study is concerned with social and political rights; the role of neighbourhood associations and other non-governmental organizations is discussed in mitigating the harmful effects of social exclusion. Most of the studies analyse economic exclusion in terms of different manifestations of poverty. Some adopt a 'target groups' approach, concentrating on such disadvantaged social groups as women, the landless, return migrants and casual workers. None of the studies (except the Peruvian) explicitly analysed the interaction between *distributional* and *relational* issues. However, as we show in Chapters 1 and 2, a proper understanding of social exclusion requires a more comprehensive approach based on the complex relationship between relational and distributional problems, since exclusion is not a single set of processes.

The studies suggest a number of tentative conclusions. First, the relative size and composition of social groups at risk of being excluded will vary among countries, depending on their socioeconomic systems. Second, the poor or the excluded groups are not homogeneous across countries. Third, the strong social networks have implications for vulnerability to deprivation and its persistence.

THE CASE OF BRAZIL

Like most other Latin American countries, Brazil also suffered from the lost decade of the 1980s. During the decade, the FDI inflows dried up and economic growth slowed down. Indebtedness and structural adjustment programmes introduced during the 1980s led to a great deal of economic and social hardship. Although per capita GDP fluctuated, between 1985 and 1990 it remained at the 1985 level. And average family income actually declined (see Barros *et al.*, 1995).

Poverty and economic inequalities provide the basic framework for analysing the economic dimension of exclusion. Brazil is known to have the highest income inequality not only in Latin America but throughout the developing countries. Maddison and associates (1992,

p. 79) note that income inequality in Brazil is 'much higher than in advanced capitalist countries, and high by the standards of Latin America and the developing world'.

1. Poverty and Inequality

Empirical estimates show that both poverty (measured by headcount ratios) and income distribution (measured by Gini coefficient or the deciles distribution of households and their income shares) increased during the 1980s (see Tables 5.5, 5.6 and 5.7). Most of the studies (for example, Lopes, 1993; Psacharopoulos *et al.*, 1993) are based on a national poverty line for Brazil, which conceals regional variations that are bound to be very important in a large country. The incidence of poverty varies from region to region and between urban and rural areas on account of differences in cost of living resulting from disparities in price levels and consumption patterns. It is, therefore, more appropriate to estimate poverty lines by the main regions of Brazil. However, since time series data on prices are available only for metropolitan areas, the Fava–Rocha poverty line has been estimated only for these areas. As nearly 32 per cent of the Brazilian population

Table 5.5 Evolution of poverty in Brazil: headcount ratios (1979–90)

Year	*National*		*Urban areas*			*Rural areas*	
	I	*II*	*III*	*IV*	*V*[a]	*VI*	*VII*
1979	39	34.1	30	23.9	–	62	55.0
1981	–	–	–	–	29.1	–	–
1983	–	–	–	–	38.2	–	–
1986	–	–	–	–	22.8	–	–
1987	40	–	34	–	25.5	60	–
1988	–	–	–	–	24.4	–	–
1989	–	40.9	–	33.2	27.9	–	63.1
1990	43	–	39	–	28.9	56	–

Estimates I, III and VI – by Altimir (1992); II, IV and VII – by Psacharopoulos *et al.* (1992); V – by Lustig (1995).
[a] Based on household surveys for metropolitan areas only.
– = not available.
Source: Lustig (1995).

Table 5.6 Persons in families with per capita incomes below the poverty line in metropolitan areas of Brazil (1981–90)

Metropolitan area	*1981*	*1983*	*1985*	*1986*	*1987*	*1988*	*1989*	*1990*
Belén	50.9	57.6	43.8	45.9	45.1	46.6	39.6	43.4
Fortaleza	54.0	56.2	36.6	30.1	37.8	35.8	40.7	41.5
Recife	55.6	56.6	47.5	39.9	42.8	43.9	47.2	48.5
Salvador	43.1	43.8	39.5	37.5	39.4	33.9	39.0	39.2
Belo Horizonte	31.3	44.1	36.1	26.4	27.7	28.9	27.2	30.3
Rio de Janeiro	27.2	34.7	36.8	23.2	25.9	25.1	32.5	32.7
São Paulo	22.0	34.4	26.9	16.9	20.0	17.5	20.9	22.2
Curitiba	17.4	29.6	24.3	10.5	10.9	10.7	13.5	12.3
Porto Alegre	17.9	29.7	23.3	16.5	18.7	21.2	21.0	21.2
All Metropolitan areas	29.1	38.2	–	22.8	25.5	24.4	27.9	28.9

– = not available.
Source: Lustig (1995).

(about 46 million people) in 1989 lived in these areas, one can assume that these poverty lines are fairly representative.

Regional variations in poverty are defined in terms of the proportion of the population in metropolitan areas living in households with per capita income below the poverty lines. Table 5.6 shows that nearly 29 per cent of the population in metropolitan Brazil was below the poverty line in 1990, thus indicating no change in the magnitude of poverty prevailing in 1981. As is to be expected, the metropolitan areas in the Northeast (Fortaleza, Recife and Salvador) show greater poverty than those in the South (Curitiba and Porto Alegre).

As we noted in Chapter 2, the aggregative measure of people below the poverty line does not tell us anything about the differences in the degree of poverty among these people. It is, therefore, more relevant, for assessing economic exclusion, to examine the depth of poverty and destitution. In Brazil, two types of poverty line have been estimated: (i) the poverty line, which indicates the minimum monthly income needed to satisfy all the basic needs of an individual, and (ii) the indigence line, which enables only the fulfilment of food basic needs of an individual. Thus, (ii) measures extreme poverty or level of destitution. Trends in the degrees of poverty (that is, people below the two poverty lines) between 1970 and 1990 are shown in Table 5.8 by urban and rural areas. Both poverty and destitution were more acute in rural than in urban areas throughout this period.

Table 5.7 Estimates of income inequality in Brazil (1960–90)

	Economically active population by personal income			*Individuals by per capita family income*		
Year	*Gini coefficient*	*Distribution ratio*[a] (1)	(2)	*Gini coeff.*	*Distribution ratio*[a] (1)	(2)
1960	0.50	3.4	34	–	–	–
1970	0.57	4.6	40	0.63	7.4	–
1979	0.58	5.1	54	0.59	5.6	51
1980	0.59	5.1	47	0.58	5.1	51
1981	0.57	4.9	51	0.58	5.2	59
1982	0.58	5.0	55	0.59	5.6	54
1983	0.59	5.4	52	0.59	5.7	55
1984	0.59	5.3	57	0.59	5.4	49
1985	0.60	5.7	66	0.59	5.7	55
1986	0.59	5.3	50	0.59	5.4	52
1987	0.60	5.6	61	0.60	6.0	62
1988	0.62	6.5	80	0.61	6.6	72
1989	0.64	7.2	82	0.63	9.1	80
1990	0.61	6.7	60	0.61	6.6	72

[a] (1) = Ratio of the income share of the top 10 per cent of the distribution to that of the bottom 40 per cent; (2) = ratio of the income share of the top 10 per cent of the distribution to that of the bottom 10 per cent.
– = not available.
Source: Barros *et al.* (1995), p. 245.

Table 5.8 Trends in poverty and destitution in Brazil (1970–90) (%)

	Households below the poverty line[a]		*Households below the indigence line*	
	Urban	*Rural*	*Urban*	*Rural*
1970	35	73	15	42
1979	30	62	10	35
1987	34	60	13	34
1990	39	56	22	–

[a] Includes households below the indigence or extreme poverty line.
– = not available.
Source: UNECLAC (1995), Table 10, p. 145.

Table 5.9 Urban poverty and destitution in Brazil by households and regions (1989) (%)

Categories/regions	*The poor*	*The destitute*
Individuals	24.7	14.3
All households	22.5	11.0
Households with black and coloured heads	31.5	18.5
Households with white heads	16.4	6.0
Households in North, Northeast, and Centre West	30.4	19.6
Households in South and Southeast	19.1	7.3

Source: Lopes (1993), cited in Singer (1997, p. 16).

Lopes (1993) estimated the proportions of the poor and destitute in urban areas of Brazil by regions for 1989 (see Table 5.9). These estimates show that extreme poverty and destitution are concentrated among the blacks and coloured people and in the North and Northeast and Centre-West regions. The bulk of the black and coloured population also lives in Northeast, which explains the high incidence of extreme poverty in that region.

An alternative measure of income inequality is the deciles distribution of households and their respective shares. By this measure also, income inequality is known to have increased in Brazil. For example, Table 1.1 (Chapter 1) shows that between 1970–5 and 1987–92, the income share of top 20 per cent of the Brazilian population increased, whereas that of the bottom 20 per cent declined. This suggests that the structural adjustment measures introduced in the 1980s hurt the poor disproportionately, whereas the rich improved their relative position. Inflation also hurts the poor badly, by eroding their average earnings. As a result of government policies to finance fiscal stimulus, inflation rose again in the late 1980s. Empirical evidence shows that 'the level of unemployment and the inflation rate are positively correlated with the level of income inequality' (Barros *et al.*, 1995, p. 249).

We need to strike a note of caution about the reliability of the Brazilian estimates of income distribution. First, the national accounts statistics are considerably underestimated because they do not account for income from informal earning activities. Second, the total income reported in the decennial demographic censuses is less than 60 per cent recorded in the national accounts (see Maddison and associates, 1992, p. 80). Third, the high and accelerating rates of inflation and their frequent fluctuations make measurement of poverty lines highly volatile. The inflation rate rose from an average of 1.6 per cent a month in 1980 to 27 per cent a month in 1989 (Barros *et al.*, 1995).

The root causes of severe inequality in income distribution and its worsening over time are to be found not only in the economic explanations (for example, a wage freeze) but also in social structures, ethnic distinctions and the uneven distribution of property ownership, as well as the educational disparities we discuss below.

2. Social Questions

Exclusion of certain groups of the population from sources of income, property and education in Brazil arises from acute economic and social disparities. Educational inequalities, property ownership and ethnic factors account for differential access of the population to income and such public goods as health services. Paradoxically, one does not find any deterioration in the social disparities over the past two to three decades. As a result of the process of democratization during the 1980s, many social services and programmes were expanded (for a discussion of these programmes, see Draibe and Arretche, 1995). Many of the social indicators have improved over time, which suggests that in contrast to the deterioration of economic inequalities, social inequalities may have declined (see Table 5.10). This may have occurred partly as a consequence of the process of democratization, which led to popular participation and innovations at the local levels of government (see below the section on political exclusion). But one has to be careful in arriving at this conclusion, since the social indicators shown in Table 5.10 do not reflect a qualitative dimension. There are indications of a decline in the quality of public social services. These aggregative indicators also conceal lack of access of the poorest target groups to many social programmes (for example, day-care nurseries and free food distribution programmes) (Draibe and Arretche, 1995, p. 98). In Brazil, social welfare benefits continue to be awarded on the basis of patron–client relationships between the government and such powerful lobbies as bureaucracies

Table 5.10 Social indicators in Brazil (1970–93)

Indicator	*1960*	*1970*	*1980*	*1990*	*1993*
Infant mortality rate (per 000 births)	116	–	87.9	–	57
Life expectancy (years)	51.6	–	60.1	–	66.5
Adult literacy rate (%)	60.5	–	73.9	–	–
Passenger cars (per 000 population)	6.6	–	67.2	–	–
Percentage of households with:					
Safe water	–	24.3	–	55.1	87.0
Sanitation	–	23.8	–	43.2	83.0
Electricity	–	38.5	–	68.5	–
Refrigerator	–	11.6	–	50.4	–
Radio	–	35.4	–	76.2	–
TV sets	–	–	–	–	56.1
Owner-occupied house	–	57.1	–	–	61.7
Percentage of private dwelling units with:					
Piped water	–	–	32.8	54.9	82.6
Sewage disposal	–	–	–	27.7	52.8
Electric lighting	–	–	47.6	68.5	97.6
Public expenditure on education (% of GDP at current prices)	–	–	1.2	0.7	3.7
Public expenditure on health (% of GDP)	–	–	1.3	1.3	2.9
Social expenditure/GDP ratio	–	–	–	9.7	10.8 (1990–1)
Social expenditure/total public expenditure	–	–	–	46.5	36.8 (1990–1)

– = not available.
Sources: Maddison *et al.* (1992); UNDP (1996); UNECLAC (1994, 1995).

and professionals. Thus the population excluded from the formal labour market, namely the rural and the urban poor, remains excluded from social rights and benefits.

Furthermore, a very small proportion of the adult population (10.5 per cent) are reported to be involved in any social conflict in Brazil despite the high levels of economic and social inequalities.[2] Such a low ratio may reflect apathy on the part of the population and disbelief in justice and fair trial. Below we discuss social problems of such disadvantaged social groups as racial and ethnic minorities, female-headed households and street children.

Racial and Ethnic Minorities

Ethnic and racial inequalities are an important source of income differences in Brazil (Lovell, 1994; Telles, 1993). In a study of the urban labour market segmentation, Telles shows that being black or of mixed race means greater loss of income compared with whites in different employment categories (namely, protected employees, protected self-employed, unprotected workers and domestic workers). The former belong to employment categories associated with low wages and poor working conditions.

Studies in the late 1970s and mid-1980s (Hasenbalg, 1979, 1985; Silva, 1978, 1985) showed that inequalities in the urban labour market were characterized by racial discrimination even a hundred years after the abolition of slavery.

A great majority of the socially excluded is made up of people excluded from the main sources of income. As we noted above, income distribution is very unequal, and poverty is known to be the main source of exclusion. Singer (1997, p. 14) states that 'people with the same skin colour may be classified socially as white, coloured or black according to their income and social status. The higher their economic and social standing, the whiter they become'. The situation is somewhat similar in the United States, where well-off blacks with high incomes and education are more easily accepted in white neighbourhoods than the poorer blacks. However, this does not necessarily suggest the absence of racial discrimination in Brazil on non-economic grounds. The point is that very few blacks and coloured people have the possibility of climbing the economic and social ladder. Using data from the Brazilian censuses for 1960 and 1980, Lovell (1994) shows that race and gender discrimination continue to persist in the Brazilian urban labour market. Although the Afro-Brazilian men and women have benefited absolutely from industrialization and growth, they remain disadvantaged relatively to the white population. Afro-Brazilian women earned much less than the white women; racial and gender inequalities have increased.

Female-Headed Households

We noted in Chapter 3 that among women as a disadvantaged group, female-headed households are generally considered particularly vulnerable. In Brazil, although these households include both poor and rich families, a majority of them are poor. Their poverty is due to higher dependency ratios and low earning power of household members (see Barros *et al.*, 1997). Much more serious is the social situation of female-headed households with children who are deprived of education and schooling, especially if the household head is illiterate. Even in the case of literate household heads, access of children to schooling is limited by the lack of earning power. Thus economic exclusion reinforces social exclusion. As children of single-parent families are known to have a lower rate of socioeconomic attainment than those in two-parent families, even controlling for income (see McLanahan and Bumpass, 1988), they are more likely to be excluded from the labour market when they grow up.

The economic and social situation of Brazilian female-headed households varies a great deal across regions. For example, examining their situation in the three metropolitan areas, Barros *et al.* (1995) found that Recife (Northeast) has more female-headed households per capita, and the households with children have higher dependency ratio. The extent of poverty among female-headed households is also greater in Recife than in Porte Alegre (South). But comparisons across regions need to take into account regional price differences, which tend to be quite marked.

'Street Children'

Working children (often known in Brazil as 'street children') are another socially disadvantaged and vulnerable group. In 1990, over 32 per cent of the children (aged 13 to 17 years) were working in urban areas and 55.5 per cent in rural areas. While the share of working children declined in rural areas between 1979 and 1990, it increased in urban areas. Fourteen per cent of the total Brazilian households had working children who generally worked long hours (in 1992 those not studying on average worked 45 hours in urban areas and 44 hours in rural areas) and earned very little (only about 35 per cent of the monthly income of adult wage earners with seven years of schooling). Disaggregating their income by per capita income quartiles of their households shows that in the lowest income quartile children barely make enough to cover their own needs (only 0.7 times the per capita poverty line in urban areas in 1990 and 0.6 times the per capita poverty line in rural areas). However, at the fourth income quartile, the children earned 1.6 times the per capita poverty line in urban areas and 2.3 times in rural areas, suggesting some positive contribution to other members of the household (see UNECLAC, 1995).

Working children are usually engaged in casual, informal and exploitative form of work carrying no legal protection or social benefits. They usually earn well below the minimum wage. Their vulnerability arises from low incomes, poor working conditions, seasonality of work, and exploitation for delinquency and crime. Children at work means lower education and greater forgone life-time earnings. For Latin America it is estimated that two years of less education is equivalent to about 20 per cent less monthly income for the duration of the working life (see UNECLAC, 1995, p. 51). Lower education and loss of income will further adversely affect future off-springs of child labour in terms of their lower educational attainment and earning capacity.

We noted earlier the economic value of children in developing societies. This is also shown by the reduction in the incidence of poverty of households with working children in Brazil and other Latin American countries (see Figure 5.1). In the absence of their earnings, the incidence of poverty is raised by 10 to 20 per cent. The working children come from very poor households and are on the streets looking for means of livelihood (see Myers, 1988).

Thus, the case of working children as a socially disadvantaged group in Brazil shows how poverty and economic exclusion are so closely intertwined with social exclusion. Economic exclusion pushes children out into the labour market to supplement their families' meagre incomes. This leads to social problems of juvenile delinquency and crime. Lack of education that results may lead them to a category of social outcastes.

3. Political Exclusion

Until the early 1980s, Brazil was under an authoritarian military regime. The shift to democracy from authoritarianism has no doubt led to the granting of personal and political freedoms. But some authors (for example, Graham, 1990) believe that despite democratic reforms, political practices have continued to deny the workers a share in political power. Graham (1990) subdivides political regimes in Brazil during the 20th century into three categories: local landed aristocracy (*cornelismo*), control of urban masses with the grant of certain social benefits (*populismo*), and military rule (*autoritarismo*). All three types of regime were characterized by the political exclusion of workers and the masses. However, some benefited from family and kinship networks which determined the patronage given by the rulers.

Figure 5.1 Households with working children and adolescents aged 13–17: incidence of poverty with and without their earnings

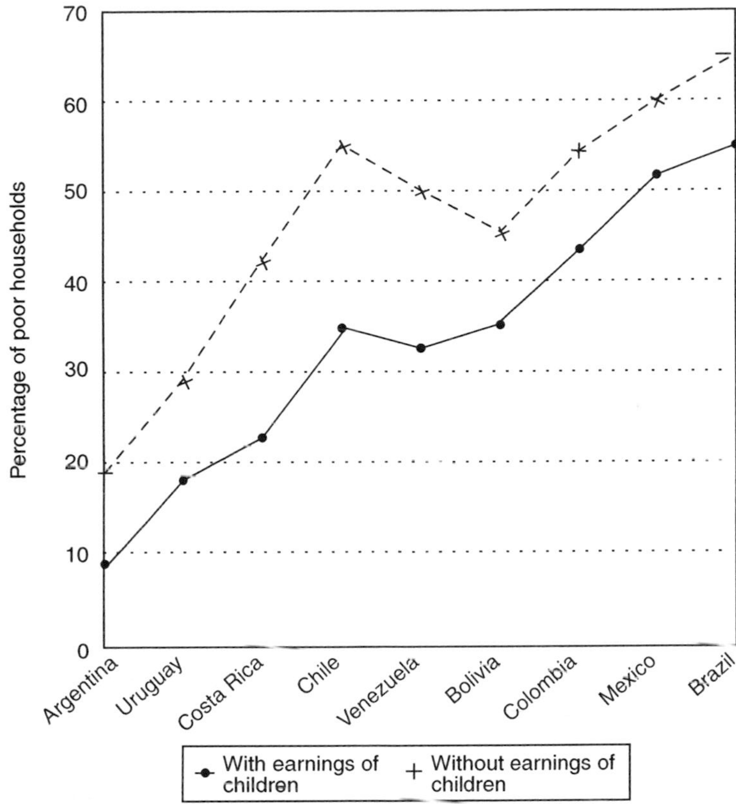

Source: UNECLAC, on the basis of special tabulations of data from household surveys in the countries.

Local urban movements emerged during the military regime as a response to political suppression. These movements attempted local collective solutions to community's problems through family and kinship networks. Women were particularly active in the urban social movements and local political struggles (Albarez, 1990). However, these movements did not provide any significant opposition to the erstwhile military regime. Several reasons are noted for the ineffectiveness of these movements: offers of favours by the state in the form of urban services as reward for political allegiance, heterogeneity of movements in terms of objectives and composition, which led to fragmentation rather than unity, strong social hierarchy and powerful individuals overshadowing the universality of rights, and élitism, which discouraged popular participation in important institutions (see Mainwaring, 1987).

Political exclusion is manifested in lack of civil liberties, discrimination against the minorities and police brutality. The extreme economic and social inequalities discussed above make it harder to build and consolidate democratic institutions (Mainwaring, 1995a; 1995b). Freedom House (New York) regularly provides rankings of political and civil liberties by countries including Brazil (see Table 5.11), and these rankings suggest that the situation in Brazil worsened in the 1990s. Considering that police brutality and rural violence are rampant in Brazil, the ranking in Table 5.11 seems overstated.[3] The methodology of ranking is also somewhat subjective and arbitrary. A country's rank is 'based on responses to a check-list and the judgements of the Survey team at Freedom House'. The scales used are 1 to 7, with 1 being free and 7 not free, and the numbers in between reflecting different degrees of freedom or lack of it.

A combined average rating of countries is also undertaken. This combined rate, the average of the two seven-category scales of political rights and civil liberties, is taken as an overall index of freedom. Brazil's index is higher than that of Argentina, Bolivia,

Table 5.11 Ranking of political and civil liberties in Brazil (1984–94)

Year	*Political rights*	*Civil liberties*	*Freedom rating*
1984	3	3	PF
1985	3	2	F
1986	2	2	F
1987	2	2	F
1988	2	3	5
1989	2	2	F
1990	2	3	F
1991	2	3	F
1992	2	3	F
1993	3	4	PF
1994	2	4	PF

F: free. PF: partly free.
Source: Freedom House; cited in Mainwaring (1995), p. 152.

Table 5.12 Brazil's ranking of liberties compared with those of other developing countries (1995)

Free			*Partly free*		*Not free*	
(1.5)	*(2.0)*	*(2.5)*	*(3.0)*	*(4.0)*	*(6.0)*	*(7.0)*
Costa Rica Uruguay	Benin Chile	Argentina Namibia Panama	Bangladesh Brazil Ecuador Honduras India Nicaragua	Colombia Senegal Sri Lanka	Algeria Egypt Indonesia	China Cuba Somalia Sudan

Note: Figures in brackets represent scales of freedom.
Source: World Freedom Survey (1997), p. 26.

Chile, Costa Rica and Uruguay, suggesting that it is less free than they are (see Table 5.12).

Apart from political violence, civil liberties in Brazil tend to be limited partly because of the weak and corrupt judicial system. The independence and autonomy of the judicial system is essential for safeguarding the Rule of Law. During the military regime the judiciary was subservient to the wishes of the dictators (Sadek, 1995). While the 1988 constitution guaranteed the judiciary's financial and administrative autonomy, in practice it is not independent of political pressures. The institution is too weak to control the political élite, as was demonstrated by delays in the ex-President Collor's judgement and the conviction of the politicians. Furthermore, there are very few judges per thousand of the population (only 7,000 for a population of over 150 million) (Freedom House, 1996, p. 155),[4] which means, *inter alia*, considerable delays in the delivery of justice.

The process of democratization did result in an increase in the number of court cases. However, it is noted that only 33 per cent of the population went to the courts to resolve disputes, suggesting a lack of trust in the Brazilian jusdicial system. Corruptness of the system accounts for this perception, particularly among the poor who believe that laws are meant for them, not the rich who can flout the law at will. Sadek (1995, p. 163) notes that 'many Brazilians would rather look for help by going to a church, to the police, to a TV or a radio programme, or to trade union than to a court'.

Economic and social inequalities discussed above reinforce political exclusion by denying the poor access to legal services and fair trial. The existence of these inequalities hinder the universal application of the law because the wealthy and influential people can bend the law to their advantage.

4. Unemployment and Precarious Jobs

In Chapter 3 we discussed some general issues concerning the growth of long-term unemployment and the precariousness of jobs in developing countries as two indicators of exclusion. Here we consider the particular case of Brazil.

A prolonged economic recession in the 1980s and 1990s and subsequent response of the corporate sector to restructuring and adjustment led to a decline in output and employment in Brazil. Between 1990 and 1992, industrial output declined by 14 per cent, and industrial employment by nearly 20 per cent (see Baltar *et al*., 1996). However, despite this, the overall unemployment rates in Brazil have remained low by regional and international standards (about an average of 4 per cent in metropolitan Brazil during 1982–92) and stable for over a decade. This has been so despite the introduction of an unemployment insurance programme that should, in principle, have induced an increase in unemployment, but in practice did not do so. This odd situation has been explained by some authors (for example, Amadeo *et al.,* 1995, p. 53) in terms of collusion between workers and employers to informalize the labour force by discontinuing labour contract (see below). Workers with unsigned contracts are cheaper than those with signed contracts because of the payment of social security benefits in the latter case. The duration of unemployment is also low compared with that in industrialized countries. For the state of São Paulo, Bivar (1993, p. 86, cited in Amadeo and Camargo, 1996, p. 139) notes that it was only 1.6 months in 1988 compared with 50 months in Belgium and 105 months in Spain. On the other hand, the frequency of unemployment (number of times a worker is unemployed during the year) is quite high.

5. Informalization of the Labour Market

In Brazil, as in France (see Chapter 4), precariousness has been growing since the early 1980s. In France this trend is characterized by the growth of temporary and part-time forms of work (see Table 4.2);

in Brazil it is manifested more in the growth of self-employment and informal jobs than temporary contracts. Indeed, during the 1980s the Brazilian labour market has been characterized by two main trends: (i) *tertiarization* of the economy, which implies a process of replacement of permanent employees (from the formal sector mostly) by self-employed workers and those engaged in micro or family firms, and (ii) *informalization*, resulting from an increase of non-standard jobs (mainly in the informal sector) and a decline in the labour absorption capacity of the private formal sector. Table 5.13 shows that between 1979 and 1990 urban informal employment increased substantially among men and less so among women. Self-employment, consisting of employers and own-account workers, also increased. But the proportion of wage earners without any contract of employment (suggesting vulnerability) increased far more significantly. Between 1979 and 1990, average incomes of those engaged in the urban informal sector declined for wage earners, unskilled independent workers and household workers. As multiples of the respective per capita poverty lines they declined from 3.6 in 1979 to 3.4 in 1990 in the case of wage earners in microenterprises, 5.2 to 3.3 in the case of independent workers and 1.1 to 0.9 in the case of household workers

Table 5.13 Employment in the Brazilian urban informal sector (%)

Category	*Men*		*Women*	
	1979	*1990*	*1979*	*1990*
Total	38.2	48.8	49.6	52.3
Employers of fewer than 5 workers[a]	6.0	6.6	1.2	2.4
Wage earners in establishments with fewer than 5 workers[b c]	12.8	21.2	7.1	12.2
Own-account and unpaid family workers[b]	19.0	20.6	19.7	22.5
Domestic employees	0.4	0.4	21.6	15.2

[a] Includes professional and technical occupations.
[b] Excludes professional and technical occupations.
[c] Workers without an employment contract.
Source: UNECLAC (1995).

(see UNECLAC, 1995, p. 141). In the early 1990s, the recession led to a decline in formal employment and growth of precarious jobs in the formal sector, as reflected in a drop in the average income of workers, an increase in labour turnover and a decline in jobs with a formal labour contract. In the 1990s, the proportion of workers with contracts is estimated to have declined by more than 6 percentage points in less than three years (see Amadeo *et al.*, 1995, p. 62).

The Brazilian labour market is characterized by flexibility on the part of the private sector in hiring and firing workers in response to fluctuating market conditions. For example, in 1988, nearly a million workers were laid off out of a total of 23.6 million (which represents a monthly turnover of 4 per cent) (Baltar *et al.*, 1996). This evolution of the Brazilian labour market has had the effect of worsening the living conditions of the population and raising the incidence of poverty. In the case of the metropolitan area of São Paulo, the average income of employees in 1990 was equivalent to 69.1 per cent of the average income of 1985, for example (SEADE, 1994).

To a large extent, exclusion from the private formal sector and consequent involvement in informal activities denies people access to adequate sources of income and formal institutions (formal goods and services markets, labour legislation, social protection, health, education and so on).

Non-standard and Involuntary Employment

Non-standard forms of employment (for example, self-employed and unregulated workers) in Brazil have been quite sizeable ever since the Second World War. It is noted that the urban informal sector, accounting for much of non-standard employment, was sizeable even during the period of 'Brazilian economic miracle' (1968–73), which recorded a very rapid industrial growth (see Telles, 1993). Does this mean that non-standard forms of employment are not so precarious or *involuntary* in Brazil?

Not all of the informal employment is *involuntary;* it also includes an element of voluntary employment. It is therefore necessary to distinguish those who are unable to find formal employment and have no other choice but to survive through working in the informal sector. In 1990, 42 per cent of the total occupied labour force were engaged in the formal sector, whereas over 29 per cent of the remaining – informal workers, self-employed or unpaid members of the owner's family – declared that they would have preferred formal labour contracts. Thus, approximately three-tenths of the total occupied labour force were involuntarily excluded from the formal sector (Singer, 1997). More precisely, the proportion of the labour force who were not formal employees and who considered themselves excluded from formal employment and wanted a job in the formal sector was 24.5 per cent in urban areas and 43.6 per cent in rural areas (IBGE, 1994).

The situation with respect to *involuntary* employment varies a great deal across different regions. Involuntary employment is concentrated much more in the Northeast (nearly 40 per cent in urban areas and nearly 57 per cent in rural areas) than in the Southeast (19 per cent in urban areas and 35 per cent in rural areas) and the South (about 20 per cent in urban areas and about 29 per cent in rural areas) (IBGE, 1994).

Job Precariousness in Greater São Paulo

The debt crisis and the deep economic recession of the early 1980s hurt the metropolitan area of São Paulo particularly badly, as its industrial structure was based on manufacturing. The absolute level of employment in manufacturing declined, and by 1983 it stood at the same level as in 1973. However, between 1984 and 1986, the Brazilian economy improved under the initial impetus of export expansion. In greater São Paulo, industrial employment regained its pre-recession level, thereby substantially reducing unemployment. But failure of the Brazilian economy to grow in the latter part of the 1980s, combined with increasing inflationary instability and fluctuating levels of output and employment, had a marked impact on the labour market in greater São Paulo. Between 1989 and 1992, industrial employment fell sharply (unemployment rose from 8.7 per cent to 15.2 per cent) and faster than between 1980 and 1983 as a result of a fall in industrial production and corporate restructuring. The result was an informalization of the employment structure and an increase in job insecurity (Baltar *et al.*, 1996).

A study covering 1989–92 period ranked precariousness (or insecurity) status of different job groups by average duration of employment and average earnings. On the basis of the AID (automatic interaction detection) statistical process, 32 groups of homogeneous jobs were determined, showing varying degrees of average instability explained by different characteristics (Troyano, 1996). The nature of the labour contract, followed by the level of skill qualifications required, were found to be the two important factors explaining precariousness.

A survey of living conditions in the metropolitan area of São Paulo was conducted by SEADE in 1991 and 1994 (see Table 5.14 for the evolution of the labour market structure in the area). This survey was based on an analytical framework very similar to the one developed by CERC in France, discussed in Chapter 4. Our intention is to examine whether there are any similarities between France and Brazil in respect of the relationships between precariousness and social and economic vulnerability.

Table 5.14 can be compared with Table 4.2 on the evolution of standard and non-standard jobs in France. Data indicate a trend reversal between formal and informal employment (public sector excluded). Indeed, formal private employment decreased by 9 per cent between 1990 and 1994, whereas informal forms of work (those without a labour contract and self-employed workers) rose considerably, by 27 per cent during the same period (and by 52 per cent between 1985 and 1994). Most of the new entrants to the labour force (which increased by 11.4 per cent) were absorbed by the informal sector. Moreover, growth of self-employment led to a decline in the share of wage earners: from 72 per cent in 1989 to 65.7 per cent in 1993 (SEADE/DIEESE, 1993). Thus an increasing number of workers have become insecure in terms of access to income.

Table 5.14 Formal and informal employment in the metropolitan area of São Paulo (000)

	1985	*1990*	*1994*
Economically active population	6,360	7,161	7,978
Formal private employment (contract)	2,903	3,405	3,099
Informal employment	1,305	1,562	1,988
Private wage employment without contract	461	530	715
Self employed	844	1,032	1,273
Others[a]	819	794	1,070
Unemployed	779	737	1,134

[a] Includes employees, non-remunerated/family workers.
Source: SEADE/DIEESE.

The methodology used by SEADE in the metropolitan area of São Paulo is based on the premise that an indicator of vulnerability in the labour market provides a good indicator of social and economic vulnerability at the individual and household levels. This survey of living conditions classified individuals into different categories according to their situation of vulnerability in the labour market: vulnerable, intermediate and non-vulnerable. This classification is a combination of three elements: (i) labour turnover, (ii) income-generation features at workplaces and (iii) non-continuity of employment. The survey estimated a household's vulnerability in the labour market by combining the employment situation of the head of the household with that of another active member who has the best labour status. Finally, the survey defined four socioeconomic groups as follows, by combining the degree of labour market vulnerability with a wide range of data on housing, education, health and income (quoted from SEADE, 1994):

> *Group A*: encompasses 20.5 per cent of the families; their social situation is the most favourable in that they have better housing, a higher level of education, better labour market status and a higher level of income;
> *Group B*: comprises 37.2 per cent of the families with an intermediate position on the social scale. Although families in this group have no housing needs, a significant percentage lack adequate schooling and/or have a vulnerable position in the labour market. Most of these families do not have income needs;
> *Group C*: comprises 19.7 per cent of the families and may also be described as having an intermediate position on the social scale. They all have housing needs, although they are better positioned in the labour market than families from group B. In terms of income and level of education, their situation is similar to that of families in group B;
> *Group D*: accounts for 22.6 per cent of the families and is made up of families in the most unfavourable situation as regards education, labour market status and income, although their housing conditions seem to be better than those of group C. Half of the families in Group D have simultaneous needs in the four aspects covered by the survey.

Table 5.15 indicates a strong correlation between access to decent income, housing or education of household members and their type of

Table 5.15 Vulnerability by socioeconomic groups in the metropolitan area of São Paulo (1990–94) (%).

Type of integration	*Socioeconomic groups*[a]				*Total in the labour market*
	A	*B*	*C*	*D*	
1990					
Vulnerable	6.6	30.0	(6.8)	96.7	35.7
Non-vulnerable	93.4	70.0	93.2	(3.3)	64.3
1994					
Vulnerable	7.5	36.3	15.0	98.9	42.8
Non-vulnerable	92.5	63.7	85.0	(1.1)	57.2

[a] For a definition of these groups, see the quotation from SEADE (1994) on page 163.
Source: SEADE (1995).

integration in the labour market. For example, we note that Groups A and D are very homogeneous according to the labour status of their members. Households from Group D do not enjoy access to the non-vulnerable segment of the labour market and are trapped in precarious forms of work. The table also shows an unfavourable evolution of the labour market in the early 1990s. The proportion of households in a situation of vulnerability in the labour market increased from 35.7 per cent in 1990 to 42.8 per cent in 1994. In particular, the worsening of the situation in the formal sector severely affected the intermediate Group C, whereas Group A was relatively unaffected; the proportion of people from C affected by vulnerability in the labour market increased from 6.8 per cent to 15.0 per cent between 1990 and 1994.

The SEADE framework relates to an analysis of precariousness and exclusion from the formal market and fundamental elements of the household's standard of living. It demonstrates the applicability of this new approach to poverty and well-being in developing countries. One of the major conclusions of this type of surveys is that access to secure jobs, which provide decent incomes and access to formal institutions, is a central element in the appraisal of the processes of exclusion affecting individuals and households. Nevertheless, in the case of Brazil the survey emphasized *distributional* aspects related to precariousness more than *relational* aspects.

CONCLUDING REMARKS

In this chapter we have shown how *distributional* and *relational* aspects are intermingled in developing countries. Unlike industrialized countries, in these countries it is poverty and low incomes that drive people to seek income and employment security through family, community and kinship networks. These networks are particularly important among very poor societies without any social security arrangements. There is another important difference between the two groups of countries. In the industrialized countries, social exclusion is manifested in long-term unemployment. This phenomenon is not important in developing countries, where people cannot afford to remain unemployed for long periods. In the absence of any social employment benefits, people are so poor that they have to eke out a living by undertaking any kind of social and economic activities in the informal sector, for example. Thus while in both industrialized and developing countries the distributional/relational issues are important, their nature and characteristics vary.

The case study of Brazil illustrates how poverty lies at the heart of the problems of social exclusion. Even race and cultural factors are influenced by this economic factor. Further it shows the importance of political exclusion in addition to the economic exclusion also prevailing in many other developing countries. While the process of democratization is underway in most developing countries today, it has not yet enabled democracy to take root in these countries. One positive feature of the process is the strengthening of existing social movements and NGOs, and the creation of new ones, but they are often too weak or too isolated to overcome the harmful effects of globalization discussed in Chapter 6.

The case of political exclusion in developing countries is more complicated than its economic and social dimensions. While many countries are democratizing, the spread of liberal and democratic political forms is often not associated with a real empowerment of the people. In most cases the interpretation of democracy has been restricted to free elections, ignoring the fundamental changes in existing power relations that are embedded in the notion of democracy and political freedom.

6 Globalization and Exclusion

In Chapters 1 to 5 we discussed the economic and social issues largely in a national context, even though the framework in Chapter 2 explicitly recognized the importance of the global dimension. The causes of exclusion are a complex interaction of both *internal* and *external* factors. The purpose of this chapter is to extend our analysis to the external factors and the global dimension of exclusion. The two main global phenomena today are (i) the emergence of a global economy involving increasing interdependence between countries of the North and South and (ii) an acceleration of the process of democratization in most developing societies briefly discussed in Chapter 5. Both these phenomena have implications for the *analytical* as well as the *normative* aspects of the concept of exclusion discussed in the earlier chapters. While globalization may alleviate poverty and exclusion in some societies which are equipped to benefit from it, it may accentuate marginalization and exclusion in others. Does globalization generate exclusion and social disintegration and thereby threaten social cohesion and sustainable growth? This question is addressed below in the context of both industrialized and developing countries.

The process of democratization makes paramount the granting of social and political rights to citizens and people. But are the implications for exclusion of the two global phenomena – globalization and democratization – consistent with each other? There may indeed be tensions in the sense that the social and political rights of citizens to participate in the process of political decision-making under democracy are being granted at the same time as the process of globalization is reducing the political autonomy of nation states and the opportunity to exercise these rights (see Gore, 1995).

Ten years ago nobody spoke about globalization, but now this term has become fashionable in both academia and the mass media. Today the literature on economic globalization and other global issues is vast and diverse but the concept remains poorly conceptualized. Thus, it is essential to be clear about the nature and definition of globalization. The phenomenon of the internationalization of economic relationships between nations is not new (Bairoch, 1997).

It was a feature of the international economy even before 1914. In terms of global trade, globalization was more highly developed at the turn of the century than it is now. In the nineteenth and early twentieth centuries, trade and foreign investments grew rapidly. Between 1870 and 1914 the world had also experienced a historic period of integration. For example, if we consider the share of exports in total GNP as an indicator of interdependence, between 1900 and 1913 the proportion increased from 18.2 per cent to 21.2 per cent for 16 major industrial countries, whereas between 1973 and 1992, it increased from 12 per cent to 17 per cent (Streeten, 1998, p. 16). Indeed, the internationalization of trade, production and finance was high before the First World War but had drastically decreased during the great depression of the 1930s as a result of protectionism all round the world.

Hirst and Thompson (1996) are sceptical of the mainstream image of a truly global economy. They show that the extreme vision of a 'borderless world' and 'the end of the nation state *à la* Ohmae (1990, 1993) is largely a myth. They emphasize the conceptual gap between the present international economy and the extreme vision of a globally integrated economy; in the former interdependence between nation states remains crucial. Thus, they conclude that global markets are not beyond regulation and control through national and international governance and they envisage an increasingly prominent role for states, international agencies, regimes and structures of governance (p. 3).

However, globalization today differs both qualitatively and quantitatively from the earlier processes. According to Giddens (1996, p. 5), the current phase of globalization is not just an extension of earlier phases of Western expansion. It is reflected in the fundamental phenomenon of the increasing impact on our lives of action at a distance. It refers both to the compression of the world and the intensification of consciousness of the world as a whole (Robertson, 1992a, p. 8). Globalization involves not just increasing interdependence but, also historically speaking, relatively new subjective and cultural aspects (however, in this chapter we are concerned mainly with economic globalization). What is new about the present phase of globalization is the manner and the extent to which both lifestyles and the policies of nation states are penetrated by global phenomena. According to Mittelman (1995, p. 273), globalization refers to multidimensional transnational processes that allow the economy, politics and culture of one country to penetrate those of another – processes that lead to the compression of the time and space aspects of social relations.

THE MAIN FEATURES OF GLOBALIZATION

There are several different ways in which globalization is defined: increasing openness of the national economies reflected in the rapid growth of trade, foreign direct investment (FDI) and other private capital flows, internationalization of production and demand, global competition, liberalization of macroeconomic (trade and investment) policies by countries, standardization of values and cultures across the world and some loss of national autonomy of governments in the formulation and implementation of national policies (for details, see Bhalla, 1998).

Transnational corporations (TNCs), with their regional and global strategies of production, investment, marketing and distribution, have become the driving forces of globalization. The power balance between the nation state and transnationals is shifting in favour of the latter. With a decline in the importance of trade unions, the state plays an increasing role in serving the business interests of corporations. This is reinforced by the fact that many countries (particularly in the developing world) are competing for FDI channeled by these corporations. The globalization of international finance and media information often bypasses control by national governments. Some authors (Ohmae, 1990, 1993; Reich, 1991) go so far as to perceive the nation state as the local authority for the global system. The job of the nation state is seen by some theorists of globalization as 'that of municipalities within states heretofore: to provide the infrastructure and public goods that business needs at the lowest possible cost' (Hirst and Thompson, 1996, p. 176).

The characteristics of the emerging global economy can now be discussed in greater detail.

Spatial Reorganization of Production

This will transform the share of world output and trade in favour of successful developing countries. The increasing internationalization of production, distribution and marketing in goods and services is one of the main features of globalization (Harris, 1993). Economic globalization has deeply changed the pattern of geographic specialization and the core–periphery relationship (Gereffi, 1996). Developing countries as a group have significantly increased their participation in the world economy, despite dramatic disparities among them. Their share in world merchandize trade has risen from

33 per cent in the mid-1980s to 43 per cent in 1995 (Quereshi, 1996, p. 31). It is predicted that if present trends continue, China will be the world's largest economy in 2020, when developing countries will account for over 60 per cent of the world output (*The Economist*, 1994a). The manufacturing sector's share of GDP in some developing countries such as China (38 per cent), Taiwan (34 per cent) or the Republic of Korea (31 per cent) was higher than in Japan (29 per cent) in 1990 (Gereffi, 1996). Nevertheless, in 1990 the G7 countries still accounted for 90.5 per cent of high-technology manufacturing in the world, and were holding 80.4 per cent of global computing power (Castells, 1996).

In the 1970s, TNCs responded to the Fordist mass production of standardized goods by decentralizing production across the world to take advantage of cheap labour and the miniaturization of new information technology. The restructuring of production processes is based on (i) flexibility in respect of labour processes, products and patterns of consumption, and (ii) the use of capital and knowledge-intensive methods of production. The two tendencies of flexible accumulation and geographical restructuring of production have been enhanced by the diffusion of radically new technologies such as computer and telecommunications technology. These technologies have accelerated global transfers of capital, labour, information and knowledge. Indeed, they have facilitated the fragmentation of production around the world. The result is a proliferation of production sites in the South for the export of manufactured goods regionally or worldwide. Production restructuring and flexibility have also been facilitated by trade and investment liberalization, particularly by developing countries, to maintain a trade friendly environment and stimulate international competitiveness. Indeed, during the 1980s most developing countries implemented reform programmes to enable their integration into the global economy. Supported by the IMF and the World Bank, these programmes were based on export promotion policies often combined with incentives for attracting FDI.

Therefore, it appears that we have reached a new stage of capitalism, where the division of the world into developed and developing countries, industrialized and industrializing nations, and core and periphery are becoming more and more obsolete (Mittelman, 1995). Growth poles fully integrated into the global economy can emerge everywhere if appropriate policies are implemented to meet the requirements of global competition.

The Growth of International Trade

A common indicator of globalization is trade as a share of GDP. During 1985–94 this ratio rose three times faster than in the preceding decade and nearly twice as fast as in the 1960s (World Bank, 1996a, p. 1). In 1993, the share of global trade in world GDP was 32 per cent (UNDP, 1996, p. 207). The international community has made considerable progress in eliminating barriers to international trade. The creation of the WTO and the acceptance of its rules by its members – 123 member countries and another 31 governments requested to join it in 1996 – have greatly contributed to the opening up of national borders. Therefore, this process of trade liberalization has played a central role in the emergence of the global economy.

The Growing Role of Transnational Corporations

According to the United Nations *World Investment Report* (1992), there were more than 37,000 TNCs and 200,000 affiliates in 1992 (compared with only 7,000 twenty years before), controlling 75 per cent of world trade. One-third of this trade is intra-firm (UNRISD, 1995, p. 27). Of the TNCs 95 per cent originate in developed countries. They control one-third of the world's private-sector assets; in 1990 they were responsible for about 40 per cent of world output (Hirst, 1997, p. 419).

TNCs exploit national differences and competition between countries to receive FDIs for their own profit-making ends. FDI is the main mechanism through which they promote globalization of production. According to UNCTAD (1996), between 1980 and 1994, FDI stock to GDP doubled. From 1983 to 1990, corporate investment across borders grew four times faster than world output and three times faster than world trade (*The Economist*, 1993). Indeed, between 1983 and 1990, FDI flows expanded at an average annual rate of 34 per cent, compared with an annual growth rate of 9 per cent in global merchandize trade (OECD, 1992).

However, despite some globalization of production discussed above, for strategic decision-making and research and development, TNCs are strongly linked to their home country. In the emerging global economy, they continue to enjoy predominant national location; their strategies are dependent on national regulations and system of innovation for core functions.

The impact of TNCs on developing countries has been the subject of debate since the early 1960s, particularly in Latin America. As we noted in Chapter 5, the dependency theory associated with Prebisch and others divided the world into the centre and periphery. The developing countries that formed the periphery were exploited by the industrial 'metropolitan' countries (the centre). The transnational capital of corporations owned or controlled primary production for export from developing countries. The small export sectors acted as 'enclaves', with little positive effects on the domestic or host economy. The monopolistic nature of the primary export activity, and the adverse terms of trade for the primary producers, meant an outflow of profits and benefits to the transnationals and industrial countries at the expense of the periphery. Thus the periphery was assumed to be in a permanent dependent relationship with the centre. In discussing the role of the transnational corporations (TRANCOS), Sunkel (1973, p. 163) states:

> The TRANCOS do in fact constitute a new economic system – both national and international ... This new system favours the development of local segments integrated into the internationalized nucleus of the capitalist system, in particular, those segments which are more directly connected with the TRANCOS, while at the same time tending to disrupt the rest of the economy and society, segregating and marginalizing significant sections of the population.

Spread of International Financial Markets

International capital flows increased up to fourteen-fold between 1972 and 1996. In 1995, approximately US$1.2 billion were exchanged every day in the currency market (*The Economist*, 1995). Daily foreign exchange trading registered grew by 50 per cent between 1992 and 1995 (Kaul, 1996, p. 3). Liberalization has caused a significant decline in domestic barriers to international capital movements over the past two decades. Chesnais (1994, p. 209) shows acceleration of the trend in the internationalization of capital since the early 1980s by calculating the percentage of GDP of cross-border operations in shares and obligations. This percentage, which was less than 10 per cent in major countries in 1980, reached 72.2 per cent of GDP in Japan, 109.3 per cent in the United States and 122.2 per cent in France. The financial markets, operating 24 hours a day, are characterized by the speculative fever of international bankers; and most foreign-exchange transactions are speculative (Eatwell, 1995). Capital mobility has increased the dominance of market forces on domestic policy. Priority is increasingly accorded to economic and monetary policies driven by market expectations in the global economy.

Decline in the Scope of Nation State Policy

In the new global context, where capital outflows immediately penalize any domestic policy that does not fit in with expectations of international bankers, governments often feel constrained by the domination of financial markets. Thus, financial market signals exercise an increasing power over governments, sharply reducing their policy-making autonomy. Market forces operating beyond national regulations are becoming increasingly powerful. UNCTAD (1996) notes how firms exert pressures on governments to provide favourable conditions for operating worldwide. Such conditions facilitate further liberalization of international trade, freedom of entry, right of establishment and national treatment, as well as freedom for international financial transactions, deregulation and privatization. Increasingly the State is facilitating restructuring and adaptation to benefit from growth opportunities made possible by globalization. It thereby promotes the process of economic globalization (Cox, 1987).

Redefinition of the Role of the State

The state is a key actor for ensuring proper integration into the global economy, by providing education, training and health care, as well as long-term investment in scientific policy, telecommunications and transportation (Boyer and Drache, 1997). State intervention is crucial to reduce uncertainty and to contribute to sustainable growth.

Globalization as an Ideology

While the paradigm of modernization during the 1950s and 1960s emphasized the complex and problematic conditions of access to modernity, the new thinking that dominates the 1990s reduces them to a question of integration into the global economy and the adoption of the 'universal values' of the market, of democracy and of the rights of individuals. In the neoliberal discourse on globalization, modernization takes the form of competitive poles of accumulation of capital on a world scale, designed to generate growth and an increase in the population's well-being – in accordance with an updated version of the 'trickle down' theory. In these conditions the only rational strategy in terms of economic and social efficiency would be to mobilize resources towards the development and consolidation of those poles of growth, subject to the constraint of international competition. The requirements of the global economy henceforward take priority over national requirements. And if national areas want to benefit from the growth potential that globalization offers, they must necessarily be restructured in such a way as to provide an environment that is as favourable as possible for adapting to the standards of internationalization.

Because it enables companies to adapt to the changing conditions of the world market, flexibility is an essential condition of the dynamics of the global economy. The greater mobility of capital and the restructuring of economic systems is, therefore, justified in the name of flexibility. That process ends – principally through redefining the State's role – in the progressive freeing of the conditions of accumulation of capital from the mechanics of social regulations which had been set up on a national basis. Thus as Peemans (1995, pp. 29–30) points out, in the 'transnational neo-modernisation', international priorities take preference over national priorities, companies and their operating standards impose themselves on the State and the private sector imposes its priorities on the public sector'.

Thus, according to the dominant thinking, integration into the global economy offers growth prospects to all on condition that they satisfy the requirements of the global economy; it is, therefore, important to favour greater liberalization in order to achieve a genuine golden age of the global economy. Those requirements concern principally material infrastructure, the control of new technologies, training of the labour force, flexibility and competitiveness. The idea of convergence is, in particular, linked to adapting the new technologies which are designed to allow the limitless accumulation of wealth and an increasing homogenization of all human societies.

The protagonists of globalization see the phenomenon as a triumph of neoliberalism and market forces. The failure of the socialist system is often interpreted as a convergence or universalization of the values of free market, democracy and human rights. Economic globalization is seen to be creating tremendous growth opportunities everywhere, thereby reducing or eliminating North–South antagonism. It is not a zero-sum game, but 'a vector of sustainable global growth if domestic policies are implemented to meet the requirements of integrated and competitive world markets' (IMF, 1997a, p. 4). Any country can adapt its macroeconomic policies and economic system and take advantage of these growth opportunities. Thus the global economy can be seen as 'a neo-liberal world of trading and mutually dependent nations that have all successfully found a niche in the structure of world commerce' (Hettne, 1995, p. 17).

Privatization, deregulation and transnationalization of capital are considered desirable even from a broad social viewpoint. Indeed, structural reforms are enhancing the role of market forces and thereby strengthening the basis for sustained and robust growth. Thus there is no conceptual difference between development and sustainable growth. Both imply beneficial integration into the global economy. Indeed, structural policy reforms designed to achieve efficiency and growth are also seen to promote poverty reduction. From this perspective, 'social development is economic development' and social targeting policies can be seen as a superb investment in future economic growth (Birdsall, 1993). The late Michael Bruno (1995, pp. 16–17), former chief economist of the World Bank, wrote:

> Growth is necessary for a persistent reduction in poverty. Adjustment is necessary for the resumption of growth. And fiscal and monetary restraint are necessary components of adjustment. These conditions, met in success stories of the past twenty-five years, cut across diverse experiences and have withstood the test of time.

Thus we are facing an environment in which radical reforming national strategies are rejected and the debate on relevant alternatives to neoliberalism is stifled. The current hegemonic thinking has a dualistic perspective which opposes rationality and irrationality, modernity and archaism, progressive forces and conservative forces, modernity and barbarity. According to that thinking there is a confrontation between, on the one hand, the forces of transnationalism, and on the other hand, a conservative block, that would be blind to the reality of the considerable material gains that globalization can generate. That hegemonic approach paralyzes the debate on the question of the rationality of globalization as a whole and of the policies that are justified in its name. During strikes in France Bourdieu (1995a) denounced the conservative revolution that produced the paradoxical situation where not only reason and modernity, but also the right vision of where to go are on the side of governments, ministers, employers or 'experts' whereas archaism, inertia and conservatism are on the side of the people, trade unions, and intellectual critics who are fighting against the disruptive social effects of globalization. It is interesting to note how that dualistic vision of the world has been the vector of a subtle conversion of intellectuals, militants, or even trade unionists, who through fear of being placed in the category of 'conservatives', have rallied to the call of those who advocate the need to implement the necessary adjustments to ensure full integration into the global economy.

As for the reformist forces, they no longer call into question globalization as such, but instead seek to reconcile its requirements with humanist values. The publication of 'Our Global Neighbourhood' by the Commission on Global Governance (1995) is a perfect illustration of that current reformist trend. The weakness of that approach lies in its lack of determination to call into question the foundations of the new world order and the dynamics of the global economy. The report fails to identify the causes of the regressive social phenomena which affect most societies.

During the 1990s the hegemonic discourse on globalization asserted itself as the only relevant perspective of restructuring under way. But its legitimacy and constrictive side – structural adjustment programmes designed to satisfy the conditions of profitable integration into the global economy – fit into the very dynamics of the global capitalist economy.

In fact the current reasoning ignores or minimizes what is involved in social exclusion, maintaining that the social problems will be resolved by growth. However, as restructuring, necessary for integration into the global economy, can have a negative short-term social impact on the poorest populations, the implementation of social policies aimed at the most underprivileged is recommended. The logic underlying such policies is to prevent the dynamics of the global economy from being disrupted by the ever-growing number of those in the world who are not positively integrated into the global economy. The policies of income redistribution in a system that generates exclusion provide no satisfactory answer to the problem of the degradation of the quality of the social fabric which ensures that each individual has his or her place in the society in which they live; those excluded find themselves thrown into a social 'no man's land' and suffer from this resultant lack of symbolic or social recognition. Yet society may be considered 'fair' even when a limited number of individuals are excluded as long as there is a 'safety net' for them. Exclusion and alienation must be exceptional, not mass phenomena (Walzer, 1995).

Globalization is not the logical and inevitable result of market forces at work and technological trends. It has been institutionalized and protected by the new international rules and regulations set by the IMF, World Bank and now the WTO. The hegemony of the discourse on globalization is resulting from the emergence of a new historic bloc (including firm managers, bankers, politicians and technocrats). Since the 1980s, neoliberal economics and conservative political forces have been on the ascendant. They have guided domestic policies towards liberalization and restructuring to ensure consistency with the norms of globalization.

The success of the ideology of globalization results from the growth opportunities and the dynamics of accumulation created by the global economy. Nevertheless, the present form of globalization – the neoliberal form – tends to increase economic and social inequality and strengthens the strong at the expense of the weak. As Freeman and Soete (1994, p. 67) note, the challenge of the emerging global economy is to 'get smarter or get poorer'. The hegemonic discourse does not take into account the undermining impact of social disintegration and exclusion on the conditions for accumulation in the future.

Our objective is not to criticize economic globalization *per se*, but to question the neoliberal paradigm that guides the actual process of globalization. The key cause of such phenomena as social disintegration is the radical restructuring of capitalism designed to restore the dominance of capital over labour on a global scale. Thurow (1996, p. 7) emphasizes the tendency of the present phase of capitalism to rip up the implicit social contracts and produce a 'vicious circle of individual disaffection, social disorganization and a consequent slow downward spiral'.

EXCLUSION AND THE NEOLIBERAL PATTERN OF GLOBALIZATION

The logic of accumulation in a global economy runs counter to the logic of human security or of reproduction supported by family and political structures. The general rise in uncertainty and risks linked to the global economy – the important role of the financial markets, the volatility of capital, the calling into question of the welfare state – lead to the disintegration of forms of social organizations which protected people against risks (or from their consequences), from one generation to the next. The neoliberal project which currently guides the globalization of the economy results in phenomena which recall those described by Polanyi (1957) in the case of the UK in the nineteenth century, that is to say, an increase of the divide between rich and poor, the disintegration of the pre-existing social fabric and greater alienation. The rise in insecurity at individual levels as well as at the societal level is apparent in several forms: (i) rise in depression, suicides, heart attacks, (ii) upsurge of religious and ethnic violence as well as civil wars, (iii) increase in urban violence and in clandestine, illegal survival strategies, (iv) growth in trade in prohibited products and mafia-type organizations at the world level. Over time the development of such phenomena represents a major danger for the global economy.

There is a dramatic paradox between the mainstream discourse on the net benefits of greater integration into the global economy on the one hand, and the reality of the rising spiral of human insecurity for the bulk of the world's population on the other. All around the world globalization is accompanied by increased impoverishment, growing inequalities, job insecurity and unemployment, the weakening of institutions and social support systems and social exclusion (Bhalla, 1998; ILO, 1995b; UNDP, 1996; UNRISD, 1995). Instead of eliminating or reducing differences, global integration has made those differences more apparent and even unacceptable (ILO, 1995b).

The impact of globalization on exclusion can be examined by analysing how the process will affect the economic situation and standard of living of the poor, and how some countries and regions that are unable to integrate into the global economy are likely to be marginalized through denial of the benefits of trade and foreign direct investment.

The protagonists of globalization assume that it will improve the allocation of resources and market efficiency, and thus accelerate economic growth. But globalization is benefiting only some regions of the world and some segments of the global population. The emerging global economy is leading to a fundamental spatial restructuring. As Gill (1995, p. 75) notes:

> the global economy is dominated by, concentrated in, and organized from, a number of mega-sized urbanized regions or world cities (and their contiguous hinterlands) which form the major centres of production and consumption and, which house the vast bulk of corporate headquarters.

At the international level, North–South or core–periphery dichotomies are becoming less and less relevant because some dynamic poles of development emerge in the South while exclusion and new poverty have emerged in the most advanced regions in the North. Furthermore, the notion of periphery is not applicable to regions that are progressively marginalized as a consequence of globalization (Veltz, 1996, p. 57).

Globalization and Exclusion Between Countries

The emerging global economy is composed of highly dynamic poles of accumulation which are interconnected into a global web. However, many countries, regions or economic sectors and populations are excluded because they cannot respond to the requirements of the global economy, owing to their lack of infrastructure, technology, transport, skilled labour, and so on. In the 1980s, the logic of poles of accumulation became mainstream; all the resources available had to be concentrated on the strengthening of such poles to take advantage of the market opportunities of the global economy. These dynamic poles of accumulation are created by a network of highly competitive enterprises that operate according to international norms.

Holm and Sorensen (1995) refer to the concept of 'uneven globalization' to describe the increasing marginalization of a large number of developing countries. It is a process that has led to the fragmentation of what is now called the 'Third World'. The success story, for example, of the four dragons, took place in a very specific international context characterized by a robust world economy. Existing uneven development between countries and regions may be further accentuated, particularly between low-wage assemblers in developing countries and high-skill producers in industrialized countries. One cannot exclude the possibility of polarization of production activity attributed to differences across regions in skill availability and market size (see Bailey *et al.*, 1993). The least-developed countries, mostly in Africa, may be particularly adversely affected. Globalization may reinforce or aggravate 'income gaps' and 'technology gaps' between nations, since all countries are not equally prepared or endowed to benefit from it.

The World Bank (1996a) notes wide disparities in global integration, and distinguishes between the strong and weak integrating countries. The weak integrators are not only in sub-Saharan Africa (as one would expect) but also in North Africa, the Middle East and middle-income countries in Latin America. Many developing countries have indeed become less integrated during the past decade. The World Bank study cited above notes that in 44 out of 93 developing countries, the trade-to-GDP ratio has declined over the past decade. The decline in their shares of world trade and international capital flows contribute to the dangers of marginalization.

There is a sharp geographical concentration of trade and FDI in the emerging global economy. Taking FDI first, in the 1980s the 'Triad' (Europe, North America and Japan) attracted 75 per cent of all FDI flows, whereas they accounted for only 14 per cent of the world population in 1990. Moreover, during this period ten developing countries received 66 per cent of total FDI flows going to all developing countries (Hirst and Thompson, 1996); these countries/regions are: Argentina, Brazil, China, Egypt, Hong Kong, Malaysia, Mexico, Singapore, Taiwan and Thailand. Their combined population plus that of the OECD countries amounts to 43 per cent of the world's population – and it is unlikely that all the populations of larger countries, such as China or Brazil, will benefit from investment inflows. Therefore, a large part of the world is excluded from the benefits of FDI, in particular, sub-Saharan Africa. FDI inflows in this region have been marginal; the FDI/GDP ratio even declined from about 2.4 per cent per annum during 1984–9 to about 1.5 per cent in 1995 (Bhalla and Berry, 1998, p. 172).

Like FDI, global trade also remains concentrated. The bulk of trade occurs between OECD industrialized countries. There is a tripolar fragmentation of trade between North America, Europe and Japan. The trade share of OECD countries (as a proportion of exports) has increased. While intraregional trade shares of some developing regions have increased, those of other regions have declined (see Bhalla and Bhalla, 1997). The share of African exports in total world exports is decreasing; from 1984 to 1989, African exports increased at a rate of 2.4 per cent a year compared with the rate in South-East Asia of approximately 14 per cent and the average rate for developing countries of 7.3 per cent (ILO, 1995b, p. 109).

Far from leading to a convergence at the global level, the above forces at work are intensifying inequalities between regions (see Table 6.1).

The world is becoming increasingly polarized. Between 1960 and 1989, the countries with the richest 20 per cent of world population increased their share of global GNP from 70.2 per cent to 82.7 per cent, whereas the countries with the poorest 20 per cent of

Table 6.1 Widening economic gaps between regions (percentages)

	Global population		*Global GNP*		*Global trade*		*Foreign direct investment*	
	1960	*1989*	*1960*	*1989*	*1960*	*1989*	*1960*	*1989*
Industrial countries	31.5	22.9	84.1	84.2	81.1	80.7	–	–
Developing countries	68.5	77.1	15.9	15.8	18.9	19.3	100	100
Least developed countries	6.8	8.4	1.0	0.5	0.8	0.4	1.7	2.2
East and South-East Asia (excl. China)	8.8	9.9	1.7	2.9	4.1	8.1	11.7	33.3
China	21.8	21.6	3.0	2.0	0.8	1.9	11.8	7.0
Sub-Saharan Africa	7.1	9.5	1.9	1.2	3.8	1.0	24.8	15.0
Latin America and the Caribbean	7.1	8.4	4.7	4.4	5.6	3.3	40.4	28.4

– = not available.
Source: UNDP (1992).

world population saw their share fall from 2.3 per cent to 1.4 per cent (UNDP, 1992, p. 34). Thus the income gap between the richest and the poorer countries has increased sharply; the top 20 per cent received 30 times more than the bottom 20 per cent in 1960, but they were receiving 60 times more in 1989 (UNDP, 1992, p. 34). In 1993, world GNP was US$23,000 billion; industrialized countries accounted for US$18,000 billion and developing countries, representing 80 per cent of world population, for only US$5,000 billion (UNDP, 1996, p. 2).

Globalization and Exclusion Within Countries

There are growing fears that societies in the new global era will produce a large group of the excluded, the permanent losers from globalization (see Chapters 3–5). Where jobs do not grow, the new social structure will have an increasing number of marginal and excluded segments depending on informal activities (legal or not) or social assistance. Where jobs do grow, there will still be a growing number of insecure working poor trapped in poverty and low-paid monotonous jobs. Despite the growth of world GNP between 1980 and 1993, 'a billion of individuals have experienced a decrease in income (per inhabitant) between 1980 and 1993' (UNDP, 1996, p. 3).

As we discussed in Chapters 3 and 4, the phenomena of new poverty and social exclusion in industrialized countries are deeply rooted in the evolution of the labour market towards precariousness and long-term unemployment. In the OECD countries, low-skilled workers have been particularly hit and their living and working conditions have deteriorated sharply during the last decade. Globalization has been blamed for this phenomenon, but a controversy surrounds the trade-led explanation of persistent and rising unemployment in industrialized countries.

The question of the impact of North–South trade on low-skilled workers in the North is the subject of serious debate (Freeman, 1997). Wood (1994) estimates that about 20 per cent of low-skilled job loss in manufacturing in the OECD countries is due to import penetration from developing countries. These estimates are based on the following arguments. First, the increased share of the South's manufactured goods exports to the North consists almost entirely of labour-intensive goods produced with unskilled labour. To the extent that comparative advantage lies with skilled labour, unskilled labour-intensive goods 'vanished' from developed-country exports, which consist increasingly of skill-intensive goods. Second, trade with developing countries and increasing global competition have induced substantial labour-saving innovations contributing to jobless growth.

Other economists (notably, Krugman, 1994, 1996; Lawrence, 1994) assert that international trade, and in particular, increasing competition from low-wage developing countries, has had little net effect on the employment of less-skilled workers and income inequality in the North. This is because trade between the North and South is at present surprisingly small. Krugman (1994, p. 116) notes that in 1990 advanced industrial countries spent only 1.2 per cent of their GDP on imports of manufactured goods from newly industrializing countries (NICs).[1]

In the short term, active labour market policies and reasonably effective social safety nets may provide some temporary relief, but not a lasting solution to social disintegration and exclusion. As we noted in Chapters 1 and 4, a growing number of individuals face economic and social deprivation whereby they are wholly or partially excluded from full social participation. Indeed, globalization can be seen as a dual process of social integration and exclusion. A three-tier hierachy is emerging in the new social order shaped by globalization. At the top of this structure are people with the training and skills to be able to take advantage of the opportunities created by the global economy in terms of jobs and consumption, for example. The second level in the hierarchy includes those who serve the global economy but are increasingly vulnerable as a result of deregulation and flexibility in the labour market. New industrial relations and forms of work threaten their monetary and social stability. The bottom layer consists of potentially surplus low-skilled or unskilled labour trapped in long-term unemployment and precarious jobs. This segment of the population at the fringes of society can be considered as a powerful means of social control in a fragmented society.

Through high rates of growth and efficiency, globalization is able to distribute high incomes to the fully integrated groups (managerial staff, so-called 'symbolic analysts' *à la* Reich and so on) and contribute to the emergence of a transnational class integrated positively into the global economy. These middle- and high-income groups tend to pursue (all around the world) a lifestyle characterized by a frenetic consumption of status-enhancing luxury goods, referred to as 'symbolic capital' by Bourdieu (1977, pp. 171–97). Therefore, the logic of the dynamic poles is a key factor in social restructuring, leading to growing fragmentation between those who are able and those who are not able to acquire 'symbolic capital'. Fragmentation also occurs among workers as a result of the rise in numbers of the working poor and precarious jobs (Peemans, 1996, p. 56).

Globalization has involved deep changes in the management of urban spaces. Indeed, we have seen a restructuring of urban spaces in major cities according to the logic of the dynamic pole of accumulation which is a logic of selection, marginalization and exclusion (Peemans, 1995, p. 32). A major change in urban social life is the endemic rise in poverty and informal activities (Harvey, 1989). It signals an end to the city as an integrated territory and as a social entity. The idea of a public sphere open to all citizens is being abandoned, and local politics are being reoriented towards a defence of communities of self-interest and consumer rights. City spaces in the global era are now privatized places of consumption (Davis, 1990), as evidenced by the proliferation of shopping and leisure projects in recent years aimed at maximizing profits (Christopherson, 1994, p. 410). As cities become arenas of exclusion and private spaces, the resulting social polarization is leading to a growing preoccupation with the need to separate different kinds of people in space. The new priority is to manage this new dualism between those who are integrated into these dynamic poles and the excluded who cannot take part in the new consumption patterns. The urban space recomposition is based on (i) the needs of the market forces in terms of adequacy measured against the norms of the global economy, and (ii) the need to provide secure enclaves open only to the well-off who are valued as consumers or producers (Amin, 1994, p. 33).

EXCLUSION VS. SUSTAINABLE GROWTH

The very relationships that create opportunities for growth also generate sharp conflicts. To understand capitalist reproduction it is, therefore, necessary to understand the social and institutional context in which accumulation occurs. The central notion here is that the crucial features of the process of capital accumulation over a long period are the product of the supporting role played by a set of social institutions (Aglietta, 1982; Boyer, 1995; Kotz *et al.,* 1995).[2] This set of institutions is referred to as a mode of regulation. Simply having the basic institutions of capitalism in place is seen to be insufficient for achieving vigorous growth. An additional set of social institutions is required to assure stability and mitigate the conflicts engendered by capitalism. Only then is rapid and sustainable growth possible.

The market appears to be bursting free from the bonds of national social regulation, to subject global society to its laws (Cox, 1995, p. 39). The result is greater social polarization, the disintegration of pre-existing social bonds and alienation, which are weakening the social consensus on growth objectives within the global economy. In the face of growing social fragmentation and vulnerability, the losers from globalization will seek to resist and to redefine both their role in the emerging new global order and the strategies of social struggle (Mittelman, 1996). Fragmented data sources from case studies and monographs exist concerning local processes and micro-conflicts related to the social impact of economic globalization (Bourdieu, 1995b). Moreover, with the growth of long-term unemployment and precarious forms of work, channels of upward social mobility are gradually being closed off, a phenomenon with crucial consequences for both the stability and the dynamic evolution of society.

On the basis of an analysis of capitalism in the nineteenth century, Polanyi (1957) developed the 'double movement' thesis: the first part of that movement is the expansion and deepening of market exchange; the second part is the reaction of self-protection on the part of society against the disruptive and destabilizing effects of the market. Thus society is transformed in accordance with the double movement, so that, in its second phase, the economy tends to be re-embedded in society. The logic of Polanyi's analysis leads us to look for the sources of opposition to the effects of economic globalization and the possible emergence of a more coherent countervailing force (Cox, 1995, p. 40). As global integration intensifies, a protective response will emerge from communities seeking to avoid being marginalized and excluded.

As Boyer and Drache argue (1997, p. 14), 'history teaches that internationalization is not an irreversible process, especially when countries are faced with the anonymous and often destructive forces of the market'. Therefore, economic policy should focus on overcoming such pressure on the 'losers' if the process of globalization is to be sustained (Kapstein, 1996). There is a serious risk of revolts against an open international economy if the undesirable social effects of the emerging global economy are ignored.

Among the many sources of disruption in global society out of which a countermovement may emerge, the most important is social fragmentation and disintegration associated with the restructuring of the condition for accumulation. As Cox (1995, p. 39) notes:

> A first consequence is that the core/periphery metaphor now applies more accurately to a social relationship as inequalities and exclusion within countries worsen. The new production organizations have a relatively small core of permanent employees and a larger number of peripheral employees whose relationship to the production network is more precarious. A second consequence is the exclusion of a large part of the population from the labour market. (See also Chapters 3 and 4.)

It is clear that the link between production and jobs has been broken in the process of restructuring of production. A large proportion of the population is becoming superfluous to the global production process, and long-term unemployment and precarious forms of work have increased sharply both in the European Union and Eastern Europe. On the other hand, in the United States income inequalities and an increase in the number of working poor are the main trends. Globalization – and with it the associated pressure towards liberalization and deregulation – is undermining any state capacity to guarantee workers' rights, and more generally, social rights (Tilly, 1995).

It is important to take account of social forces challenging the social implications of the neoliberal model of globalization through the resurgence of identities (religion, ethnicity, and gender, for example) and an emphasis on locality. The 'new regionalism' should be seen as a manifestation of the second movement (noted above), or, in other words, the self-protection of society. This time round, the social reaction against global market expansion will not be at the level of the nation state, but at the level of the region (Hettne, 1995). However, not all of these forces are progressive, and the danger is that a countermovement could be ethnonationalist, or neo-fascist, reactionary or, more generally, extremist (Gill, 1996). In particular, the growing discontent with rising inequalities and social disintegration has contributed to the development of fundamentalist movements. As McMichael (1996, p. 215) argues, the fundamentalist movements have two main features. First, they articulate the uncertainties and distress brought about by the social decay that populations experience as a result of the limits of developmentalism and the increasing selectivity of globalization. Second, they often take the form of a nationalist resurgence against perceived threats to their culture. The combination frequently involves contesting the universalist assumptions of global development, presenting alternative ways of organizing social life at a national or local level.

Far from converging towards a fully integrated world and a global society there is a trend towards 'a discontinuous space where differences flourish in a multiplicity of places' (Sachs, 1992, p. 112). Territorially oriented development based on local cultural identity and the mobilization of local resources will probably emerge as a defensive reaction to preserve developmental objectives and a social control of such development (the Chiapas movement can be seen as a good example of this kind of new social movement). Therefore, the tendency towards social disintegration is accompanied by a new emphasis on territorial issues and a reaffirmation of identities. Thus paradoxically, globalization engenders territorial demands and conflicts.

Transition Economies, Liberalization and Sustainable Growth

The transition economies have rapidly made great strides towards market economies. The key measures adopted to integrate into the global economy included trade liberalization, opening of new businesses, achieving price stability, privatization and a system of property rights. According to the cumulative liberalization index (CLI) developed by de Melo *et al.* (1996), Hungary and Poland are advanced reformers which are now experiencing relatively robust economic growth.[3] The foreign trade of the transition economies continued to expand rapidly in both value and volume. The expansion of foreign trade has been a key driving force underlying rapid growth. Indeed, the share of foreign trade in GDP increased significantly between 1989 and 1995. In Poland for example, exports of goods and services rose from 19 to 25 per cent, and imports from 15 to 23 per cent between 1989 and 1995. In particular, the importation of inputs processed in Poland and their reexport accounted for an increasing share of foreign trade. One of the most remarkable features of the transition economies is the rapidity with which they (particularly, Poland and Hungary) have liberalized trade. Moreover, in 1995 the net capital flows into Eastern Europe tripled, from US$10.6 billion in 1994 to just over US$31 billion. Most of the funds (nearly 90 per cent) went to just three countries namely, the Czech Republic, Hungary and Poland (UNECE, 1997). As most of the funds were private capital, this distribution seems to confirm the view that foreign investors are attracted to economies when reforms and stabilization policies are in place and are credible, and when the prospects for growth seem reasonably bright.

All these achievements lead the World Bank (1996c) to highlight the point that with continued and sustained reforms, the group of advanced reformers can achieve successful long-term economic growth considerably above the world average. In Chapter 4 we approach the great transformation in Poland and Hungary rather differently. We have shown that although achieving economic growth through greater openness, liberalization and deregulation may not be difficult, *sustaining* it is much more problematic in a context of social polarization. The processes of global economic and social deprivation highlight the fragility of the new conditions of accumulation and the lack of a stable basis for sustained, robust and long-term growth. Bienefeld (1995, p. 103) notes: 'The alleged irreversibility of globalization will be increasingly challenged as more people experience its costs and recognize that these are not due to minor or temporary disturbances affecting a small monority, but are part of an open ended and long-term challenge to the majority's quality of life.'

We have focused on the indicator that best combines the *distributional* and *relational* aspects of social exclusion, that is, the employment situation. Indeed, long-term unemployment and precariousness of employment are expressions of social vulnerability which have seriously affected the transition economies including Poland and

Hungary (see Chapter 4). Major changes in the employment structure, growing tension in the labour market, the rise of labour and income insecurity have all increased the risk of cumulative deprivation and then of exclusion.

Fostering economic growth by continuing to pursue more liberal pro-market policies is not the most appropriate approach to solving the social problems of transition. Indeed, targeting policies based on the trickle down hypothesis do not adequately answer the new social question, that is, the loss of social cohesion. Therefore, the integration of Eastern Europe into the global economy and its convergence to the norms of global markets is far from being the 'end of history'. We believe that it is the start of a 'second movement' characterized by multi-layered social reactions against the disruptive impact of global market expansion.

CONCLUSION

In the 1980s, the mainstream idea was that economic growth implied flexibility and competitiveness. The requirements were, in particular, (i) access to technological sources, and the ability to use and adapt them, (ii) human capital formation through the adaptation of education and vocational training, (iii) labour market flexibility, and (iv) redefinition of the role of the state towards supporting private sector competitiveness and facilitating economic globalization. Nevertheless, sustainable growth does not flow automatically from those requirements; it requires a stable social basis and consensus on growth objectives.

A critical feature of the process of capitalist accumulation is that it takes place in an environment of conflict (Kotz *et al.*, 1995) generated by the capitalist relations of production and exchange. Such conflict takes two forms: class conflict and competition. Thus, the crucial priority for sustainable growth is to stabilize class conflict and channel it in directions that are not unduly disruptive of accumulation.

If in the flexible regime of accumulation a growing segment of the population is excluded from participation in the market system, they are still at its inside fringe. Thus, social disintegration can have a 'boomerang effect' on the conditions of accumulation. There is a dramatic need for an institutional framework capable of overcoming the conflicts because the social disruptive impact of economic globalization will not continue unchallenged. For Rodrik (1997, p. 2), 'the most serious challenge for the world economy in the years ahead lies in ... ensuring that international economic integration does not contribute to domestic social disintegration'. Indeed, the contradictions of globalization in the 1990s, are already giving rise to a countermovement. The question of the quality of the social bond between the individual and society is central from that perspective.

Thus, one can question the global optimism shared by the élite all around the world. This optimism is based on the development and diffusion of new information technology and the integration of countries into the global economy.

To conclude, social exclusion can be a very useful approach and an analytical and operational framework for research and policy-making. Policy guidelines flowing from such an approach suggest that a restoration of sustainable growth will require the creation of a new set of social institutions capable of overcoming the conflict, coordination and agency problems endemic to capitalist economies. The main issue is the ability of social movements to bargain and struggle to implement new forms of social regulation on accumulation, and restoring social bonds to preserve social cohesion. By showing the fragility of the basis for the accumulation of wealth in the global economy and the problematic character of its sustainability, the social exclusion approach should make it possible to deny the legitimacy of the dominant argument on globalization – in its current form – and the policies implemented in its name.

Notes

Preface

1. Speech by the Prime Minister, Tony Blair, for the Social Exclusion Unit Launch – 'Bringing Britain Together' – Stockwell Park School, London, 8 December 1997.

1 Defining Exclusion

1. In the core of the text of Lenoir (1974), the term 'exclusion' is very rarely used, and generally it is replaced by the term 'lack of social adaptability'. This lack of conceptualization and the socio-economic context (it is the end of the golden age and those processes affecting certain groups are still marginal) explained why the notion of exclusion had little success in the French debate during the 1970s. A debate on inequalities seemed more relevant than the one based on social exclusion concerning the socio-historic realities at that time.
2. These organizations are of different types – semi-official, popular and even illegal (see Howell, 1994). The semi-official organizations, like the Self-employed Workers' Association, have emerged to assist the state in maintaining its control over decentralized economic activities. Such organizations act as a 'bridge between the state and people' and represent people's participation in decision-making.
3. The experience of China under post-Mao reforms shows that even in the absence of full political freedom, the growth of social organizations and the increased role of trade unions make it easier to control or alleviate social exclusion. The introduction of market reforms and the somewhat diminished role of the state in China have given new and different functions to the trade unions. For example, the tremendous growth of contract labour in China has led to an increase in the number of disputes between workers and management. Trade unions are increasingly involved as arbiters of such disputes.
4. In particular, in recent years the idea of a 'solidarity bank' (widely based on the successful experience of low-income developing countries, notably Bangladesh), which could support initiatives for overcoming exclusion, has been spreading in Western Europe.

2 Towards an Analytical and Operational Framework

1. In making a plea for integrating social and economic programmes, Maxwell (1996) distinguishes between two notions of competitiveness:

'(a) cost minimisation, and (b) long-run success of society in generating economic growth and well-being of its citizens'. These two notions may not be in harmony. A continued reliance on cost minimization alone will generate social, economic and political costs which may eventually 'poison the prospects of a successful knowledge-based economy'.

2. Kuwait is perhaps the only exception where the state provides welfare for all Kuwaiti citizens. However, non-Kuwaiti residents are excluded from this public provision.
3. However, the UNDP methodology of constructing the political freedom index is not very clear. It is also not clear whether Dasgupta and UNDP use the same methodology and sources of data for estimating political and civil liberties.

3 Unemployment, Precarious Jobs and Exclusion

1. It is noted that women's job tenure is higher in France because of the availability of full-time and free child care services to children aged 3 to 6, and public policy supporting flexitime and leave in case of children's illness (see OECD, 1993, p. 122).
2. There is a clear distinction between these two types of temporary work in French- and Spanish-speaking countries but this distinction is less clear in English-speaking countries (OECD, 1993).
3. For example, several US insurance companies despatch their insurance claims to Ireland, American Airlines undertakes routine data processing in Barbados and Swissair has transferred its accounting and data-processing department to Mumbai (Bombay, India). Many labour-intensive activities in South-East Asia are moving to labour-cheap countries like China and Vietnam.
4. Over 11 million workers belonged to these two categories. When both are included, roughly 2 to 5 percentage points are added to the unemployment rate in the OECD area.
5. For example, in Manila the owners of informal transport enterprises (the *jeepney* and tricycle operators) are not poor, since they invested a substantial amount of capital. However, the drivers of *jeepneys* are poor and vulnerable by virtue of (i) insecure or irregular labour force status and (ii) lack of protection through legal restraints or lack of collective organizations (Alonzo, 1989).
6. Writing on vulnerable workers in Coimbatore (Kerala, India), Harriss (1989, p. 235) notes that 'scheduled caste people are most likely to be found working in moulding shops where work is particularly unpleasant and low-skilled, or in casting gangs where the work is physically hard and somewhat dangerous'. He also notes that the politically and economically dominant upper castes are more strongly represented among permanent wage workers than short-term wage workers suffering from instability.
7. The poor rural families in India and Thailand are known to send wives and daughters to cities to provide financial support to them through prostitution (see Standing, 1989).

4 Exclusion in Developed Countries

1. The Social Exclusion Unit aims at: (a) improving understanding of the key characteristics of social exclusion and the impact on it of government policies, and (b) promoting solutions, making recommendations for changes in policies, machinery or delivery mechanisms. During its first year of operation, its three main priorities are: (i) to reduce school truancy, (ii) to reduce or eliminate the numbers of people sleeping rough in towns and cities, and (iii) developing integrated approaches to the problems of the worst housing estates, including crime, drugs, unemployment, community breakdown, bad schools and so on. In his inaugural speech on 8 December 1997, Prime Minister Tony Blair underlined the central theme of national renewal, Britain rebuilt as one nation, in which each citizen is valued and has stake; in which no-one is excluded from opportunity and chance to develop their potential; in which we make it, once more, our national purpose to tackle social division and inequality' ('Bringing Britain Together', Stockwell Park School, South London, 8 December 1997). The unit consists of a network of ministers from various government departments (Environment, Transport and the Regions, Social Security, Education and Employment, Health, Home Office, Trade and Industry, and the Treasury). The Unit plans to 'draw extensively on outside expertise and research, and lock into relevant external networks to hear views from local authorities, business, voluntary organizations and other organizations/individuals with experience of dealing with exclusion'.
2. Under RMI, the average monthly income allowance in metropolitan France in June 1996 was 1905 francs, whereas the poverty line is fixed at FF 3316 francs.
3. Integration activities have been decentralized to the '*départements*' (French administrative areas), public authorities, local politicians, social workers, associations, and so on, which work together to develop integration opportunities for the RMI recipients. The RMI legislation has created a new institutional framework to support the objectives of social and professional integration – the Conseil Départemental d'Insertion (Departmental Council of Integration) and the Commission Locale d'Insertion (Local Commission for Integration). For example, the integration contract formulated by the recipient and the social worker who supports him or her is signed by the Departmental Council and the Chairman of the Local Commission for Integration. In France, two-thirds of the annual new labour contracts correspond to atypical forms of work (see Brunhes, 1993).
4. To measure household standard of living, Institut National de la Statistique et des Etudes Economiques (INSEE) in France sums up all the different categories of income received by households and adjusts it for the varying sizes of households. The total household income is divided by the number of household members, giving different weights to each member depending on whether he or she is an adult or a child. The weights given are as follows: first adult, 1.0; second and subsequent adults, 0.7; children under 15, 0.5.

5. A survey by the INSEE of underprivileged households showed that in 1993–4 the number of heads of households looking for a job was three times higher for low-income households than for the total number of households (17.2 per cent as against 6 per cent) and 39 per cent of the heads of households belonging to the first decile were part-time or temporary workers.
6. The labour force surveys provide data unaffected by changes in unemployment benefits. Indeed, the registered unemployed do not include those who are really out of work but are no longer entitled benefit, or are not for some reason registered, whereas the labour force surveys do not cover those unemployed who have some kind of job or do not actively seek a job. However, in the cases of Poland and Hungary the two indicators are close to each other and display the same trend.
7. The outflow rate is defined as the average outflow from unemployment as a proportion of the number of unemployed. In Poland and Hungary, it ranged between 4 and 6 per cent at the beginning of the 1990s.
8. It appears that one out of every two persons exiting the unemployment register leaves the labour force rather than being (re)integrated into the active population (Boeri, 1994, p. 16).

5 Exclusion in Developing Countries

1. Case study examples in this section are drawn from ILO (1993b).
2. Between 1983 and 1988, the following distribution of social conflicts were reported: labour disputes (18.7 per cent); divorce (18.0 per cent); criminal problems (17.2 per cent); inheritance (10.3 per cent); neighbourhood problems (10.2 per cent); debt problems (9.1 per cent); notice of eviction (8.5 per cent); alimony cases (5.2 per cent); and land tenure disputes (3.0 per cent) (IBGE, 1990; cited in Sadek, 1995).
3. A Human Rights Watch report (1991) notes that a very few trials and convictions occurred in the cases of 1566 murders of rural workers, Indians, lawyers, nuns and priests that were tabulated by the Pastoral Land Commission from 1964 through 1989. Furthermore, there are frequent cases of serious human rights abuses in the form of torture and extrajudicial killings. US (1997) notes that state police killed 19 landless workers in southern Para in April 1996; at least 10 of these victims were summarily executed. In São Paulo, police killed 119 citizens in the first six months of 1996. Disappearance and killing of street children is also quite common. According to Freedom House (1996), two former street children who campaigned against child violence were murdered in December 1995. It notes the results of research at the University of São Paulo which show that up to five street children are murdered every day, that their killers are rarely caught and that most of these victims are of African origin.
4. In Brazil in 1988, there were 31 555 inhabitants to one judge, compared with 3,443 in Germany, 7,692 in Italy and 7,142 in France (Lombard, 1988; cited in Sadek, 1995, pp. 164–5).

6 Globalization and Exclusion

1. According to Krugman's estimates in 1994, capital flows to the Third World since 1990 had reduced real wages in the advanced countries by about 0.15 per cent – hardly the devastation that many people envisage. While it is true that tens and even hundreds of thousands of workers in advanced countries have lost their jobs to low-wage imports, the total labour force in the industrialized countries is more than 400 million; almost every effort to explain why more than 30 million of these workers do not have jobs finds that Third World competition plays little if any role (Krugman, 1996, p. 195). Indeed, if it was the case then a protectionist response would easily solve the problem. Rather, the main cause of problem is the technological change, which is strongly skill-biased. The reality is that informational economy will create some new jobs but these will be far too few to absorb the millions of people displaced by the new technology revolution (Rifkin, 1995).
2. According to the French School of Regulation and social structure of accumulation, economic processes are embedded in society, and they result from its mode of regulation. Indeed, a key assertion of the 'regulation approach' is that a long period of vigorous capital accumulation (or long swings) depends on the existence and effective functioning of a set of social institutions (Aglietta, 1982; Boyer, 1990; Boyer and Saillard, 1995).
3. This index is defined to represent the duration as well as the intensity of reform from 1989 onward. Indeed, this index is used to classify countries into reform groups, based on their cumulative experience with economic liberalization. The CLI is calculated as the sum of a country's Liberalization Index (LI), that is, the weighted average (with weights of 0.3, 0.3 and 0.4 respectively) of a 0 to 1 ranking of liberalization in the following areas: (a) internal markets (liberalization of domestic prices and abolition of state trading monopolies); (b) external markets (currency convertibility and liberalization of foreign trade regime); and (c) private sector entry (privatization and banking reform).

Bibliography

The items listed below *include contributions relevant to the book but not specifically cited in the text.*

Aborn, M. and J. Demko (1984) 'Can There Be Social Indicators for the Observance of Human Rights?', in *Proceedings of the Social Statistics Section, American Statistical Association*.

Adams, R.J., G. Betcherman and B. Bilson (1995) *Good Jobs, Bad Jobs, No Jobs* (Toronto: CD Howe Institute).

Adelman, Irma and Cynthia Taft Morris (1965) 'A Factor Analysis of the International Relationship Between Social and Political Variables and Per Capita Gross National Product', *Quarterly Journal of Economics*, November.

Adelman, Irma and Cynthia Taft Morris (1972) 'The Measurement of Institutional Characteristics of Nations: Methodological Considerations', *Journal of Development Studies*, April.

Afsa, C. (1997) 'RMI, chômage et activité', *Solidarité Santé* Paris, no. 1.

Aglietta, M. (1982) *Regulation and the Crisis of Capitalism* (New York: Monthly Review Press).

Aglietta, M. (1997) 'Postface', in *Régulation et crises du capitalisme*, third edition (Paris: Éditions Odile Jacob).

Akerloff, G. (1970) 'The Market for "Lemons": Quality, Uncertainty and the Market Mechanism', *Quarterly Journal of Economics*, August.

Akerloff, G. (1976) 'The Economics of Caste and the Rat Race and Other Woeful Tales', *Quarterly Journal of Economics*, vol. 90.

Albarez, Sonia E. (1990) *Engendering Democracy in Brazil: Women's Movements in Transition Politics* (New Jersey: Princeton University Press).

Aldeghi, I. (1996) 'Les Nouveaux Arrivants au Revenue Minimum d'Insertion: profils, parcours antérieurs rapport a l'emploi et à la famille', *Rapport CREDOC*, no. 173.

Alesina, A. and R. Perotti (1994) 'The Political Economy of Growth: A Critical Survey of the Recent Literature', *World Bank Economic Review*, vol. 8, no. 3.

Allain, D. (1993) 'Que sont devenus les premiers bénéficiaires du RMI?', *Problèmes Economiques*, no. 2356.

Allen, J. and N. Henry (1996) 'Fragments of Industry and Employment', in R. Crompton, D. Gallie and K. Purcell (eds), *Changing Forms of Employment* (London: Routledge).

Alonzo, R. (1989) 'Trends in Poverty and Labour Market Outcomes', in G. Rodgers (ed.), *Urban Poverty and the Labour Market* (Geneva: International Institute for Labour Studies.

Altimir, O. (1994) 'Income Distribution and Poverty Through Crisis and Adjustment', *CEPAL Review* (Santiago), no. 52.

Alvarez, Sonia E. (1990) *Engendering Democracy in Brazil: Women's Movements in Transition Politics* (Princeton University Press).

Amadeo, E.J., R.P. Barros, J.M. Camargo and R. Mendonca (1995) 'Brazil', in G. Màrquez (ed.), *Reforming the Labour Market in a Liberalized Economy* (Washington DC: Interamerican Development Bank (IDB)).

Amadeo, E.J. and J.M. Camargo (1996) 'Labour Flexibility, Productivity and Adjustment', in José B. Figueiredo (ed.), *Las instituciones laborales frente a los cambios en America Latina* (Labour Institutions and Process of Change in Latin America) (Geneva: International Institute for Labour Studies).

American Correctional Association (1990) *Report on the State of the Nation's Prisons*, Washington, DC.

Amin, A. (1994) 'Post-Fordism: Models, Fantasies and Phantoms of Transition', in A. Amin (ed.), *Post-Fordism: A Reader* (Oxford: Basil Blackwell).

'Analyses de réseaux et structures relationnelles – études réunis et présentés par Emmanuel Lazega' (1995), Special Issue, *Revue française de sociologie*, October–December.

Anand, S. and A. Sen (1993) *Human Development Index: Methodology and Measurement*, UNDP Occasional Paper no. 8 (New York: UNDP).

Andersen, J.G. (1996) 'Marginalization, Citizenship and the Economy', in E.O. Eriksen and J. Loftager (eds), *The Rationality of the Welfare State* (Oslo: Scandinavian University Press).

Andorka, R. (1994a) 'Hungary: Disenchantment after Transition', *The World Today*, vol. 50.

Andorka, R. (1994b) 'Anciennes et nouvelles inégalités sociales en Hongrie', *Revue d'Etudes Comparatives Est-Ouest*, 4, Dec.

Andorka, R. (1995) 'Recent Changes in Social Structure, Human Relations and Values in Hungary', *Social Compass*, vol. 42, no. 1.

Andorka, R. and Z. Speder (1994) *Poverty in Hungary: Some Results of the First Two Waves of the Hungarian Household Panel Survey in 1992 and 1993* (Tilburg: the Netherlands) (mimeo.).

Aponte, R. (1990) 'Definitions of the Underclass: A Critical Analysis', in H. Ganz (ed.), *Sociology in America* (Newbury Park: Sage).

Appasamy, P., S. Guhan, R. Hema, M. Majumdar and A. Vaidyanathan (1996) *Social Exclusion From a Welfare Rights Perspective in India*, Research Series no. 106 (Geneva: International Institute for Labour Studies).

Arrighi, G. (1970) 'Labour Supplies in Historical Perspective: A Study of the Proletarianization of the African Peasantry in Rhodesia', *Journal of Development Studies*, no. 3.

Atkinson, A.B. (1995) *Incomes and the Welfare State* (Cambridge University Press).

Auletta, K. (1982) *The Underclass* (New York: Random House).

Avenel, C. (1997) 'La question de l'underclass des deux cotés de l'Atlantique', *Sociologie du Travail*, no. 2/97.

Bagguley, P. and K. Mann (1992) 'Idle, Thieving Bastards: Scholarly Representations of the "Underclass"', *Work, Employment and Society*, vol. 6, no. 1.

Bailey, P., A. Parisotto and G. Renshaw (eds) (1993) *Multinationals and Employment: The Global Economy of the 1990s* (Geneva: ILO).

Bairoch, P. (1997) 'Globalization: Myths and Realities: One Century of External Trade and Foreign Investment', in R. Boyer and D. Drache (eds), *States Against Markets – The Limits of Globalization* (London: Routledge).

Baltar, Paulo Eduardo de Andrade, Claudio Salvadori Dedecca and Wilnes Henrique (1996) 'Mercado da trabalho, precarizacao e exclusao no Brasil (The Labour Market Insecurity and Exclusion in Brazil)', in José B. Figueiredo (ed.), *Las instituciones laborales frente a los cambios en América Latina* (Geneva: International Institute for Labour Studies).

Bane, M.J. and D.T. Ellwood (1986) 'Slipping Into and Out of Poverty: The Dynamics of Spells', *Journal of Human Resources*, vol. 12.

Banks, D.L. (1989) 'Patterns of Oppression: An Exploratory Analysis of Human Rights Data', *Journal of the American Statistical Association*, September.

Bardhan, P. (1996) 'Efficiency, Equity and Poverty Alleviation: Policy Issues in Less Developed Countries', *Economic Journal*, September.

Barros, R., L. Fox and R. Mendonca (1997) 'Female-Headed Households, Poverty, and the Welfare of Children in Urban Brazil', *Economic Development and Cultural Change*, January.

Barros, R., R. Mendonca and S. Rocha (1995) 'Brazil: Welfare, Inequality, Poverty, Social Indicators, and Social Programs in the 1980s', in Nora Lustig (ed.), *Coping with Austerity: Poverty and Inequality in Latin America* (Washington, DC: Brookings Institution).

Barry, N. (1990) 'Markets, Citizenship and the Welfare State: Some Critical Reflections', in D. Green (ed.) *Citizenship and Rights in Thatcher's Britain* (London: Institute of Economic Affairs).

Becker, Gary S. (1974) 'A Theory of Social Interactions', *Journal of Political Economy*, November–December.

Becker, Gary S. (1976) 'Altruism, Egoism, and Genetic Fitness: Economics and Sociobiology, *Journal of Economic Literature*, September.

Becker, H. (1985) *Outsiders – Etudes de sociologie de la déviance* (Paris: Metaille).

Bédui, M. and G. Ridha (1996) *Les politiques de lutte contre l'exclusion sociale en Tunisie*, International Institute of Labour Studies (IILS) Discussion Paper no. 88.

Benabon, R. (1994) 'Theories of Persistent Inequalities – Human Capital, Inequality and Growth: A Local Perspective', *European Economic Review*, vol. 38.

Benoit, G. and D. Gallie (1994) *Long-term Unemployment* (London: Pinter).

Ben-Porath, Y. (1980) 'The F-Connection: Families, Friends and Firms and the Organization of Exchange', *Population and Development Review*, March.

Bequele, A. and J. Boyden (1988) *Combating Child Labour* (Geneva: ILO).

Berghman, J. (1994) *The Measurement and Analysis of Social Exclusion in Europe: Two Paradoxes for Researchers*, paper presented at the Seminar on the Measurement and Analysis of Social Exclusion, Bath, England, 17–18 June.

Berghman, J. (1995)'Social Exclusion in Europe: Policy COntext and Analytical Framework', in G. Room (ed.), *Beyond the Threshold: The Measurement and Analysis of Social Exclusion* (Bristol: Policy Press).

Berry, A., M.T. Mendez and J. Tenjo (1997) 'Growth, Macroeconomic Stability and the Generation of Productive Employment in Latin America', in A.R. Khan and M. Muqtada (eds), *Employment Expansion and Macroeconomic Stability under Increasing Globalization* (London: Macmillan).

Berry, S. (1988) 'Concentration Without Privatization: Some Consequences of Changing Patterns of Rural Land Control in Africa', in R.E. Downs and S.P. Reyna (eds), *Land and Society in Contemporary Society* (Hanover and London: University Press of New England).

Betcherman, G. (1995) 'Inside the Black Box: Human Resource Management and the Labor Market', in R.J. Adams *et al.*, *Good Jobs, Bad Jobs, No Jobs*, op. cit.

Betcherman, G. and G.S. Lowe (1997) *The Future of Work in Canada – A Synthesis Report* (Ottawa, Canadian Policy Research Networks (CPRN) Inc.).

Bhalla, A.S. (1995) *Uneven Development in the Third World*, Second (revised and enlarged ed)(London: Macmillan), Chapter 9 on Access to Health and Chapter 10 on Access to Education.

Bhalla, A.S. (ed.) (1998) *Globalization, Growth and Marginalization* (London: Macmillan).

Bhalla, A.S. and Albert Berry (1998)'Regional Perspectives: An Overview', ibid.

Bhalla, A.S. and P. Bhalla (1997) *Regional Blocs: Building Blocks or Stumbling Blocks?* (London: Macmillan).

Bhalla, Ajit and Frédéric Lapeyre (1997) 'Social Exclusion: Towards an Analytical and Operational Framework', *Development and Change*, July.

Bienefeld, M. (1995) 'Capitalism and the Nation State in the Dog Days of the Twentieth Century' in R. Millband and L. Panitch (eds) *The Socialist Register – 1994* (New York: Merlin).

Birdsall, N. (1993) 'Social Development is Economic Development', *Policy Research Working Papers WPS 1123* (Washington DC: World Bank).

Birdsall, N. and R. Sabot (1993) *'Vicious Circles: Human Capital, Growth and Equity in East Asia'* (Washington, DC: World Bank).

Bivar, W. (1993) *Estimativas da duração do desemprego no Brasil*, San Francisco, International Centre for Economic Growth Occasional Paper no. 26.

Blanchard, O., S. Commander and F. Coricelli (1994) 'Unemployment and the Labour Market in Eastern Europe' in T. Boeri (ed.), *Unemployment in Transition Countries: Transient or Persistent?*(Paris: OECD).

Blank, Rebbeca, M. (1990) 'Are Part-time Jobs Bad Jobs?', in G. Burtless (ed.), *A Future of Lousy Jobs?: The Changing Structure of US Wages* (Washington, DC: Brookings Institution).

Boeri, T. (1994) 'Labour Market Flows and the Persistence of Unemployment in Central and Eastern Europe', in T. Boeri (ed.), *Unemployment in Transition Countries: Transient or Persistent?* (Paris: OECD).

Boltho, A. (1992) 'Growth, Income Distribution and Household Welfare in the Industrialized Countries since the First Oil Shock', *Innocenti Occasional Papers* (Florence, UNICEF).

Boltvinik, Julio (1994) 'Poverty Measurement and Alternative Indicators', in R. van der Hoeven and R. Anker (eds), *Poverty Monitoring – An International Concern* (London: Macmillan).

Boschi, Renato R. (1987) 'Social Movements and the New Political Order in Brazil', in John Wirth *et al.* (eds), *State and Stability in Brazil-Continuity and Change* (Boulder: Westview).

Bouget, D. and H. Nogues (1993) 'L'Evaluation des politiques de lutte contre les exclusion sociales', in M. Ferra (ed.), 'The Evaluation of Social Policies: Experiences and Perspectives', *Quaderni della Revisita 'Il Politico'*, no. 38.

Boullay, V. du (1997) Le Revenu Minimum d'Insertion, *Solidarité Santé*, no. 1.

Bourdieu, P. (1977) *Outline of a Theory of Practice* (Cambridge University Press).

Bourdieu, P. (1995a) 'je suis ici pour dire notre soutien ...' *Libération*, Paris 14 décembre.

Bourdieu, P. (ed.) (1995b) *La Misère du monde* (Paris: Gallimard).

Bourdieu, P. (1998) 'Contre la destruction d'une civilisation (Intervention à la gare de Lyon lors des grèves de décembre 1995) *Contre-Feux*, Paris (Liber-Raisons d'agir).

Bourgeois, L. (1931) *Solidarité* (Paris: Armand Colin).

Bourguignon, F. (1989) *Optimal Poverty Reduction, Adjustment and Growth: An Applied Framework'*, World Bank Human Resources Division, Technical Department, Latin America and the Caribbean Region, December.

Bourguignon, F. (1993) *Growth, Distribution, and Human Resources: A Cross-Country Analysis,* (Paris: EHESS and DELTA) (Document 93-13), June.

Bowles, S. and H. Gintis (1995) 'Escaping the Efficiency–Equity Trade-off: Asset Redistribution', in G. Epstein and H. Gintis (eds), *Macroeconomic Policy After the Conservative Era* (Cambridge University Press).

Boyer, R. (1990) *The Regulation School: A Critical Introduction* (New York: Columbia University Press).

Boyer, R. (1991) *Markets Within Alternative Coordinating Mechanisms: History, Theory and Policy in the Light of the Nineties* (mimeo.) (Paris: CEPREMAP).

Boyer, R. (1994) 'Quelles réformes à l'Est? Une approche régulationniste', *Problèmes Economiques*, no. 2374.

Boyer, R. (1995) 'Avant propos' in R. Boyer and Y. Saillard (eds) *La théorie de la régulation: l'état des savoirs* (Paris: La Découverte).

Boyer, R. and D. Drache, (1997), 'Introduction', in Boyer and Drache, *States Against Markets – The Limits of Globalization*, op. cit.

Boyer, R. and Y. Saillard (eds) (1995) *Handbook on Regulation of Economics* (Armonk: Sharp).

Brecher, Jeremy, John Brown Childs and Jill Cutler (eds) (1993) *Global Visions – Beyond the New World Order* (Boston: South End Press).

Breen, R., D.F. Hannan, D. Rottman and C.T. Whelan (1990) *Understanding Contemporary Ireland: State, Class and Development in the Republic of Ireland* (London: Macmillan).

Breman, J. (1996) *Footloose Labour: Working in India's Informal Economy* (Cambridge University Press).

Brown, P. and R. Crompton (eds) (1994) *Economic Restructuring and Social Exclusion* (London: UCL (University College London) Press).

Bruegel, I. and A. Hegewisch (1994) 'Flexibilization and Part-Time Work in Europe', in Brown and Crompton, *Economic Restructuring and Social Exclusion*, op. cit.

Brunhes, B. (1993) *Choisir l'emploi* (Paris: La Documentation Française).

Bruno, M. (1995) 'Development Issues in a Changing World: New Lessons, Old Debate, Open Questions', in *Proceedings of the World Bank*

Annual Conference on Development Economics 1994 (Washington, DC: World Bank).

Brus, W. and K. Laski (1989) *From Marx to the Market: Socialism in Search of an Economic System*, (Oxford: Clarendon Press).

Bryson, Alex and Michael White (1996) *From Unemployment to Self-employment – The Consequences of Self-employment for the Long-term Unemployed* (London: Policy Studies Institute).

Buarque, C. (1993) *The End of Economics? Ethics and the Disorder* of *Progress* (London: Zed Books).

Buchanen, J.M. (1965) 'An Economic Theory of Clubs', *Economica*, vol. 32.

Büchtemann, C.F. and S. Quack (1990) 'How Precarious is "Non-standard" Employment? Evidence for West Germany', *Cambridge Journal of Economics*, September.

Buck, N. (1992) 'Labour Market Inactivity and Polarisation: A Household Perspective on the Idea of an Underclass', in D.J. Smith (ed.), (1992) *Understanding the Underclass* (London: Policy Studies Institute).

Buck, N. (1996) 'Social and Economic Change in Contemporary Britain: the Emergence of an Urban Underclass', in E. Mingione (ed.), *Urban Poverty and the Underclass – A Reader* (Oxford: Basil Blackwell).

Bulletin d'Information de la Délégation interministérielle du RMI (1993) 'Le RMI: un bilan contrasté', *Problèmes Economiques*, no. 2.391.

Burchell, B. (1989) 'The Impact on Individuals of Precariousness in the United Kingdom Labour Market', in Gerry and Janine Rodgers, *Precarious Jobs in Labour Market Regulation – The Growth of Atypical Employment in Western Europe* (Geneva: ILO).

Burtless, G. (1990) *A Future of Lousy Jobs? The Changing Structure of US Wages*, (Washington, DC: Brookings Institution).

Cacciamali, Maria Cristina (1996) 'The "Black Market" for Labour in Greater São Paulo: Characteristics and Trends 1985–1992', in J. Figuereido (ed.), *Las instituciones laborales frente a los cambios en América Latina* (Geneva: International Institute for Labour Studies).

Callan, T., B. Nolan and C.T. Whelan (1993) 'Resources, Deprivation and Measurement of Poverty', *Journal of Social Policy*, vol. 22, no. 2.

Cannan, C. (1997) 'The Struggle Against Social Exclusion: Urban Social Development in France', *IDS Bulletin*, April.

Cardoso, E. (1992) '*Poverty and Inequality in Brazil: Comments on Barros, Ricardo et al.: Welfare, Inequality, Poverty and Social Conditions in Brazil in the Last Three Decades*, paper presented at the Brookings Institution Conference, 15–17 July, Washington, DC (Unpublished).

Cardoso, F.H. (1973) *Dependency Revisited* Austin, Institute of Latin American Studies (University of Texas).

Carneiro, F. (1997) 'The Changing Informal Labour Market in Brazil: Cyclicality versus Excessive Intervention', *Labour*, vol. 3, no. 22.

Cartaya, V., R. Magallanes and C. Dominguez (1997) *Venezuela: Exclusion and integration – A Synthesis in the Building?*', Discussion Paper Series no. 90 (Geneva: International Institute for Labour Studies).

Casey, B. (1991) 'Survey Evidence on Trends in "Non-standard" Employment', in A. Pollert (ed.), *Farewell to Flexibility* (Oxford: Basil Blackwell).

Castel, R. (1990) 'Extreme Cases of Marginalisation: From Vulnerability to Disaffiliation', paper presented to a Conference on 'Poverty, Marginalisation and Social Exclusion in the Europe of the 1990s', organised under the auspices of the European Commission, Alghero, Sardinia.

Castel, R. (1991) 'De l'indigence à l'exclusion: la désaffiliation', in Jacques Danzelot (ed.), *Face à l'exclusion: Le modèle français* (Paris: Esprit).

Castel, R. (1992) 'De l'exclusion comme état à la vulnérabilité comme processus', in J. Affichard and J-B. de Foucauld (eds), *Justice Sociale et Inégalités* (Paris: Esprit).

Castel, R. (1995a) *Les Métamorphoses de la question sociale* (Paris: Fayard).

Castel, R. (1995b) 'Les Pièges de l'exclusion', *Lien Social et Politique*, no. 34.

Castel, R. and J-F. Laé (1992) 'La Diagonale du pauvre', in R. Castel and J.-F. Laé (eds), *Le Revenu Minimum d'Insertion – une dette sociale* (Paris: L'Harmattan).

Castells, M. (1971) *Problemas de investigacion en sociologia urbana* (Mexico: Siglo XXI Editores).

Castells, M. (1989) *The Informational City: Information Technology, Economic Restructuring, and the Urban-Regional Process* (Oxford: Basil Blackwell).

Castells, M. (1996) *The Rise of the Network Society* (Oxford: Basil Blackwell).

Castillo, Yépez del I. (1994) 'A Comparative Approach to Social Exclusion: Lessons from France and Belgium', *International Labour Review*, vol. 133, no. 5–6.

Centre d'Etude des Revenus et des Coûts (CERC) (1993) *Précarité et Risques d'Exclusion en France* (Paris: La Documentation Française).

Chesnais, F. (1994) *La Mondialisation du Capital* (Paris: Syros).

Christopherson, S. (1994) 'The Fortress City: Privatized Spaces, Consumer Citizenship', in Amin, *Post Fordism: A Reader*, op. cit.

Cingranelli, D.L. (ed.) (1988) *Human Rights – Theory and Measurement* (New York: St Martin's Press).

Cohen, B. and W.J. House (1996) 'Labor Market Choices, Earnings, and Informal Networks in Khartoum, Sudan', *Economic Development and Cultural Change*, April.

Coleman, James S. (1988) 'Social Capital and the Creation of Human Capital', *American Journal of Sociology*, vol. 94 (supplement).

Coleman, James S. (1990) *Foundations of Social Theory* (Cambridge, MA.: Belknap Press of Harvard University).

Collier, Paul (1995) 'The Marginalisation of Africa', *International Labour Review*, vol. 134, no. 4–5.

Commissariat Général au Plan – Rapport présidé par P. Nasse (1992) *Exclus et Exclusion-Connaître les populations et comprendre les processus* (Paris: Commissariat Général au Plan/La Documentation Française).

Commission on Global Governance (1995) – *Our Global Neighbourhood* (Oxford University Press)

Conseil de l 'Europe (1998) Opportunité et risque: les tendances de l 'exclusion sociale en Europe, Strasbourg: Conseil de l 'Europe

Cornelius, P. and B. Weder (1996) 'Economic Transformation and Income Distribution: Some Evidence from the Baltic Countries', *IMF Staff Papers*, vol. 43, no. 3, p. 602.

Cornia, G. (1996) 'Public Policy and Welfare Conditions during the Transition: an Overview', *MOCT-MOST Economic Policy in Transitional Economies*, vol. 6, no. 1.

Council of the European Communities (1989a) Resolution of the Council and Ministers for Social Affairs, 29 September, *Official Journal of the European Communities*, C277/1, Brussels.

Council of the European Communities (1989b) 'Resolution on Combating Social Exclusion', *Official Journal of the European Communities*, C277/1, Brussels.

Council of the European Communities (1991) 'Working Time, Employment and Production Capacity: Reorganization/Reduction of Working Time', *Social Europe*, Supplement 491, pp. 13–15.

Cox, R. (1987) *Production, Power and World Order: Social Forces in the Making of History* (New York: Columbia University Press).

Cox, R. (1995) 'Critical Political Economy', in B. Hettne *et al.* (eds), *International Political Economy – Understanding Global Disorder* (London: Zed Books).

Crompton, R., D. Gallie and K. Purcell (1996) 'Work, Economic Restructuring and Social Regulation', in R. Crompton, D. Gallie and K. Purcell (eds), *Changing Forms of Employment* (London: Routledge).

Dagnino, E. (1993) 'An Alternative World Order and the Meaning of Democracy', in Brecher *et al.*, *Global Visions – Beyond the New World Order*, op. cit.

Dahrendorf, R. (1988) *The Modern Social Conflict: An Essay in the Politics of Liberty*, (London: Weidenfeld Nicolson).

Dahrendorf, R. (1989) *The Underclass and the Future of Britain*, Tenth Annual Lecture, St George's House, Windsor Castle, 27 April.

Dahrendorf, R. (1992) 'Footnotes to the Discussion', in D.J. Smith (ed.), *Understanding the Underclass* (London: Policy Studies Institute).

Dahrendorf, R. *et al.* (1995) *Report on Wealth Creation and Social Cohesion in a Free Society* (Commission on Wealth Creation and Social Cohesion), London.

Dale, A. and C. Bamford (1988) 'Flexibility and the Peripheral Workforce', *Occasional Papers in Sociology and Social Policy*, no. 11, Department of Sociology, Surrey University.

Dasgupta, P. (1986) 'Positive Freedom, Markets and the Welfare State', *Oxford Review of Economic Policy*, vol. 2, no. 2.

Dasgupta, P. (1990) 'Well-Being and the Extent of its Realisation in Poor Countries', *Economic Journal*, vol. 100, no. 400, supplement.

Dasgupta, P. (1993) *An Inquiry into Well Being and Destitution* (Oxford: Clarendon Press).

Davidson, I. (1989) 'Inequality Grows in "Socialist" France', *Financial Times*, 24 November.

Davidson, M.J. and J. Earnshaw (1991) *Vulnerable Workers: Psychological and Legal Issues* (Chichester: J. Wiley).

Davis, M. (1990) *City of Quartz: Excavating the Future in Los Angeles* (London: Verso).

Dawes, L. (1993) *Long-term Unemployment and Labour Market Flexibility* (Leicester: University Centre for Labour Market Studies).

Deleeck, H. (1991) *Indicators of Poverty and Social Security* (Luxembourg, Office of Statistical Services of the European Communities (EUROSTAT)).

Délégation Interministérielle au Revenu Minimum d'Insertion (1989), *Bulletin d'Information*, no. 7 (Paris).

Deninger, K. and L. Squire (1996) 'A New Data Set Measuring Income Inequality', *World Bank Economic Review*, vol. 10, no. 3.

Desai, M. (1995) 'Poverty and Capability: Towards an Empirically Implementable Measure', in Meghnad Desai, *Poverty, Famine and Economic Development*, The Selected Essays, vol. II (Aldershot: Edward Elgar).

Desai, M. and A. Shah (1988) 'An Economic Approach to the Measurement of Poverty', *Oxford Economic Papers*, October.

Desai, M., A. Sen and J. Boltvinik (1992) *Social Progress Index – A Proposal* (Bogota: United Nations Development Programme (UNDP)).

Domanski, H. (1994) 'The recomposition of social stratification in Poland', *Polish Sociological Review*, *vol. 4*, no. 108.

Donzelot, J. (1996) 'Les transformations de l'intervention sociale face a l'exclusion, in S. Paugam (ed.), *L'Exclusion: l'état des savoirs* (Paris: La Découverte).

Donzelot, J. and Ph. Estèbe (1994) *L'Etat animateur* (Paris: Esprit).

Dore, R. (1986) *Flexible Rigidities: Industrial Policy and Structural Adjustment in the Japanese Economy*, 1970–80 (London: Athlone Press).

Dore, R. (1997) 'Jobs and Employment – Good Jobs, Bad Jobs and No Jobs', *Journal of Industrial Relations*, vol. 28, no. 4.

Draibe, S.M. and M.T.S. Arretche (1995) 'Involving Civil Society: Brazil', in D. Raczynski (ed.), *Strategies to Combat Poverty in Latin America* (Washington, DC: Interamerican Development Bank).

Dubar, C. (1996) 'Socialisation et processus' in S. Paugam (ed.), *L'Exclusion: l'état des savoirs* (Paris: La Découverte).

Duffy, K. (1995) *Social Exclusion and Human Dignity in Europe* (Strasbourg: Council of Europe).

Eatwell, J. (1995) 'The International Origins of Unemployment', in J. Michie and J. Grieve-Smith (eds.), *Managing the Global Economy* (Oxford University Press).

Economist, The (1993) 'A Survey of Multinationals', 27 March.

Economist, The (1994a) 'The Global Economy – War of the Worlds'. (By Pam Woodall), 1 October 1994.

Economist, The (1994b) 'For Richer, For Poorer', 5 November.

Economist, The (1995) Currencies in a Spin', 11 March.

Elbaum, M. (1995) 'Justice sociale, inégalités et exclusion', *Revue de l'OFCE*, no. 53.

Elmeskov, J. (1993) *High and Persistent Unemployment: Assessment of the Problem and Its Causes*, Economics Department Working Paper no. 132 (Paris: OECD).

Epstein, G. and H. Gintis (1995) *Macroeconomic Policy After the Conservative Era* (Cambridge University Press).

Erickson, K.P. (1977) *The Brazilian Corporative State and Working Class Politics* (Berkeley: University of California Press).

Esping-Andersen, G. (1990) *Three Worlds of Welfare Capitalism* (London: Polity Press).

Esping-Andersen, G. (1994) *After the Golden Age: the Future of the Welfare State in the New Global Order*, Occasional Paper no. 7 (Geneva: United Nations Research Institute for Social Development (UNRISD)).

Eurobarometer (1994) *The Perception of Poverty and Social Exclusion in Europe 1994* (Brussels: European Commission).

European Bank for Reconstruction and Development (EBRD) (1995).

European Commission (1992) *Towards a Europe of Solidarity*, Communication from the Commission 542 (Brussels).

European Commission (1993) *Medium-term Action Programme to Combat Exclusion and Promote Solidarity: A New Programme to Support and Stimulate Innovation* (1994–9); and Report on the Implementation of the Community *Programme for the Social and Economic Integration of the Least Privileged Groups*, Brussels, Communication from the Commission 435.

European Commission (1994a) *Growth, Competitiveness, Employment – The Challenge and Ways Forward into the 21st Century*, White Paper (Brussels: Office for Official Publications of the European Communities).

European Commission (1994b) *European Social Policy – The Way Forward for Europe*, COM(94)333, Brussels.

European Commission (1994c) *Social Protection in Europe*, Brussels.

European Commission (1996) *Employment in Europe 1996* (Brussels: European Commission).

Euvrard, F. and S. Paugam (1991) 'Les Allocataires du Revenu Minimum d'Insertion', *Problèmes Economiques*, no. 2232.

Evans, M., S. Paugam and J.A. Prélis (1995) *Channel Vision: Poverty, Social Exclusion and the Debate on Social Welfare in France and Britain*, London School of Economics (LSE) Discussion Paper, Welfare State Programme, no. 115, October.

Evason, E. and R. Wood (1995) 'Poverty, Deregulation of Labour Markets and Benefit Fraud', *Social Policy and Administration*, vol. 29, no. 1.

Evers, Hans-Dieter and Ozay Mehmet (1994), 'The Management of Risk: Informal Trade in Indonesia', *World Development*, January.

Falk, R. (1992) 'Democratising, Internationalising and Globalizing – A Collage of Blurred Images', *Third World Quarterly*, vol. 13, no. 4.

Falk, R. (1993) 'The Making of Global Citizenship', in Brecher *et al.*, *Global Visions-Beyond the New World Order*, op. cit.

Faria, V. (1994a) *Social Exclusion in Latin America: An Annotated Bibliography*, Discussion Paper no. 70 (Geneva: International Institute for Labour Studies).

Faria, V. (1994b) *The Current Social Situation in Brazil: Dilemmas and Perspectives*, Kellog Institute Working Paper, Democracy and Social Policy series no. 1, Spring (Indiana: University of Notre Dame).

Faria, V. (1995) 'Social Exclusion and Latin American Analyses of Poverty and Deprivation', in C. Gore, Gerry Rodgers and José B. Figuereido (eds), *Social Exclusion: Rhetoric, Reality, Responses* (Geneva: International Institute for Labour Studies).

Faria, V. and M.H. Guimaraes Castro (1990) 'Social Policy and Democratic Consolidation in Brazil', in Lawrence S. Graham and Robert H. Wilson (eds), *The Political Economy of Brazil: Public Policies in an Era of Transition* (Austin: University of Texas Press).

Fassin, D. (1996a) 'Exclusion, underclass, marginalidad. Figures contemporaines de la pauvreté urbaine en France, aux États-Unis et en Amérique latine', *Revue française de sociologie*, vol. 36, no. 1.

Fassin, D. (1996b) 'Marginalidad et marginados: La construction de la pauvreté urbaine en Amérique latine', in S. Paugam (ed.) *L'Exclusion: l'état des savoirs* (Paris: La Découverte).

Fenton, N., P. Golding and A. Radley (1993) *Beyond the Welfare State* (London: John Libbey).

Ferge, Z. and J.E. Kolberg (eds) (1992) *Social Policy in a Changing Europe* (Boulder: Westview Press).

Figueiredo, José B. (1996) *Las institutuciones laborales frente a los cambios en América Latina* (Geneva: International Institute for Labour Studies).

Figueroa, A., T. Altamirano, D. Sulmont (1996) *Social Exclusion and Equality in Peru*, Research Series no. 104 (Geneva: International Institute for Labour Studies).

Fontaine, P.M. (ed.) (1985) *Race, Class and Power in Brazil* (Los Angeles: UCLA Center for Afro-American Studies).

Foster, J., J. Greer and E. Thorbecke (1984) 'A Class of Decomposable Poverty Measure', *Econometrica*, vol. 53, no. 3.

Fragonard, B. (1993) *Cohésion sociale et prévention de l'exclusion* (Paris: Commissariat Général au Plan).

Freedom House (1996) *Freedom in the World – 1995–1996*; Annual Survey of Political Rights and Civil Liberties (New York).

Freedom House (1997) 'World Freedom Survey', *Freedom Review*, January-February.

Freeman, C. and L. Soete (1994) *Work for All or Mass Unemployment* (London: Pinter).

Freeman, R. (1997) 'Does Globalization Threaten Low-skilled Western Workers?', in J. Philipott (ed.), *Working for Full Employment* (London: Routledge).

Freund, J. (1993) 'Préface' in M. Xiberras, *Les théories de l'exclusion* (Paris: Méridiens Klincksieck).

Fukuyama, F. (1995a) 'Social Capital and the Global Economy', *Foreign Affairs*, vol. 74, no. 5.

Fukuyama, F. (1995b) *Trust – The Social Virtues and the Creation of Prosperity* (London: Hamish Hamilton).

Furtado, Celso (1995) *Globalisation et exclusion: le Brésil dans l'ordre mondial émergeant* (Paris: Editions Publisud).

Galbraith, J.K. (1996) 'Commentary', *New York Times*, 13 July.

Gallie, D. (1994) 'Are the Unemployed an Underclass? Some Evidence from the Social Change and Economic Life Initiative', *Sociology*, vol. 28, no. 3.

Gallup (1995) *Gallup Political and Economic Index* (London: Gallup House).

Galtung, J. (1995) On the Social Costs of Modernisation-Social Disintegration, Atomie/Anomie and Social Development, Geneva, *UNRISD Discussion Paper*.

Gans, J.H. (1996) 'From "Underclass" to "Undercaste": Some Observations About the Future of the Post-Industrial Economy and its Major Victims', in E. Mingione (ed.), *Urban Poverty and the Underclass – A Reader* (Oxford University Press).

Garreton, M. Manuel Antonio (1994) 'Human Rights in Processes of Democratisation', *Journal of Latin American Studies*, February.

Gay, R. (1990) 'Neighbourhood Associations and Political Change in Rio de Janeiro', *Latin American Research Review*, vol. XXV, no. 1.

Geertz, Clifford (1978) 'The Bazar Economy: Information and Change in Peasant Marketing', *American Economic Review*, May.

Gereffi, G. (1996) 'The Elusive Last Lap in the Quest For Developed-Country Status', in J.E. Mittleman (ed.), *Globalization: Critical Reflections* (Boulder: Lynne Rienner).

Geyer, F. (1996) '*Alienation, Ethnicity, and Post-Modernism: Three Problems for the Next Century* (Haifa, Israel: School of Education, University of Haifa).

Ghai, D. (1994) 'Structural Adjustment, Global Integration and Social Democracy', in R. Prendergast and F. Stewart (eds), *Market Forces and World Development* (London: Macmillan).

Giddens, A. (1996) 'Anthony Giddens on Globalization', *UNRISD News*, no. 15.

Gilbert, A. and P. Ward (1984a) 'Community Action by the Urban Poor: Democratic Involvement, Community Self-help or a Means of Social Control?', *World Development*, August and September.

Gilbert, A. and P. Ward (1984b) 'Community Participation in Upgrading Irregular Settlements: The Community Response', *World Development*, September.

Gill, S. (1994) 'Globalizing Elites in the Emerging World Order', in Y. Sakamoto (ed.), *Global Transformation* (Tokyo: UNU Press).

Gill, S. (1995) 'Theorizing the Interregnum: The Double Movement and Global Politics in the 1990s', in B. Hettne (ed.), *International Political Economy-Understanding Global Disorder* (London: Zed Books).

Gill, S. (1996) 'Globalization, Democratization and the Politics of Indifference', in J.E. Mittelman (ed.), *Globalization: Critical Reflections* (Boulder: Lynne Rienner).

Goodman, A., P. Johnson and S. Webb (1997) *Inequality in the UK* (Oxford University Press).

Gordon, D. (1988) 'The Global Economy: New Edifice or Crumbling Foundations?', *New Left Review*, March/April.

Gordon, S. (1997) *Poverty and Social Exclusion in Mexico*, Discussion Paper Series no. 93 (Geneva: International Institute for Labour Studies).

Gore, C. (1993) 'Entitlement Relations and "Unruly" Social Practices: A Comment on the Work of Amartya Sen', *Journal of Development Studies*, April.

Gore, C. (1994) *Social Exclusion and Africa South of the Sahara: A Review of the Literature*, IILS Discussion Paper DP/62, Geneva.

Gore, C. (1995) 'Introduction: Markets, Citizenship and Social Exclusion', in Gerry Rodgers, Charles Gore and José Figueiredo (eds), *Social Exclusion: Rhetoric, Reality, Responses* (Geneva: International Institute for Labour Studies).

Gore, C. (1996) *Social Exclusion and the Design of Anti-Poverty Strategy in Developing Countries*, Draft Working Paper for the Policy Forum on Social Exclusion, New York, 22–24 May.

Gore, C. and J.B. Figueiredo (1997) *Social Exclusion and Anti-Poverty Policy: A Debate*, (International Institute for Labour Studies Research Series no. 110, Geneva).

Gorostiaga, X. (1993) 'Latin America in the New World Order', in Brecher *et al.*, *Global Visions – Beyond the New World Order*, op. cit.

Gorz, A. (1988) *Critique of Economic Reason* (London: Verso).

Gorz, A. (1994), 'Revenu Minimum et Citoyenneté', *Futuribles*, February.

Graham, Lawrence S. and Robert H. Wilson (eds) (1990) *The Political Economy of Brazil: Public Policies in an Era of Transition* (Austin: University of Texas Press).

Graham, Richard (1990) 'Dilemmas for Democracy in Brazil', in Graham and Wilson, ibid.

Gregory, M. and C. Greenhalgh (1997) 'International Trade, Deindustrialization and Labour Demand: An Input-Output Study for the UK (1979–90)', in J. Borkakoti and C. Milner (eds), *International Trade and Labour Markets* (London: Macmillan).

Griffin, K. and A.R. Khan (1992) *Globalization and the Developing World* (Geneva: United Nations Research Institute for Social Development (UNRISD).

Gros-Jean, C. and C. Padieu (1995) 'Les Exclus: Comment sortir de l'approche en catégories, *Revue Française des Affaires Sociales*, no. 2–3.

de Haan, A. and Simon Maxwell (eds) (1998) 'Poverty and Social Exclusion in North and South', *IDS Bulletin*, January.

Hantrais, Linda (1995) *Social Policy in the European Union* (New York: St Martin's Press).

Harriss, J. (1986) *Vulnerable Workers in the Urban Labour Markets of South and Southeast Asia* (Norwich: University of East Anglia School of Development Studies).

Harriss, J. (1989) 'Vulnerable Workers in the Indian Urban Labour Market', in Gerry Rodgers (ed.), *Urban Poverty and the Labour Market* (Geneva: ILO).

Harris, R.G. (1993)'Globalization, Trade and Finance', *Canadian Journal of Economics*, November.

Harvey, D. (1989) *The Conditions of Postmodernity* (Oxford: Basil Blackell).

Hasenbalg, Carlos A. (1979) *Discriminação e desigualdades raciais no Brasil* (Rio de Janeiro: Graal).

Hasenbalg, Carlos A. (1985) 'Race and Socioeconomic Inequalities in Brazil', in Fontaine, *Race, Class and Power in Brazil*, op. cit.

Hashem, M.H. (1996) *Goals for Social Integration and Realities of Social Exclusion in the Republic of Yemen*, Research Series no. 105 (Geneva: International Institute for Labour Studies).

Heady, C. (1997) 'Labour Market Transition and Social Exclusion', *Journal of European Social Policy*, vol. 7, no. 2.

Heath, A. (1992) 'The Attitudes of the Underclass', in D.J. Smith (ed.), *Understanding the Underclass* (London: Policy Studies Institute).

Heller, P. (1996) 'Social Capital as a Product of Class Mobilization and State Intervention: Industrial Workers in Kerala, India', *World Development*, June.

Hellwig, D.J. (ed.) (1992) *African-American Reflections on Brazil's Racial Paradise* (Philadelphia: Temple University).

Herpin, N. (1993) 'Exclusion sociale et pauvreté: L'urban underclass chez les sociologues américains', *Revue française de sociologie*, July-September.

Hettne, B. (1995) 'Introduction: The International Political Economy of Transformation' in B. Hettne (ed.), *International Political Economy-Understanding Global Disorder* (London: Zed Books).

Hillman, A. (1992) 'Socialist Clubs: A Perspective on the Transition', *European Journal of Political Economy*, vol. 9.

Hirata, H. and J. Humphrey (1991) 'Workers' Response to Job Loss: Female and Male Industrial Workers in Brazil', *World Development*, vol. 19, no. 6.

Hirst, P. (1997) 'The Global Economy – Myths and Realities', *International Affair Contents*, vol. 3, no. 3.

Hirst, P. and G. Thompson (1996) *Globalization in Question* (Cambridge: Polity).

Holloway, Thomas (1993) *Policing Rio – Repression and Resistance in a 19th Century City* (Stanford University Press).

Holm, H. and G. Sorensen (eds) (1995) *Whose World Order – Uneven Globalization and the End of the Cold War* (Boulder: Westview).

Honig, M. (1974) AFDC Income, Recipients Rates, and Family Dissolution', *Journal of Human Resources*, vol. 9.

Horton, S., R. Kanbur and D. Mazumdar (1991) 'Labour Markets in an Area of Adjustment. Evidence from 12 Developing Countries', *International Labour Review*, vol. 130, nos. 5–6.

Howell, J. (1994) 'Refashioning State-Society Relations', *European Journal of Development Research*, June.

Humana, C. (1983) *World Human Rights Guide* (London: Hutchinson).

Humana, C. (1986) *World Human Rights Guide* (London: Economist Publications).

Human Rights Watch (1991) *Rural Violence in Brazil: An America's Watch Report* (New York and Washington, DC), February.

Humphrey, J. (1994) 'Are the Unemployed Part of the Urban Poverty Problem in Latin America?', *Journal of Latin American Studies*, October.

Hungary, Ministry of Labour (1997) *Labour Force Survey*, Budapest.

Hungary, Central Statistical Office (1993) *Household Income Survey* (cited in Andorka and Speder, *Poverty in Hungary*, op. cit.), Budapest.

Hutton, W. (1995) *The State We're In* (London: Vintage).

IBGE (Brazilian Institute of Geography and Statistics)(1990) *Participacao Politico-social 1988*, vol. I, *Justica e Vitimizacao* (Rio de Janeiro).

IBGE (Brazilian Institute of Geography and Statistics) (1994) *Mapa do mercado de trabalho no Brazil* (Rio de Janeiro).

Illner, M. (1996a) 'Post-communist Transformation Revisited', *Czech Sociological Review*, vol. 4, no. 2.

Illner, M. (1996b) The Changing Quality of Life in a Post-Communist Country: The Case of the Czech Republic, Working Paper presented at the World Conference on the Quality of Life, Prince George, August 22–25.

Inack, S.I. (1997) *L' Exclusion sociale au Cameroun*, Discussion Paper Series no. 89 (Geneva: International Institute for Labour Studies).
Institute for Fiscal Studies (IFS) (1995) *Poverty: Two Views* (London).
Institut National de la Statistique et des Etudes Economique (INSEE) (1994) Le Travail à Durée Limitée, *Les Dossiers* Thématiques no. 1 (Paris).
ILO (1987) "Other Urban Incomes: Vulnerable Groups in Developing Countries", Chapter 6 in *World Labour Report no. 3* (Geneva).
ILO (1993a) *Part-Time Work*, Report V (1), International Labour Conference, 80th Session, Geneva.
ILO (1993b), *World Labour Report 1993* (Geneva).
ILO (1995a) *World Labour Report 1995* (Geneva).
ILO (1995b) *World Employment 1995: An ILO Report* (Geneva).
ILO (1997) *World Employment Report* (Geneva)
IMF (1997a) 'Forces of Globalization Must be Embraced', *IMF Survey*, vol. 26, no. 10.
Independent (London) (1997) 'Growth in Temporary Jobs', 21 February.
IMF (1997b) World Economic Outlook. I – Global Economic Prospects and Policies, (Internal document) (Washington, DC) May.
INSEE (1988) *Situations défavorisées* 1986–87 (Paris).
INSEE (1994) *Le travail à durée limitée*, Les dossiers thématiques, no. 1 (Paris).
Ion, J. (1995) 'L'Exclusion une problématique française?', *Lien Social et Politique – Revue interdisciplinaire des Sciences Humaines consacrée aux thèmes du lien social, de la sociabilité, des problèmes sociaux et des politiques publiques (RIAC)* Montréal, Lien Social et Politique, no. 34.
Jagannathan, N. Vijay (1987) *Informal Markets in Developing Countries* (New York: Oxford University Press).
James, Ralph, C. (1960) 'The Casual Labour Problem in Indian Manufacturing', *Quarterly Journal of Economics*, February.
Jargowrski, P.A. and M.J. Bane (1991) 'Ghetto Poverty in the United States, 1970–1980', in C. Jenks and P. Peterson (eds), *The Urban Underclass* (Washington, DC: Brookings Institution).
Jarvis, S. and S. P. Jenkins (1996) *Changing Places: Income Mobility and Poverty Dynamics in Britain*, Working Paper of the ESRC Research Centre on Micro-social Change, paper 96–19 (Colchester: University of Essex).
Jatoba, J. (1989) 'Urban Poverty, Labour Markets and Regional Differentiation in Brazil', in G. Rodgers (ed.), *Urban Poverty and the Labour Market* (Geneva: International Institute for Labour Studies).
Jellinek, Lea (1991) *The Wheel of Fortune – The History of a Poor Community in Jakarta* (London: Allen & Unwin).
Jencks, C. (1992) *Rethinking Social Policy: Race, Poverty and the Underclass* (Cambridge, MA: Harvard University Press).
Jencks, C. and P.E. Peterson (1991) *The Urban Underclass* (Washington, DC: Brookings Institution).
Jordan, B. (1996) *A Theory of Poverty and Social Exclusion* (Cambridge: Polity).
Jordan, B. and M. Redley (1994) 'Polarization, Underclass and the Welfare State', *Work, Employment and Society*, vol. 8, no. 2.
Jordan, B., M. Redley and S. James (1994) *Putting the Family First: Identities, Decisions, Citizenship* (London: UCL Press).

Kaijage, F. and A. Tibaijuka (1996) *Poverty and Social Exclusion in Tanzania*, Research Series no. 109 (Geneva: International Institute for Labour Studies).

Kanbur, R. (1994) 'The Human Development Report 1990', and the World Development Report 1990" in R. van der Hoeven and R. Anker (eds), *Poverty Monitoring: An International Concern* (London: Macmillan).

Kannappan, S. (1981) 'Income Distribution and Urban Labor Markets in Brazil', *Luso-Brazilian Review*, vol. 18, no. 1 (Summer).

Kannappan, S. (1985) 'Urban Employment and the Labour Market in Developing Nations', *Economic Development and Cultural Change*, July.

Kannappan, S. (1986a) 'The Economic Significance of Social Structure for Urban Labour Markets with Special Reference to India', *Proceedings of the Industrial Relations Research Association*, Madison.

Kannappan, S. (1986b) *An Integrated View of Rural and Urban Labour Markets in the Process of Economic Growth and Welfare*, paper presented at the Eighth World Economic Congress of the International Economic Association, New Delhi, 1–5 December.

Kannappan, S. (1988) 'Urban Labour Markets in the Development Process', *World Bank Research Observer*, July.

Kannappan, S. (1995) 'The Economics of Development: The Procrustean Bed of Mainstream Economics', *Economic Development and Cultural Change*, July.

Kapstein, E. (1996) 'Workers and the World Economy', *Foreign Affairs*, vol. 75, no. 3.

Katz, M.B. (1989) *The Undeserving Poor: From the War on Poverty to the War on Welfare* (New York: Pantheon).

Katz, M.B. (1993) 'The Urban "Underclass" as a Metaphor of Social Transformation', in M.B. Katz (ed.), *The Underclass Debate – Views from History* (Princeton University Press).

Kaul, I. (1996) *Globalization and Human Development: Policy Lessons and Options for the Future*, paper presented at the VIIIth EADI General Conference, Vienna, 11–14 September.

Kennett, P. (1994) 'Exclusion, Post-Fordism and the "New Europe", in P. Brown and R. Compton, *Economic Restructuring and Social Exclusion* (London:UCL Press).

Khan, A. (1994) *Overcoming Unemployment* (Geneva: ILO).

Klitgaard, R. and J. Fedderke (1995) 'Social Integration and Disintegration: An Exploratory Analysis of Cross-Country Data', *World Development*, March.

Kofman, E. and G. Youngs (eds) (1996) *Globalization: Theory and Practice* (London: Pinter).

Kolarska-Bobinska, L. (1992) 'Civil Society and Social Anomy in Poland', in B. Deacon, (ed.) Social policy, Social Justice and Citizenship in Eastern Europe (Aldershot: Avebury).

Koltay, J. (1994) 'Unemployment and Employment Policy in Central and eastern Europe: Similarities and Differences', *Acta Economica*, vol. 46, no. 3–4.

Kornai, J. (1992) *The Socialist System* (Princeton University Press).

Kornai, J. (1997) 'Political Economy of the Hungarian Stabilization and Austerity Program', in M. Blejer and M. Skreb, *Macroeconomic Stabilization in Transition Economies* (Cambridge University Press).

Kotz, G. (1995) 'The Regulation Theory and the Social Structure of Accumulation Approach', in D. Kotz, T. McDonough and M. Reich (eds), *Social Structures of Accumulation* (Cambridge University Press).

Kotz, G., T. McDonough and M. Reich (eds) (1995) *Social Structures of Accumulation* (Cambridge University Press).

Krueger, Alan B. (1993) 'How Computers Have Changed the Wage Structure: Evidence from Micro Data, 1984–1989', *Quarterly Journal of Economics*, February.

Krugman, P. (1994) 'Does Third World Growth Hurt First World Prosperity?', *Harvard Business Review*, July–August.

Krugman, P. (1996) *Pop Internationalism* (Cambridge, MA: MIT Press).

Krugman, P. and R. Lawrence (1994) 'Trade, Jobs and Wages', *Scientific American*, April.

Kurzewski, J. (1994) 'Poland's Seven Middle Classes', *Social Research*, vol. 61, no. 2.

Lafore, R. (1992) 'La pauvreté saisie par le droit', in R. Castel and J.-F. Laé (eds), *Le Revenu Minimum d'Insertion – une dette sociale*, op. cit.

Lamounier, B. (1989) 'Brazil: Inequality Against Democracy', in Larry Diamond, Juan J. Linz and Seymour Martin Lipset (eds.), *Democracy in Developing Countries: Latin America*, vol. 4 (Boulder: Lynne Rienner).

Lasker, B. (1950) *Human Bondage in Southeast Asia* (Westport, CT: Greenwood).

Lautier, R. (1991) 'Les ouvriers n'ont pas la forme: informalité des relations de travail et citoyenneté en Amérique latine', in B. Lautier, C. de Miras and A. Morice (eds), *L'État l'informel* (Paris: L'Harmattan).

Lawrence, R.Z. (1994) 'Trade, Multinationals, and Labor', *Faculty Research Working Paper Series, JFK School of Government, Harvard University* (Cambridge MA:), July.

Lee, R. (1995) 'Look After the Pounds and the People Will Look After Themselves: Social Reproduction, Regulation and Social Exclusion in Western Europe', *Environment and Planning*, vol. 27.

Leibfried, S. and P. Pierson (1992) 'Prospects for Social Europe', *Politics and Society*, vol. 20, no. 3.

Lenoir, R. (1974) *Les Exclus: un français sur dix* (Paris: Le Seuil).

Lewis, O. (1965) 'The Culture of Poverty', *Scientific American*, vol. 215, no. 4.

Lewis, G.W. and D.T. Ulph (1988) 'Poverty, Inequality and Welfare', *Economic Journal*, vol. 98.

Libération (1998) 'Chômeurs: pourquoi les Français sont solidaires', 19 January.

Lim, D. (1978) 'Sweat Labour Wages in Malaysian Manufacturing', *Economic Development and Cultural Change*, October.

Lin, Nan (1995) *Social Resources and Social Action* (New York: Cambridge University Press).

Lipietz, A. (1996) *La Société en Sablier* (Paris: La Découverte).

Lipietz, A. (1997) 'The Post-Fordist World: Labour Relations, International Hierarchy and Global Ecology, *RIPE*, vol. 4, no. 1.

Lipton, M. and N. Maxwell (1992) *The New Poverty Agenda: An Overview*, Institute of Development Studies (IDS) Discussion Paper no. 306, Brighton, August.

Lister, R. (1990) *The Exclusive Society: Citizenship and the Poor* (London: Child Poverty Action Group).

Loi no. 88–1088 du 1er décembre 1988 relative au RMI (1988), *Journal Officiel*, 3 décembre.

Lombard, P. (1988) *Le Crépuscule des Juges* (Paris: Edition Robert Laffont).

Lomnitz, L.A. (1977) *Networks and Marginality – Life in a Mexican Shantytown* (New York: Academic Press).

Lopes, Juarez R. Brandão (1993) Brazil *1989 – um estudo sociôeconomico da indigênce e da probeza urbanas*, *Campinas Paper Series* (Cadernos), Núcleo de Estudos de Politicas Públicas (NEPP), Universidade Estadual de Campinas.

Lovell, Peggy A. (1994) 'Race, Gender and Development in Brazil', *Latin American Research Review*, vol. 29, no. 3.

Lustig, N. (ed.) (1995) *Coping with Austerity: Poverty and Inequality in Latin America*, (Washington, DC: Brookings Institution).

Lyons, B. and J. Mehta (1997) 'Contracts, Opportunities and Trust: Self- interest and Social Orientation', *Cambridge Journal of Economics*, March.

Mac-Clure, O. (1994) '*Exclusion en Chile? De la desintegracion a la integración*, ILO Multidisciplinary Team for Argentina, Brazil, Chile, Paraguay and Uruguay (Santiago).

McDonough, P. (1981a) 'Development Priorities among Brazilian Elites', *Economic Development and Cultural Change*, April.

McDonough, P. (1981b) *Power and Ideology in Brazil* (Princeton: Princeton University Press), Chapter 2 on 'Networks'.

McLanahan, S. and L. Bumpass (1988) 'Intergenerational Consequences of Family Disruption', *American Journal of Sociology*, July.

McMichael, P. (1996) *Development and Social Change* (London: Pine Forge Press).

McNitt, A.D (1988) 'Some Thoughts on the Systematic Measurement of the Abuse of Human Rights', in D.L. Cingranelli, *Human Rights – Theory and Measurement*, op. cit.

Maddison, A. and associates (1992) *The Political Economy of Poverty, Equity and Growth: Brazil and Mexico* (Oxford University Press).

Magdoff, H. (1992) 'Globalization – To What End?', in R. Miliband and L. Panitch (eds), *New World Order? The Socialist Register* (London: Merlin).

Maier, F. (1991) 'Part-time Work, Social Security Protections and Labour Law: An International Comparison', *Politics and Policy*, vol. 19.

Mainwaring, S. (1987) 'Urban Popular Movements, Identity and Democratization in Brazil', *Comparative Political Studies*, July.

Mainwaring, S. (1995a) Political Parties and Democratization in Brazil', *Latin American Research Review*, vol. 30, no. 3.

Mainwaring, S. (1995b) 'Democracy in Brazil and the Southern Cone: Achievements and Problems', *Journal of Interamerican Studies and World Affairs*, Spring.

Mann, K. (1991) *The Making of an English Underclass* (Oxford University Press).

Marris, R. (1996) *How to Save the Underclass* (London: Macmillan).

Marshall, A. (1989) 'The Sequel of Unemployment: The Changing Role of Part-time and Temporary Work in Western Europe', in Gerry Rodgers and Janine Rodgers (eds), *Precarious Jobs in Labour Market regulation – The Growth of Atypical Employment in Western Europe* (Geneva: ILO).

Marshall, A. (1992) *Circumventing Labour Protection: Non-standard Employment in Argentina and Peru*, International Institute for Labour Studies Research Series no. 88 (Geneva).

Marshall, G., S. Roberts, C. Burgoyne and D. Routh (forthcoming) *Social Class and Underclass in Britain and the United States* (Oxford: Nuffield College).

Marshall, T.H. (1950) *Citizenship and Social Class* (Cambridge University Press).

Marshall, T.H. (1964) *Class, Citizenship and Social Development* (New York: Doubleday).

Marshall, T.H. and T. Bottomore (1992) *The New Poverty Agenda: An Overview*, Institute of Development Studies (IDS) Discussion Paper no. 306.

Martin, C. (1994) 'Diversité des trajectoires post-désunion. Entre le risque de solitude, la défense de son autonomie et la recomposition familiale', *Population*, no. 6.

Massé, P. (1991) *Le Plan ou l'Anti-Hasard* (Paris: Hermann).

Mateju, P. (1996) 'In Search of Explanations for Recent Left-Turns in Post-Communist Countries', *International Review of Comparative Public Policy*, vol. 7.

Matutinovic, I. (1998) 'Quality of Life in Transition Countries: Central East Europe with special reference to Croatia', *Social Indicator Research*, no. 43.

Maxwell, Judith (1996) *Social Dimensions of Economic Growth*, Eric J. Johnson Memorial Lecture, Edmonton,University of Alberta, 25 January.

Maxwell, Simon (1998) 'Comparisons, Convergence and Connections – Development Studies in North and South', *IDS Bulletin*, January.

Mazumdar, K. (1996) 'An Analysis of Causal Flow Between Social development and Economic Growth: The Social Development Index', *American Journal of Economics and Sociology*, July.

Melo, M. de, C. Denizer and A. Gelb (1996) 'Patterns of Transition from Plan to Market', *World Bank Economic Review*, vol. 10, no. 3.

Melo, M. de, C. Denizer and A. Gelb (1997) 'From Plan to Market: Patterns of Transition' in M. Blejer and M. Skreb, *Macroeconomic Stabilisation in Transition Economies* (Cambridge University Press).

Merrick, T.W. (1976) 'Employment and Earnings in the Informal Sector in Brazil: The Case of Belo Horizonte', *Journal of Developing Areas*, vol. 10, no. 3.

Middleton, S., K. Ashworth and R. Walker (eds), *Family Fortunes* (London: CPAG).

Milanovic, B. (1996) 'Income Inequality and Poverty during the Transition: A Survey of the Evidence', *MOCT-MOST Economic Policy in Transitional Economies*, vol. 6, no. 1.

Mingione, E. (1991) *Fragmented Societies: A Sociology of Economic Life Beyond the Market Paradigm* (Oxford: Basil Blackwell).

Mingione, E. (ed.) (1996a) *Urban Poverty and the Underclass – A Reader* (Oxford: Basil Blackwell).

Mingione, E. (1996b) 'Urban Poverty in the Advanced Industrial World: Concepts, Analysis and Debates', in ibid.

Mittelman, J. (1995) 'Rethinking the International Division of labour in the Context of Globalization', *Third World Quarterly*, vol. 16, no. 2.

Mittelman, James E. (ed.) (1996) *Globalization: Critical Reflections* (Boulder: Lynne Rienner).

Monde Le (1998a) '*Le niveau de vie autorisé par les minimas sociaux a fortement baissé*', 17 January.

Monde Le (1998b) '*Dix indicateurs sur la vie des quartiers*', 13 February.

Monde Le (1998c) '*Selon une etude de l'INSEE, la pauvreté change de visage mais son taux se stabilise*' (par Jerome Fenoglio), 2 avril.

Morduch, J. (1994) 'Poverty and Vulnerability', *American Economic Review – Papers and Proceedings*, May.

Morley, Samuel A. (1995) *Poverty and Inequality in Latin America: The Impact of Adjustment and Recovery in the 1980s* (Baltimore: Johns Hopkins University Press).

Morris, L. (1992a) 'The Social Segregation of the Long-term Unemployed in Hartlepool', *Sociological Review*, May.

Morris, L. (1994) *Dangerous Classes: The Underclass and Social Citizenship* (London: Routledge).

Morris, L. (1995) *Social Divisions, Economic Decline and Social Structural Change* (London: UCL Press).

Morris, L. and S. Irwin (1992) 'Unemployment and Informal Support: Dependency, Exclusion or Participation?', *Work, Employment and Society*, June.

Mundell, R. (1997) 'The Great Contractions in Transition Economies', in M. Blejer and M. Skreb, *Macroeconomic Stabilization in Transition Economies* (Cambridge University Press).

Murphy, Raymond (1988) *Social Closure:The Theory of Monopolization and Exclusion* (Oxford University Press).

Murray, Charles (1984) *Losing Ground:American Social Policy 1950–1980* (New York:Basic Books).

Murray, Charles (1990) *The Emerging Underclass* (London: Institute for Economic Affairs).

Murray, Richard (1996) *Poverty and Social Exclusion in North and South*, Seminar Series, Brighton, Institute of Development Studies, University of Sussex.

Musgrave, P. and 0. Galindo (1988) 'Do the Poor Pay More? Retail Food Prices in Northeast Brazil', *Economic Development and Cultural Change*, October.

Myers, W. (1988) 'Alternative Services for Street Children: The Brazilian Approach', in Bequele and Boyden, *Combating Child Labour*, op. cit.

Myrdal, G. (1963) *Challenge to Affluence* (New York: Random House).
Nagy, G. and E. Sik (1993) *Report on the First Wave Results of the Hungarian Household Panel Survey*, Budapest.
Nasse, P. (1992) *Exclus et exclusion: Connaitre les populations, comprendre les processus* (Paris: Commisariat Général au Plan).
National Office of Statistics (1994) *Social Policy at Social Conditions in Poland 1939–1993* (Warsaw : GUS).
Nolan, B. and C. Whelan (eds) (1996) *Resources, Deprivation and Poverty* (Oxford: Clarendon Press).
North, D.C. (1981) *Structure and Change in Economic History* (New York: W.W. Norton).
North, D.C. (1986) 'The New Institutional Economics', *Journal of Institutional and Theoretical Economics*, vol. 142.
North, D.C. (1989) 'Institutions and Economic Growth: An Historical Introduction', *World Development*, vol. 17, no. 9.
North, D.C. (1990) *Institutions, Institutional Change and Economic Performance (*New York: Cambridge University Press).
Nun, J. (1969) 'Sóbrepoblación relativa, ejercito industriale de reserva y masa marginal', *Revista latinoamericano de sociología*, vol. 5, no. 2.
Nussbaum, M.C. and A. Sen (1993) *The Quality of Life* (Oxford: Clarendon Press).
O'Brien, D., J. Wilkes, A. de Haan and S. Maxwell (1997) Poverty and Social Exclusion in North and South, *IDS Working Paper 55*, May (Brighton: Institute of Development Studies).
OECD (1991, 1993, 1994, 1996, 1997) *Employment Outlook*, Paris, July.
OECD (1992) *International Direct Investment: Policies and Trends in the 1980s*, Paris.
OECD (1994a) *The Jobs Study: Evidence and Explanations*, Part I on 'Labour Market Trends and Underlying Forces of Change', Paris.
OECD (1994b) *New Orientations for Social Policy*, Social Policy Studies, no. 12, Paris.
OECD (1994c) *Societies in Transition*', Paris.
OECD (1997a) *Poland*, Paris.
OECD (1997b) *Short-term Economic Indicators*, Paris, January.
O'Higgins, M. and S. Jenkins (1990) 'Poverty in the EC: Estimates for 1975, 1980 and 1985', in R. Teekens and B. Van Praag (eds) *Analysing Poverty in the European Community* (Luxembourg: EUROSTAT) Chapter 11.
Ohmae, K. (1990) *The Borderless World* (New York: Collins).
Ohmae, K. (1993), 'The Rise of the Region State', *Foreign Affairs*, Spring.
Oman, C. (1994) *Globalization and Regionalization: The Challenge for Developing Countries* (Paris: OECD Development Centre).
Olson, M. (1965) *The Logic of Collective Action: Public Goods and the Theory of Groups*, (Cambridge: Harvard University Press).
Osmani, S.R. (1991) 'Social Security in South Asia', in Ehtisham Ahmed, Jean Drèze, John Hills and Amartya Sen (eds), *Social Security in Developing Countries* (Oxford: Clarendon Press).
Oxhorn, P. and G. Ducatenzeiler (1994) *Social Policies as Political Strategies: Processes of Inclusion and Exclusion*, paper prepared for the XIII

International Congress of the Latin American Studies Association, Atlanta, March.

Parkin, Frank (1979) *Marxism and Class Theory: A Bourgeois Critique* (New York: Columbia University Press).

Paugam, S. (1991) *La Disqualification sociale – essai sur la nouvelle pauvreté* (Paris: Presse Universitaire de France).

Paugam, S. (1993) *La société française et ses pauvres: l'expérience du revenu minimum d'insertion* (Paris: Presse Universitaire de France), coll. 'Recherches politiques' (seconde édition, 1995).

Paugam, S. (1994) *Précarité et risque d'exclusion en Europe*, paper presented at a Meeting on Understanding Social Exclusion: Lessons from Transnational Research Studies, Policy Studies Institute, London, 24 November.

Paugam, S. (1995) 'The Spiral of Precariousness: A Multidimensional Approach to the Process of Social Disqualification in France', in G. Room (ed.), *Beyond the Threshold: The Measurement and Analysis of Social Exclusion* (Bristol: Policy Press).

Paugam, S. (ed.) (1996) *L'exclusion: l'état des savoirs* (Paris: La Découverte).

Paugam, S., J-P. Zoyem and J-M. Charbonnel (1993) *Précarité et risque d'exclusion en France*, Document du CERC no. 109 (Paris: La Documentation Française).

Paugam, S., J.A. Prelis and J-P. Zoyem (1994) *Appréhension de la pauvreté sous l'angle de la disqualification sociale*, Paris, CERC, Report for EUROSTAT/DGV of the European Commission.

Payne, J. and C. Payne (1993) 'Unemployment and Peripheral Work', *Work, Employment and Society*, December.

Peacocke, C. (1989) 'What are Concepts?', *Midwest Studies in Philosophy*, vol. 14.

Peacocke, C. (1993) *A Study of Concepts* (Cambridge MA: MIT Press).

Peattie, Lisa (1974) 'The Concept of Marginality as Applied to Squatter Settlements', in W.A. Cornelius and F.M. Trueblood (eds), *Latin American Urban Research*, vol. 4 (Beverly Hills: Sage).

Peemans, J. Ph. (1995) 'Modernisation, globalisation et territoires: l'évolution des regards sur l'articulation des espaces urbains et ruraux dans les processus de développement', *Revue Tiers Monde*, vol. xxxvi, no. 141.

Peemans, J. Ph. (1996) L'Utopie globalitaire', *Les Nouveaux Cahiers de l'Institut Universitaire d'Etudes du Développment (IUED)*, no. 5.

Penz, G.P. (1986) *Consumer Sovereignty and Human Interests* (Cambridge: Cambridge University Press).

Pereira, A.W. (1992) 'Agrarian Reform and the Rural Workers' Unions of the Pernambuco Sugar Zone, Brazil 1985–1988', *Journal of Developing Areas*, January.

Perlman, J.E. (1976) *The Myth of Marginality: Urban Poverty and Politics in Rio de Janeiro* (Berkeley: University of California Press).

Phongpaichit, P. *et al.* (1996) *Challenging Social Exclusion: Rights and Livelihood in Thailand*, Research Series no. 107 (Geneva: International Institute for Labour Studies)

Piven, F.F. and R.A. Cloward (1977) *Poor People's Movements: Why They Succeed and How They Fail* (New York: Pantheon).

Poland, National Office of Statistics (1994) *Social Policy and Social Conditions in Poland 1989–93* (Warsaw: GUS).
Polanyi, K. (1957) *The Great Transformation* (Boston: Beacon).
Pollert, A. (ed.) (1991) *Farewell to Flexibility* (Oxford: Basil Blackwell).
Prebisch, R. (1950) *The Economic Development of Latin America and its Principal Problems* (New York: United Nations).
Psacharopoulos, G., S. Morley, A. Fizbein, H. Lee and Bill Wood (1993) 'Poverty and Income Distribution in Latin America: The Story of the 1980s', *Regional Studies Program Report no. 27*, Washington DC: World Bank.
Purdy, D. (1995) 'Citizenship, Basic Income and the State', *New Left Review*, vol. 208.
Putnam, R. (1993a) 'The Prosperous Community: Social Capital and the Public Life', *The American Prospect*, Spring.
Putnam, R. (1993b) *Making Democracy Work – Civic Traditions in Modern Italy* (Princeton University Press).
Quereshi, Z. (1996) 'Globalization: New Opportunities, Tough Challenges', *Finance and Development*, March.
Ravaillon, M. (1988) 'Expected Poverty Under Risk-induced Welfare Variability', *Economic Journal*, December.
Ravaillon, M. (1996) 'Issues in Measuring and Modelling Poverty', *Economic Journal*, September.
Reich, R. (1991) *The Work of Nations – A Blueprint for the Future* (London: Simon & Schuster).
Reszke, I. (1996) 'Stereotypes of the Unemployed in Poland', *Polish Psychological Review*, vol. 3, no. 115.
Rieger, E. and S. Liebfried (1995) *The Welfare State and Globalization: Conflicts Over Germany's Competitiveness*, paper presented at the Summer School, ZeS, University of Bremen, 25 July–5 August.
Rifkin, J. (1995) *The End of Work: The Decline of the Global Labor Force and the Dawn of the Post-Market Era* (NewYork: Tarcher and Putman's Sons).
Riveros, Luis (1990) 'Recession, Adjustment, and the Performance of Urban Labour Markets in Latin America', *Canadian Journal of Development Studies*, vol. 11, no. 1.
Robbins, D. (1990) *Marginalisation and Social Exclusion*, Report to the European Commission, Brussels.
Robbins, D. (1994)'Towards a Europe of Solidarity: Combating Social Exclusion", *Social Europe*, Supplement 4/93, Brussels, European Commission.
Robertson, R. (1992a) *Globalization* (London: Sage).
Robertson, R. (1992b) *Social Theory and Global Culture* (London: Sage).
Rodgers,G. (1989) 'Precarious Work in Western Europe: The State of the Debate', in Gerry Rodgers and Janine Rodgers (eds), *Precarious Jobs in Labour Market Regulation – The Growth of Atypical Employment in Western Europe* (Geneva: ILO).
Rodgers, G. (1994) 'Overcoming Exclusion: Livelihood and Rights in Economic and Social Development', *Discussion Paper* DP/72/1994 (Geneva: International Institute for Labour Studies).

Rodgers, G. (ed.) (1995) *The Poverty Approach and the ILO: Issues of Concept and Action*, (Geneva: International Institute for Labour Studies).

Rodgers, G. and J. Rodgers (1995) '*The Labour-Employment Nexus*', contributions to the Interamerican Development Bank (IDB) Mission on Brazilian Social Reform and Poverty Alleviation in an Urban Context: the Case of Fortaleza, November (mimeo.).

Rodgers, G., C. Gore and J. Figueiredo (eds) (1995) *Social Exclusion: Rhetoric, Reality, Responses* (Geneva: International Institute for Labour Studies).

Rodrik, D. (1997) *Has Globalization Gone Too Far?* (Washington DC: Institute for International Economics).

Room, G. (1994) *Poverty Studies in the European Union: Retrospect and Prospect*, paper presented at a Meeting on Understanding Social Exclusion: Lessons from Transnational Research Studies, Policy Studies Institute, London, 24 November.

Room, G. (ed.) (1995a) *Beyond the Threshold: The Measurement and Analysis of Social Exclusion* (Bristol: Policy Press).

Room, G. (1995b) 'Poverty in Europe: Competing Paradigms of Analysis', *Policy and Politics*, vol. 3, no. 2.

Room, G. *et al.* (1990) *'New Poverty' in the European Community* (London: Macmillan).

Room, G. *et al.* (1991, 1992 and 1993) *Observatory on National Policies to Combat Social Exclusion*, Brussels, Commission of the European Communities, DG V.

Rosanvallon, P. (1994) *La Nouvelle question sociale* (Paris: Le Seuil).

Rubery, J. (1989) 'Precarious Forms of Work in the United Kingdom', in Gerry Rodgers and Janine Rodgers (eds), *Precarious Jobs in Labour Market Regulation – The Growth of Atypical Employment in Western Europe*, op. cit.

Rural Violence in Brazil (1991) An Americas Watch Report, New York/Washington DC, February.

Rutkowski, J. (1995) *Labour Market Transition and Changes in the Wage Structure: The Case of Poland*, Polish Policy Research Group Discussion Paper 32 (Warsaw University).

Rutkowski, J. (1997) 'Low wage employment in transitional economies central and eastern Europe', *MOCT-MOST*, vol. 7, no. 1.

Ruttan, V.W. and Hayami, Y. (1985) *Agricultural Development: An International Perspective* (Baltimore: Johns Hopkins University Press) (revised and expanded edition).

Sachs, Ignacy (1996) *Developing in a Liberalized and Globalizing World Economy: An Impossible Challenge?*, Royal Danish Ministry of Foreign Affairs 1996 Copenhagen Seminar for Social Progress, Document no. 4, Havreholm Castle, 4–6 October.

Sachs, J. (1989) 'Social Conflict and Populist Policies in Latin America', *National Bureau of Economic Research (NBER) Working Paper* no. 2897.

Sachs, J. (1991) 'Crossing the Valley of Tears in East European Reform', *Challenge*, September–October.

Sachs, J. (1993) *Poland's Jump to the Market Economy* (Cambridge, MA: MIT Press).

Sachs, J. (1995) 'Consolidating Capitalism', *Foreign Policy*, no. 98.

Sachs, W. (1992) 'One World', in W. Sachs (ed.) *The Development Dictionary* (London: Zed Books).

Sadek, M.T. (1995) 'Institutional Fragility and Judicial Problems in Brazil', in M. D'Alva Kinzo and V. Bulmer-Thomas (eds), *Growth and Development in Brazil- Cardoso's Real Challenge* (London: Institute of Latin American Studies, University of London).

Sagi, M. (1993) '*Dismantling the Welfare State*, Paper prepared for the European Research Conference 'From European Societies to European Society', St. Martin, Germany, 22–26 Nov. 1992.

Salonen, T. (1993) *Margins of Welfare* (Torna: Hällestad Press).

Sassen, S. (1996) 'Service Employment and the New Inequality', in E. Mingione (ed.) (1996a) *Urban Poverty and the Underclass–A Reader* (Oxford: Basil Blackwell).

Sawyer, R. (1988) *Children Enslaved* (London: Routledge).

Scott, A.M. (1979) 'Who are the Self-Employed?', in R. Bromley and C. Gerry (eds), *Casual Work and Poverty in Third World Cities* (New York: John Wiley).

Scoville, J.G. (1989) 'The Informal Sector, Vulnerability, and Labour Market Analysis for the Traditional Sector: The King is Dead; Long Live the King', *Conference on Labour and Economic Development*, Conference Series no. 11 (Taipei: Chung-hua Institution for Economic Research).

Scoville, J.G. (ed.) (1991) *Status Influences in Third World Labor Markets: Caste, Gender, and Custom* (New York: de Gruyter).

Scoville, J.G. (1996) 'Labour Market Underpinnings of a Caste Economy: Foiling the Coase Theorem', *American Journal of Economics and Sociology*, October.

SEADE (State Data Analysis System Foundation) (1994) *Survey of Living Conditions in the Metropolitan Area of São Paulo*.

SEADE (State Data Analysis System Foundation)(1995) *Pesquisa de condiçoes de Vida na Regiao Metropolitana de São Paulo*, Primeiros Resultados, São Paulo.

SEADE/DIEESE (1985, 1990, 1993, 1994) *Pesquisa de Emprego e Desemprego na Grande São Paulo*. Estudo especial. O mercado de trabalho da Grande São Paulo.

Seers, D. (1969) 'The Meaning of Development', *International Development Review*, vol. 11, no. 4.

Sen, A.K. (1973) *On Economic Inequality* (Oxford: Clarendon).

Sen, A.K. (1975) *Employment, Technology and Development* (Oxford: Clarendon).

Sen, A.K. (1976) 'Poverty: An Ordinal Approach to Measurement', *Econometrica*, March.

Sen, A.K. (1977) 'Starvation and Exchange Entitlements: A General Approach and its Application to the Great Bengal Famine', *Cambridge Journal of Economics*, vol. 1.

Sen, A.K. (1981) *Food and Famines: An Essay on Entitlement and Deprivation* (Oxford: Clarendon).

Sen, A.K. (1983a) 'Development: Which Way Now?', *Economic Journal*, December.

Sen, A.K. (1983b) 'Poor, Relatively Speaking', *Oxford Economic Papers*, July.

Sen, A.K. (1984) 'Rights and Capabilities', in Amartya Sen, *Resources, Values and Development* (Oxford: Basil Blackwell).

Sen, A.K. (1985a) 'A Sociological Approach to the Measurement of Poverty: A Reply to Peter Townsend', *Oxford Economic Papers*, December.

Sen, A.K. (1985b) *Commodities and Capabilities* (Amsterdam: North-Holland).

Sen, A.K. (1989) 'Development as Capability Expansion', *Journal of Development Planning*, no. 19.

Sen, A.K. (1990) 'Individual Freedom: A Social Responsibility', *New York Review of Books*, 14 June.

Sen, A.K. (1992a) *Inequality Reexamined* (Oxford: Clarendon Press).

Sen, A.K. (1992b) 'Progress and Social Deficit: Some Methodological Issues' in Desai, Sen and Boltvinik, *Social Progress Index – A Proposal*, op. cit.

Sen, A. (1998) 'Mortality as an Indicator of Economic Success and Failure', *Economic Journal*, January.

Sen, Amartya and Jean Drèze (1989) *Hunger and Public Action* (Oxford: Oxford University Press).

Sernau, S. (1994) *Economies of Exclusion: Underclass, Poverty and Labour Market Change in Mexico* (Westport, CT: Praeger).

Sernau, S. (1996) 'Economies of Exclusion – Economic Change and the Global Underclass', *Journal of Developing Societies*, June.

Shaw, A. *et al.* (1995) *Moving Off Income Support? Obstacles, Opportunities, Choices,* Loughborough Centre for Research in Social Policy, Working Paper no. 246.

Silva, Nelson do Valle (1978) *White-Nonwhite Income Defferentials: Brazil – 1960*, Ph.D. Dissertation (Ann Arbor: University of Michigan).

Silva, Nelson do Valle (1985) 'Upgrading the Cost of Not Being White in Brazil', in P.M. Fontaine (ed.), *Race, Class and Power in Brazil* (Los Angeles: UCLA Center for Afro-American Studies).

Silver, H. (1994) 'Social Exclusion and Social Solidarity: Three Paradigms', *International Labour Review*, vol. 133, no. 5–6.

Silver, H. (1995) 'Three Paradigms of Social Exclusion' in Rodgers *et al.* (eds), *Social Exclusion: Rhetoric, Reality, Responses*, op. cit.

Silver, H. (1996) 'Culture, Politics and National Discourses of the New Urban Poverty', in Mingione, *Urban Poverty and the Underclass, op. cit.*

Singer, P. (1997) *Social Exclusion in Brazil*, Discussion Papers Series no. 94 (Geneva: International Institute for Labour Studies).

Sklair, L. (1991) *Sociology of the Global System: Social Change in Global Perspective* (Baltimore: Johns Hopkins University Press).

Social Justice (1993) 'Global Crisis, Local Struggles', *Social Justice*, special issue , vol. 20, nos. 304.

Smith, D.J. (ed.) (1992a) *Understanding the Underclass* (London: Policy Studies Institute).

Smith, D.J. (1992b) 'Defining the Underlcass', in Smith, ibid.

Smith, D.J. (1997) *Job Insecurity vs. Labour Market Flexibility* (London: Social Market Foundation).

Sola, L. (1994) 'The State, Structural Reform, and Democratization in Brazil', in William C. Smith, Carlos H. Acuna and Eduardo Gamara (eds), *Democracy, Markets and Structural Reform in Latin America: Argentina, Bolivia, Brazil, Chile and Mexico* (New Brunswick, NJ: Transaction Press).

Spicker, P. (1997) 'Exclusion', *Journal of Common Market Studies*, vol. 35, no. 1.

Spyropoulos, G. (1996) 'Encadrement social de la mondialisation de l'économie', *Droit Social*, no. 6, June.

Srinivasan, T.N. (1994) 'Data Base for Development Analysis: An Overview', *Journal of Development Economics*, June.

Standing, G. (1984) *Labour Circulation and the Labour Process* (London: Croom Helm).

Standing, G. (1987) 'Vulnerable Groups in Urban Labour Processes', *ILO World Employment Programme (WEP) Research Working Papers*, Geneva, no. 13.

Standing, G. (1989) 'Global Feminization Through Flexible Labour', *World Development*, July.

Standing, G. (1995) 'Labour Insecurity Through Market Regulation: Legacy of the 1980s, Challenge for the 1990s', in Katherine McFate, Roger Lawson and William Julius Wilson (eds), *Poverty, Inequality, and the Future of Social Policy* (New York: Russell Sage Foundation).

Stevens, B. and W. Michalski (1994) 'Long-term Prospects for Work and Social Cohesion in OECD Countries: An Overview of the Issues', in OECD, *Societies in Transition*, Paris.

Streeten, P. (1994) 'Human Development: Means and Ends', *American Economic Review-Papers and Proceedings*, May.

Streeten, P. (1998) 'Globalization: Threat or Salvation?', in Bhalla, *Globalization, Growth and Marginalization*, op. cit.

Strobel, P. (1996) 'From Poverty to Exclusion: A Wage-earning Society or Society of Human Rights?', *International Social Sciences Journal*, no. 148.

Sugden, R. (1993) *Welfare, Resources, and Capabilities: A Review of Inequality Reexamined*, by Amartya Sen, *Journal of Economic Literature*, December.

Sunkel, O. (1973) 'Transnational Capitalism and National Disintegration in Latin America', *Social and Economic Studies*, March.

Sunkel, O. (1993) *Development From Within – Towards a Neo-Structuralist Approach to Latin America* (Boulder: Lynne Rienner).

Sunkel, O. (1995) 'Uneven Globalisation, Economic Reform, and Democracy: A View from Latin America', in Hans-Henrik Holm and Georg Sorenson (eds), *Whose World Order? Uneven Globalization and the End of the Cold War* (Boulder: Westview).

Swaminathan, Madhura (1991) *Understanding the Informal Sector: A Survey*, UN/UNU World Institute for Development Economic Research (WIDER) Working Paper, Helsinski.

Tabard, N. (1993a) 'Quartiers Pauvres, quartiers riches, position dans la hiérarchie spatiale', Paris, *INSEE Working Paper* no. F/9311-2.

Tabard, N. (1993b) 'Des quartiers pauvres aux banlieues aisées: une représentation sociale du territoire', *Economie et Statistique*, no. 270 (Paris: INSEE).

Tannen, M.B. (1991) 'Labour Markets in Northeast Brazil: Does the Dual Market Model Apply?', *Economic Development and Cultural Change*, April.

Tanzi, V. (1997) 'Economic Transformation and the Policies for Long-Term Growth', in M. Blejer and M. Skreb, (eds), *Macroeconomic Stabilization in Transition Economies* (Cambridge University Press)

Taylor, M. (1982) *Community, Anarchy and Liberty* (Cambridge University Press).

Taylor, C. and D. Jodice (1983) *World Handbook of Political and Social Indicators*, vol. 3 (New Haven, CT: Yale University Press).

Tchernina, N. (1996) *Economic Transition and Social Exclusion in Russia*, Research Series no. 108 (Geneva: International Institute for Labour Studies).

Telles, E.E. (1992) 'Who Gets Formal sector Jobs?', Determinants of Formal – Informal Sector Participation in Brazilian Metropolitan Areas', *Work and Occupation*, May.

Telles, E.E. (1993) 'Urban Labour Market Segmentation and Income in Brazil', *Economic Development and Cultural Change*, January.

Tendulkar, S.D. and K. Sundaram (1994) *Social Exclusion: Mechanisms Processes, and Labour Market Outcomes – An Indian Case Study*, paper presented at the Asian Sub-Regional Symposium on Social Exclusion and Extension of Social Protection, Pattaya, Thailand, 22–25 November.

Thalineau, A. (1997) 'Les effets sociaux de la pensée politique sur l'insertion: l'exemple du RMI', *L'Homme et la Société*, no. 125.

Thomas, V. (1987) 'Differences in Income and Poverty within Brazil', *World Development, February.*

Thurow, L. (1996) *The Future of Capitalism* (London: Nicholas Brealey).

Tickell, A. and J. Peck (1995) 'Social Regulation after Fordism: Regulation Theory, Neoliberalism and the Global-Local Nexus', *Economy and Society*, vol. 24, no. 3.

Tilak, J.B.G. (1987) *The Economics of Inequality in Education* (New Delhi: SAGE Publications).

Tilly, C. (1995) 'Globalisation Threatens Labor's Rights', *International Labor and Working Class History*, no. 47.

Touraine, A. (1992) 'Inégalités de la societé industrielle, exclusion du marché', in J. Affichard and J.B. de Foucauld (eds), *Justice sociale et inégalités* (Paris: Editions Esprit).

Townsend, P. (1979) *Poverty in the United Kingdom* (Harmondsworth: Penguin).

Townsend, P. (1987) 'Deprivation', *Journal of Social Policy*, vol. 16, pt 2.

Townsend, P. (1993) *The International Analysis of Poverty* (Hemel Hempstead: Harvester Wheatsheaf).

Townsend, P. (1995) 'Poverty in Eastern Europe: The Latest Manifestation of Global Polarization', in Gerry Rodgers and Ralph van der Hoeven (eds), *The Poverty Agenda: Trends and Policy Options* (Geneva: International Institute for Labour Studies).

Troyano, A.A. (1996) 'Precarizacao do mercado de trablho na regiao metropolitana de São Paulo, 1989–1992 (Labour Market Insecurity in Greater São Paulo)', in José B. Figueiredo (ed.), *Las instituciones laborales frente a los cambios en América Latina* (Geneva: International Institute for Labour Studies).

Turnham, D., B. Salome and A. Schwarz (eds) (1990) *The Informal Sector Revisited* (Paris: OECD).

UNICEF (1993) Public policy and social conditions, *Regional Monitoring Report*, No. 1, Florence, UNICEF.

United Nations (1992) *World Investment Report* (New York).

United Nations (1997) '*Summary of the Economic Survey of Europe 1996–97*' (Geneva) (internal document).

United Nations Conference on Trade and Development (UNCTAD) (1996) *Promoting Growth and Sustainable Development in Globalizing and Liberalizing World Economy*, Pre-conference Text, TD/367, 3 April.

UNDP (several years) *Human Development Report* (Oxford: University Press).

United Nations Economic Commission for Europe (UNECE)(1997) *Economic Survey of Europe 1996–97* (Geneva: United Nations).

UNECLAC (1994) *Statistical Yearbook for Latin America and the Caribbean* (Santiago).

UNECLAC (1995) *Social Panorama of Latin America* (Santiago).

UNICEF (1992) '*Childhood and Urban Poverty in Brazil: Street and Working Children and their Families*', Florence Innocenti Occasional Papers, the Urban Child Series.

UNICEF (1993) *Public Policy and Social Condition*, Regional Monitoring Report no. 1, (Florence), November.

UNICEF (1995) '*Poverty, Children and Policy: Responses for Brighter Future', Regional Monitoring Report no. 2*, International Child Development Centre, Florence.

UNRISD (1995) *States of Disarray: The Social Effects of Globalization* (Geneva: UNRISD).

United States Department of Labor, Bureau of Labor Statistics (1986) *Re-employment Increases Among Displaced Workers* (Washington, DC), 14 October.

United States Department of State (1997) *Brazil Country Report on Human Rights Practices for 1996* (Washington DC), January.

Valereyberghe, P. (1992) *RMI, le pari de l'insertion*, Rapport de la Commission Nationale d'Evaluation du RMI (Paris).

Van Praag, A.M.J. and R. Teekens (1992) *Analysing Poverty in the European Community* (Brussels: European Commission).

Vecernik, J. (1995) 'Incomes in Central Europe: Distributions, Patterns and Perceptions', *Journal of European Social Policy*, vol. 6, no. 2.

Vecernik, J. (1997) 'Vox Populi – What Do People in Central and Eastern Europe Think of their Reforms?' (Washington, DC: World Bank (internal document).

Veit, Wilson, J. (1994) *Dignity Not Poverty – A Minimum Income Standard for the UK* (London: Institute for Public Policy Research).

Velloso, Joao Paulo dos Reis (1994) 'Governance, the Transition to Modernity, and Civil Society', in Colin I. Bradford, Jr (ed.), *Redefining the State in Latin America* (Paris: OECD).

Veltz, P. (1996) *Mondialisation, villes et territoires* (Paris: Presse Universitaire de France).

Viveret, P. (1992) 'Evaluation et visibilité des enjeux', in R. Castel and J-F. Laé (eds), *Le Revenu Minimum d'Insertion – une dette sociale*, op. cit.

Vos, K. de and A. Hagenaars (1988) *A Comparison Between the Poverty Concepts of Sen and Townsend* (Rotterdam: Erasmus University).

Wacquant, L. (1996) 'L'underclass urbaine dans l'imaginaire social et scientifique américain', in S. Paugam (ed.), *L'Exclusion: l'état des savoirs*, op. cit.

Walker, R., A. Shaw and L. Hull (1995) 'Responding to the Risk of Unemployment', in *Risk, Insurance and Welfare* (London: Association of British Insurers).

Wallis, J.J. and D.C. North (1986) 'Measuring the Transaction Sector in the American Economy, 1870 –1970', in S.L. Egerson and R.E. Gallman (eds.), *Long-term Factors in American Economic Growth* (University of Chicago Press).

Walsh, T.J. (1990) 'Flexible Labour Utilisation in the Private Services Sector', *Work, Employment and Society*, vol. 4.

Walter, T. (1988) *Basic Incomes, Freedom From Poverty, Freedom to Work* (London: Marion Boyars).

Walzer, M. (1995) 'Exclusion, Injustice et Etats Démocratiques', in J. Affichard and J.B. Foucauld (eds), *Pluralisme et équité, la justice sociale dans les démocraties* (Paris: Editions Esprit).

Waterman, P. (1996) 'Beyond Globalism and Developmentalism: Other Voices in World Politics', *Development and Change*, vol. 27.

Weber, M. (1922) Economy and Society [1968] ed. G. Roth and C. Wittich (New York: Bedminster Press).

Wilkie, James W. *et al.* (ed.) (1995) *Statistical Abstracts of Latin America* (Los Angeles: University of California).

Williamson, O. (1981) 'The Economics of Organization', *American Journal of Sociology*, vol. 87, no. 3, November.

Wilson, W.J. (1987, 1990) *The Truly Disadvantaged: The Underclass, the Ghetto and Public Policy* (University of Chicago Press).

Wilson, W.J. (1989a) 'The Underclass', *Annals of the American Academy of Political and Social Science*, vol. 501.

Wilson, W.J. (1989b) *The Ghetto Underclass: Social Science Perspective* (Newbury Park, CA: Sage).

Wilson, W.J. (1992) 'Another Look at the 'Truly' Disadvantaged', *Political Science Quarterly*, vol. 106, no. 4.

Wilson, W.J. (1996a) *When Work Disappears: The World of the New Urban Poor* (New York, Knopf).

Wilson, W.J. (1996b) *Jobless Ghettos: The Disappearance of Work and Its Impact on Urban Life in America* (New York: Knopf).

Winant, Howard (1992) 'Rethinking Race in Brazil', *Journal of Latin American Studies*, February.

Wolf, Charles Jr (1990) *Markets or Governments – Choosing Between Imperfect Alternatives* (Cambridge, MA: MIT Press).

Wolfe, Marshall (1995) 'Globalisation and Social Exclusion: Some Paradoxes' in Gore, Rodgers and Figuereido, *Social Exclusion: Rhetoric, Reality, Responses*, op. cit.

Wood, Adrian (1994) *North-South Trade, Employment and Inequality* (Oxford: Clarendon Press).

Wood, Adrian (1997) 'Openness and Wage Inequality in Developing Countries: The Latin American Challenge to East Asian Conventional Wisdom', *World Bank Economic Review*, January.

World Bank (1994) 'Unemployment in Eastern Europe', *Development Brief no. 25* (Washington, DC). (internal document).

World Bank (1995) *Poland* (Washington, DC).

World Bank (1996a) *Global Economic Prospects and the Developing Countries* (Washington, DC).

World Bank (1996b) *Hungary* (Washington, DC).

World Bank (1996c) *World Development Report* (New York: Oxford University Press).

World Bank (1997) *World Development Indicators*, Washington DC.

World Development (1993), Special Section on '*State, Market and Civil Organizations: New Theories, New Practices and Their Implications for Rural Development*', April.

World Development (1996) Special Section on '*Government Action, Social Capital and Development: Creating Synergy Across the Public-Private Divide*', June.

World Freedom Survey (1997) *Freedom Review*, January–February.

Wrésinski, J. (1987) Grande pauvreté et précarité économique et sociale, *Rapport au Conseil Economique et Social, Journal Officiel de la République Française*.

Xibberas, M. (1993) *Théories de l'exclusion sociale* (Paris: Méridiens Klincksieck).

Ying, B. (1993) *Las dos caras de las comunidades: entre la denuncia y la autogestión* (Caracas: Universidad Central de Venezuela); thesis work for graduation in Social Communication.

Zioklowski, M. (1994) 'The Pragmatic Shift in Polish Social Consciousness: With or Against the Tide of Rising Post-Materialism?', *Polish Sociological Review*, vol. 4, no. 108.

Zucker, L. (1986) 'Production of Trust: Institutional Sources of Economic Structure, 1840–1920', *Research in Organizational Behaviour*, vol. 8.

Zürn, M. (1995) 'The Challenge of Globalization and Individualization: A View from Europe', in Holm and Sorensen, *Whose World Order – Uneven Globalization and the End of the Cold War*, op. cit.

Author and Name Index

Subject Index